DEVOTIONS

FOR

WORKING

WOMEN

A Daily Inspiration to Live a Successful
and Balanced Life

BY

MARCIA MALZAHN

Cover photo by Marcia Malzahn

ISBN 13: 978-1-931945-67-7
ISBN 10: 1-931945-67-5

Library of Congress Catalog Number: 2006934415

Printed in the United States of America

First Printing: October 2006

11 10 09 08 07   5 4 3 2 1

Andover,
Minnesota

Expert Publishing, Inc.
14314 Thrush Street NW
Andover, MN 55304-3330
1-877-755-4966
www.expertpublishinginc.com

*I dedicate this book to all the working women
who seek to balance their lives and who have made many
sacrifices in order to achieve success.*

*Whether it's by choice or by need,
whether the office is inside or outside the home, in these days
almost every woman works in every country.*

Acknowledgements

I want to thank the following people who are dear to my heart and have helped me succeed throughout my working life.

I want to thank my parents, Orlando and Marcia Flores, who always believed in me and pushed me to be successful at everything I did. They taught me to always fight for what I want and to never give up. They also taught me to have faith in God, to know that He will never leave me nor forsake me, and that He loves me, no matter what.

I want to thank my husband, Tim, who has always been there for me. He has always encouraged me to go beyond the call of duty at every job I've held. He believes in me and challenges me to learn continually. He also jumps in with the chores at home when my job demands more of my time. He loves me for who I am and I love him dearly too.

I want to thank my three sisters, Martha Mooneyham, Isa Tyler, and Maria Painter, who are all working women themselves and love me for who I am and not for what I am or the titles I hold. They celebrate my successes and lift me up when I fall. Thank you to my two brothers, Orlando Flores and Juan Flores, who also believe in me, look up to me, and are always concerned for my well-being.

I want to thank all my friends from Financial Women International that have encouraged me through the years, believed in me, and supported me. They have been an inspiration in my life and an inspiration for this book.

Lastly, but definitely not least, I want to thank the managers who impacted my life during the course of my career. Reid Evenson, Jeanne Crain, Diane Jamar, and Pastor Mac Hammond have contributed to my success one way or another. Thank you for believing in me, trusting me, and always challenging me to do better and be the best that I can be.

Thank you to all the women that work who inspired me to write this book. It is my heart's desire that by reading this devotional, you will be encouraged and inspired to continue to fight and never give up knowing God loves *you* and He is with you *always*.

Introduction

As a working woman, you encounter many challenges to balancing life every day. This inspirational book will motivate, encourage, and inspire you to be successful and balanced in every area of your life. It will give you practical examples and tips on living in a way that positively impacts those around you. This book will demonstrate how simple your life can be when you follow basic principles from the Master of balance, our loving God the Father. It will also inspire you to never give up, knowing you are not alone. You have God and the people He has put in your life to help accomplish what He's called you to do.

This devotional covers several traits that define a true leader:

- *Character* is the most important thing other people see in you.

- The Word of God gives you the *encouragement* you need on a daily basis to be a woman of integrity.

- *Obedience* to His Word and your *trust* in Him provides you with the gift of *wisdom*.

- When He sees your *faithfulness* to His teachings, you give Him an opportunity to bless you beyond your wildest dreams.

- When you strive to live a life of *holiness*, God can use you to influence other people.

- When you have *thankfulness* in your heart and acknowledge Him in all you have and are, He shows you His amazing love for you.

- It is only by *faith* through grace that you receive the gift of salvation; you cannot earn it by your own deeds.

- *Success* comes when you love God above all things and love others with His love.

- *Balance* is a gift from God that you can obtain by asking Him to help you achieve it on a daily basis and by following His ways.

- True *leadership* is comprised of all the traits above.

How to read this devotional book:

The devotions are printed in alphabetical order by topic and then in alphabetical order by title within each topic. The index contains both the devotional number and the page number so you can find them easily.

You can read this book in three ways: 1) You can read one devotional per day in order; 2) You can read one or several devotions on a certain topic; or 3) You can look up in the index a specific topic and read devotionals within that topic. This book is very flexible and is meant for you to enjoy as you (a busy working woman) have the time to read.

In this book, pronouns are capitalized when referring to God to honor and respect His name. When you see a reference to scripture within the devotional text, it is there to illustrate the scripture basis for the comment. Both quotes and paraphrases are supported by the scripture verses and the version of the Bible they were taken from. Each devotional has one primary verse, which is the one that stood out as I was reading the Bible. As each devotional unfolded, more supporting scriptures came to me that gave additional information or supported the main subject. The additional scripture verses will be noted in parentheses with the verse number. They are found in the same chapter as the main verse.

Join me in this journey as a fellow working woman to discover your full potential and become successful and balanced in every area of your life.

BALANCE

BALANCE IS A DAILY PRAYER

Psalm 119:133 (NLT)

*Guide my steps by your word,
so I will not be overcome by any evil.*

Psalm 25:4 (NLT)

*Show me the path where I should walk, O Lord; point out the right
road for me to follow.*

With so many important things in our lives to manage, we long for balance. Balancing our lives is a daily prayer. With God's guidance, our personal discipline, and careful planning we *can* achieve balance in our lives. In His Word we not only find the truth, but also the strength and wisdom needed to help us complete and accomplish all God has called us to do.

When we pray we have to ask for the balance we need—on a daily basis. His Word says in John 16:24 (NKJV), "Ask, and you will receive." Just as we ask God for our health, our jobs, or for wisdom, balance is a precious gift, but we can only achieve it by working together with God.

Therefore, ask Him to help you balance your daily life, and once He shows you the path you should walk, be sure to follow His lead.

BALANCING YOUR PHYSICAL, EMOTIONAL, AND SPIRITUAL LIFE IS CRUCIAL

Isaiah 40:29 (NLT)

He gives power to those who are tired and worn out;
he offers strength to the weak.

How often do you feel tired, worn out, and weak? This would be a great verse to memorize and repeat on those days. We all experience physical, emotional, and spiritual weariness in our lives. Some days we may just be physically tired, but we move on because we are not mentally or spiritually exhausted. Those times we just need to rest, go to bed earlier that night, take a break from work, or simply change activities.

Dealing with emotional weariness is more difficult because when we are emotionally exhausted, it also affects our physical well-being. In those times, we also need to rest, do some exercise to relieve the stress, and spend time with the Lord. Just being in His presence will refresh our minds.

Spiritual burnout is the most dangerous because when we stop fighting in the spirit, everything else stops and dies away. Remember, we are first of all spiritual beings that live in a human body. Just as our body needs rest and food, our spirit does too. If we are spiritually starving, we will die spiritually.

We must avoid burnout in any area, but most importantly, we must avoid it in these three areas (physical, emotional, and spiritual) at the same time. In order to avoid that situation, we must have balance in our lives. Balance starts with a daily prayer asking the Lord to help us balance that day—one day at a time.

Put God in control of your life—every area and every moment. Spend time with Him. He yearns for that time. You will then be refreshed in every area. "But those who wait on the Lord will find new strength. They will fly high on wings like eagles. They will run and not grow weary. They will walk and not faint" (v. 31).

BUILD AND KEEP YOUR HOUSEHOLD

Proverbs 14:1 (NLT)

A wise woman builds her house; a foolish woman tears hers down with her own hands.

Proverbs 31:17 (NLT)

She is energetic and strong, a hard worker.

Proverbs 31:27 (NLT)

She carefully watches all that goes on in her household and does not have to bear the consequences of laziness.

As working women, we have many responsibilities. Sometimes we don't know how to prioritize the major ones such as keeping and running our households and our jobs. But when we have our priorities right—God first, our family second, and our job third—God will give us the grace to successfully manage our careers and our households.

A job should not be used as an excuse to not keep our households. As a wife and/or mother, we have the responsibility to establish a clean and orderly household for our family. We are to be a blessing to our children and an ally (not a burden) to our husbands. The good news is, when our house is in order, we will be more focused and productive—even if our office is in the home.

Even though you are responsible for properly maintaining your household, it doesn't mean you have to do it all yourself. Wise women learn to delegate. For example: assign tasks and chores to your kids, ask your husband for help, or consider hiring a cleaning service (if you can afford it). It doesn't matter how you get it done; what matters is that you properly care for your home. When you purpose in your heart to build and keep your household, God will honor your efforts and will help you every step of the way.

CHOOSE TO STORE TREASURES IN HEAVEN

Matthew 6:21, 24 (NLT)

Wherever your treasure is, there your heart and thoughts will also be… No one can serve two masters. For you will hate one and love the other, or be devoted to one and despise the other. You cannot serve both God and money.

What is our treasure? We all have treasures in the natural realm and in the spiritual realm. Jesus tells us not to focus our life on storing the treasures of earth, such as money, because it will go away. Instead, we are to focus on storing spiritual treasure in heaven where it will never go away. Verses 22 and 23 say, "Your eye is a lamp for your body. A pure eye lets sunshine into your soul. But an evil eye shuts out the light and plunges you into darkness."

Our eyes are what we use to focus on natural things. Spiritually, we focus on things with the eyes of our heart. If we focus on earthly treasure, we will end up storing and serving it. If we focus on heavenly treasure, our eyes will bring light unto our soul and we will be serving God. When we put God first and live our life for Him (our thoughts are focused on Him, our eyes are fixed on Him), He will give us the true treasures of heaven.

Therefore, don't focus your eyes on your job or career or the money it can produce. Instead, focus on God and seek Him above all. Then He will give you the job and career of your dreams.

DON'T GET DISTRACTED WITH THE THINGS OF THIS LIFE

2 Timothy 2:3-4 (NLT)

Endure suffering along with me, as a good soldier of Christ Jesus. And as Christ's soldier, do not let yourself become tied up in the affairs of this life, for then you cannot satisfy the one who has enlisted you in his army.

Part of being a soldier in the army of Jesus is to endure suffering just as He did. We also cannot get distracted with the everyday things of life because then we can't fulfill the plan God has for us. We are to remain focused on the calling God has given each one of us.

There are many distractions in our lives. Sometimes our job can be a distraction because it can become the focus of our lives instead of an avenue to fulfill the calling. Every job we have is preparation for the high calling and God's plan for our lives Therefore, we need to ask God to keep us balanced and focused on the important things.

Ask God for wisdom and discernment on a daily basis so you don't get distracted and so you can be a good soldier.

KEEP GOD AT THE TOP OF YOUR PRIORITIES

1 John 5:21 (NLT)

Dear children, keep away from anything that might take God's place in your hearts.

The King James Version of this verse says, "Little children, keep yourselves from idols." With so many things this world offers us, we have to be careful and guard our hearts at all times from things that have the potential of taking God's place in our hearts. We all have desires and dreams we want to pursue in our lives. Most of them are placed by God in us. However, even when those desires and dreams are from God, we have to be careful they don't occupy our entire life. These dreams can become our idols if that's what we pursue day and night and if we spend all of our resources on them. Things that can move us away from God are not only natural things such as money, success, fame, popularity, hobbies, or even our children; they can be also our desires, dreams, and our idols (including people we idolize). In other words, anything that takes priority over God in our lives can become our idol.

To refocus, always go back to the Word. Matthew 6:33 (KJV) says, "Seek ye first the kingdom of God and his righteousness and all these things shall be added unto you." The key is to put God first in your life. Everything else falls into place after Him.

LORD, TEACH US TO MANAGE OUR TIME

Psalm 90:12 (NLT)

*Teach us to make the most of our time,
so that we may grow in wisdom.*

Time is a valuable resource. No matter who we are, we are all given the same amount of time every day, and it is up to us to use it and manage it wisely.

We often get frustrated when we waste our time because we like to be in control of our lives and that includes our calendar. Therefore, part of our daily prayer needs to include asking God to help us manage our time wisely.

Ask God to help you balance your life one day at a time. You are then allowing Him to take control of your busy schedule, cancel appointments, and rearrange things throughout your day as He wills. When you give up that control to the Lord, He will make sure your life is balanced. Just remember to give Him priority in your schedule.

You also need to be flexible. Sometimes the Lord will ask you to stop doing an activity and pray for somebody or for a particular situation. The best example is when God reminds you of someone you haven't seen in a while. It may be the Holy Spirit nudging you to pray for that person. You need to quickly obey Him and do what He's asking you to do. If you are to be used of Him, you have to be willing to be flexible and obey His leading. This is how you make the most of your time on a daily basis.

LOVE GOD, NOT THE WORLD

1 John 2:15 (NLT)

*Stop loving this evil world and all that it offers you,
for when you love the world, you show that you do not have the love of
the Father in you.*

It is okay for us working women to have a career. It is okay to love our career and what we do. However, it is not okay to love it above God. Anything we place above God becomes our god and will separate us from Him.

The world can offer you big opportunities and promise you grandiose jobs, titles, salaries, corner offices with a view, great benefits, and perks. These are all okay things to have. You just can't make them a priority in your life. The same world can take away everything in an instant, leaving you with nothing.

When we set our eyes on Jesus and seek God's Kingdom first, all those things will be added to us (Matthew 6:33 KJV). The difference is that He makes us rich in every way and does not add sorrow to it (Proverbs 10:22 KJV).

I encourage you to examine your priorities and put God first, then your family, then your career. This will show those around you that you have the love of the Father in you.

PURSUE A GODLY LIFE

I Timothy 6:11-12 (NLT)

But you, Timothy, belong to God; so run from all these evil things, and follow what is right and good. Pursue a godly life, along with faith, love, perseverance, and gentleness.
Fight the good fight for what we believe. Hold tightly to the eternal life that God has given you, which you have confessed so well before many witnesses.

These were Paul's final instructions to Timothy in his first letter. Put your name in the verse instead of Timothy's and believe those are God's personal instructions for your life. Never forget you are a child of God. You belong to Him. Always do what is right and good. Ask God for wisdom to discern every situation.

Pursue a godly life at all cost. Don't ever give up running from evil and fighting the fight of life and for what you believe. Your reward is eternal life with God. Confess your salvation over and over. This will remind you of what Jesus did on the cross for you and will give you the strength and grace to live this life with joy and success until you die or until Jesus comes again.

10

PUT GOD FIRST IN YOUR LIFE

Matthew 6:33 (KJV)

But seek ye first the kingdom of God, and his righteousness; and all these things shall be added unto you.

Have you ever caught yourself pursuing your own agenda instead of God's? Sometimes it's hard to get our mind off our own needs, but that is exactly what God wants us to do. Instead, we need to focus on the Lord and put *Him* first in our lives. Why? Because when we make God our number one priority, He will see to it that all our needs are met.

When our priorities are out of order, our life is out of balance. But once we redirect our priorities to put Him first, all the other things fall into place. He will give our careers more meaning, He will improve our relationships with loved ones, and He will improve the quality of our life.

Remember, as a Christian woman, your priorities should be as follows: First, God; second, your family (if you're married, your husband and then your children); and then your job and career. Always seek God first.

REST IS A GIFT FROM GOD

Hebrews 4:9-10 (NLT)

So there is a special rest still waiting for the people of God.
For all who enter into God's rest will find rest from their labors, just
as God rested after creating the world.

Exodus 23:12 (NLT)

Work six days, and rest on the seventh.
This will give your ox and your donkey a chance to rest.
It will also allow the people of your household, including your slaves
and visitors, to be refreshed.

Did you know God commands us to rest? He created us to be able to work six days and rest the seventh. He Himself gave us the first example in the Book of Genesis when—after spending six days creating the entire universe—He rested on the seventh. If God wanted to rest, what makes us think we don't need to?

Unfortunately, we don't allow ourselves to rest enough. We keep going and going until there is nothing left of ourselves to give. We push until we burn out physically *and* spiritually. Our bodies and minds need rest. Proper rest refreshes and strengthens our body; it reenergizes our minds so we can think clearly again. Not only that, when we clear our minds from the daily pressures and stresses of life, the Lord can speak to us in order to refresh, renew, and strengthen our spirit.

We can experience a special peace and rest in God—but only when we obey and do His will. Rest is a blessing and a gift from God. Are you getting enough of it?

12

SPEND TIME WITH THE LORD IN PRAYER

1 Peter 4:7 (NLT)

*The end of the world is coming soon. Therefore,
be earnest and disciplined in your prayers.*

In this verse, Peter is talking to all of God's chosen people, therefore, he includes us. No matter how successful we are or want to become in business, we cannot prosper without prayer. The Bible says we are to pray earnestly and we are to do it on a consistent basis. Prayer is what connects us to God, our Father. Through prayer we get close to Him, and He gets close to us. Through prayer we get to know the person of God, we receive His blessings, and the revelation of His Word.

We are to live our lives as if Christ is coming back today and as if the end of the world (the church dispensation) is ending soon. The signs of the end of times are evident in these last days. Therefore, spend time with the Lord, and schedule Him in your life as the most important appointment of your day. Just as you protect the time you have allocated for a customer or vendor meeting, or the time you allot for a special training, you need to protect the time you set aside to be with your Father. The meetings with the Lord and your time in prayer will help you succeed in all the areas of your life.

TAKE CARE OF YOUR BODY

I Corinthians 6:19 (KJV)

What? know ye not that your body is the temple of the Holy Ghost which is in you, which ye have of God, and ye are not your own?

The Bible tells us that our bodies are the temples of the Holy Spirit. In this verse, Paul is referring to sexual immorality; however, we must take care of our temples in all areas. God gave us our physical bodies and, just as with everything else He gives us, we must be good stewards and take care of them. This means we must eat right, exercise, get enough rest, and maintain a healthy lifestyle to ensure our bodies last a long time.

As temples of the Holy Spirit, we need to remember our bodies are not our own. Our bodies are the vessels God gave us for Him to use in this earth. We must honor God with our bodies by having the discipline to take care of them. If we don't, we may not only limit our ability to let God work through us but also limit our influence as Christians throughout the earth.

WE MUST PRESS ON DAILY

Philippians 3:14 (KJV)

I press toward the mark for the prize of the high calling of God in Christ Jesus.

When we ask God to put in our hearts what He wants us to desire, He will not only give us those desires but the steps or "marks" along the way to achieve them. Our lives must be a daily press in every area and toward every mark God reveals to us. He will give us one mark at a time, so we must press toward that one mark until it is done. Then He will reveal the next mark so we can move on to that next one and so on. We must continue the press until we achieve the high calling of God in our lives. Every time we achieve or complete a mark, God has a reward for us. He helps us along the way and enjoys rewarding us.

Don't be complacent. Continue the press until you see God's high calling in your life realized.

WORK HARD, BUT NOT TO AN EXTREME. GOD WILL GIVE YOU REST.

Psalm 127:2 (NLT)

It is useless for you to work so hard from early morning until late at night, anxiously working for food to eat;
for God gives rest to his loved ones.

Many women work too hard, work long days, and end up exhausted, with nothing left to give their families, and get burned out. For some women, it has caused them their health or their marriage. They end up having a nervous breakdown, heart disease, and many other illnesses or disorders.

God wants us to have a balanced life. He is a God of order and balance. We are to be diligent and work hard, but then we need to trust God and know "He gives rest to his loved ones." As we pray and ask the Lord on a daily basis to balance our day, we will accomplish everything He wants us to do for that day and be satisfied. We can pray David's prayers: "Guide my steps by your word, so I will not be overcome by any evil… Show me the path where I should walk, O Lord; point out the right road for me to follow" (Psalm 119:133, 25:4 NLT).

God rested on the seventh day, and we should too. Don't work so much that you miss life going by right before your eyes. Make time to be with your family and loved ones. This will actually give you renewed energy to go back and work hard again. Set a goal to work more efficiently and effectively versus working long hours.

Remember, the Bible says it is useless to work so hard unless God is in it. He will give you rest.

YOUR SLEEP SHALL BE SWEET

Psalm 4:8 (KJV)

I will both lay me down in peace, and sleep: for thou, Lord, only makest me dwell in safety.

Proverbs 3:24 (KJV)

When thou liest down, thou shall not be afraid: yea, thou shall lie down, and thy sleep shall be sweet.

When we are so busy with work, home, kids, and everything else we manage to get ourselves into, it may be hard to fall asleep when it's finally time to go to bed.

If you find yourself thinking, worrying, or running lists of things to do in your head when you're trying to go to sleep, get up and write down everything that is on your mind. This way you won't forget it. Then reach for your Bible and read the above scriptures. These are promises of God to you. He promises you can trust Him and He will take care of you and all the things that concern you. You are safe with Him, and He promises your sleep will be sweet, peaceful, and safe.

CHARACTER

17

ARE YOU A CHRIST-LIKE MENTOR?

I King 2:1-4 (NKJV)

Now the days of David drew near that he should die, and he charged Solomon his son, saying: "I go the way of all the earth; be strong, therefore, and prove yourself a man. And keep the charge of the Lord your God: to walk in His ways, to keep His statutes, His commandments, His judgments, and His testimonies, as it is written in the Law of Moses, that you may prosper in all that you do and wherever you turn; that the Lord may fulfill His word which He spoke concerning me, saying, 'If your sons take heed to their way, to walk before Me in truth with all their heart and with all their soul,' He said, 'you shall not lack a man on the throne of Israel.'"

David was Solomon's mentor and in this passage, he was giving him final instructions. Just as David did with Solomon, we will, during the course of our lives, have opportunities to mentor other people. Mentoring is not something to be taken lightly. God will put people in our path He wants us to train and coach. So, the question today is: Are you ready to be a mentor?

Let's follow Jesus' example as a mentor to His disciples. Jesus had many qualities as a mentor. He taught His disciples with easy-to-understand parables. He led them by example, imparted to them, encouraged them, and mentored them so they could go out and teach others later in the same way. He loved them, prayed for them, and listened to them. On the other hand, the responsibility of His disciples was to learn, imitate, and eventually become like their mentor.

It is the same for us today. Our main goal in life is to imitate Jesus and become more like Him. As we do, He teaches us how to help others.

Ask God to help you follow Jesus' example and become a Christ-like mentor.

18

ARE YOU A COMPETENT WORKER?

Proverbs 22:29 (NLT)

Do you see any truly competent workers? They will serve kings rather than ordinary people.

Do you consider yourself a competent worker? *The American Heritage Dictionary* defines competent as someone who is "properly or sufficiently qualified; capable, adequate for the purpose, to be suitable, legally qualified or fit to perform an act." Today's companies are all looking for competent employees in the various areas of their business and at every level. The Bible tells us competent workers have a special assignment—they will work for kings rather than ordinary people. People who work for kings or presidents of countries are hand picked and chosen for each task.

I want to be considered a competent employee. But I also know that in order to become competent, we must make sacrifices and train ourselves. To fit the description of a competent person, we must undergo training, we must be disciplined, invest of our time, money, and effort, and be willing to make changes.

You could also apply these principles in your spiritual life. Do you feel competent to do God's work on earth? Just as it takes time, hard work, effort, and discipline in the business arena, it takes the same to learn the things of God. You will then feel competent to fight the enemy and do God's work, which is to win people to His Kingdom. When you work for God, you indeed work for the King of Kings.

19

ARE YOU A MATURE BELIEVER?

Hebrews 5:14 (NLT)

*Solid food is for those who are mature, who have trained themselves
to recognize the difference between right and wrong and
then do what is right.*

The Bible says that mature believers have trained themselves, meaning it takes effort and sacrifice to train yourself in the things of God. How? By reading and meditating on His Word, by spending time with the Lord, getting to know Him and learning from Him. We also mature by going through painful experiences and seeking God with all our hearts.

The next part of the verse says they have trained themselves "to recognize the difference between right and wrong." When we do the things mentioned above, we acquire God's wisdom. And only with His wisdom we can know clearly what is right and what is wrong.

The last part of the verse says that first they recognize between right and wrong, "and then do what is right." Once you know what the right thing to do is, then ask God to give you boldness to do it. As you can see, we can apply this concept every day at the workplace.

The questions for you today are: Do you consider yourself a mature believer? Do you always do what's right once you clearly know what is right and wrong? Or do you compromise your heart because you are afraid of the consequences?

20

ARE YOU AN UPRIGHT CITIZEN?

Proverbs 11:11 (NLT)

Upright citizens bless a city and make it prosper, but the talk of the wicked tears it apart.

As individuals, we each contribute to the prosperity and well-being of our community and city. The Bible says that upright citizens bless a city and make it prosper. How do we become the kind of person or citizen who is a blessing to their city? I believe one of the first things we need to do is watch what we say about the city, state, and country we live in. What are we saying about the people and the place we live in? Are we tearing it apart with our words? Are we gossiping about our neighbors? Verse 12 says, "It is foolish to belittle a neighbor; a person with good sense remains silent."

There are many things you can do to be a godly citizen and bring blessing and prosperity to your city and country. At the top of the list is to have a personal relationship with the Lord and have your priorities right—God first, then your family, then your job, then everything else.

Ask God for direction on how to get involved in your community. Some of you may be called to serve in public office. Others can volunteer at the local food shelf and help the poor. There are other things you need to do as well, such as developing a good relationship with your neighbors, knowing who your political leaders are, keeping your city clean, and voting during elections. Voting is crucial for the well-being of a nation. Exercise your right to vote for the candidate that shares your same values. Vote for those whose values align with the Word of God.

One thing you should not do is talk bad about your city or nation. The tongue destroys everything you build with the work of your hands. Instead, be a citizen that blesses your city and makes it prosper.

21

Are You Honest All Around?

Proverbs 11:3, 5 (NLT)

Good people are guided by their honesty; treacherous people are destroyed by their dishonesty... The godly are directed by their honesty; the wicked fall beneath their load of sin.

Are you an honest person in every area of your life? The word honest means being a person of integrity, upright, not deceptive, genuine, equitable, fair, truthful, and sincere, among other things (paraphrasing from *The American Heritage Dictionary*).

Sometimes we are honest in some areas of our lives but not quite in others. In order to be successful in every area we must be honest in every area. That is what being a person of integrity is. We must be *consistently* honest with ourselves, our family, friends, co-workers, employees, customers, vendors, and most importantly, with God. He knows us. We don't have to pretend in front of Him. He loves us just the way we are because He created us. Honesty gives us freedom and peace.

Therefore, if you struggle with being honest in some areas of your life, ask God to help you and reveal to you what those areas are so you can start working on them. Honesty in your life will bring direction.

ARE YOU KNOWN AS A WOMAN OF INTEGRITY?

Proverbs 10:9 (NLT)

People with integrity have firm footing, but those who follow crooked paths will slip and fall.

Christian working women must be known by their integrity. Integrity means to adhere to a strict ethical code. A person of integrity is a sound person, undivided, and complete (paraphrasing from *The American Heritage Dictionary*).

When we base our lives on the Word of God, we have a rock solid foundation on which to stand. We are solid, unmovable, because we know what the Lord says. The Word is our ethical code. It's the moral code of conduct we follow. God has given us the Bible as our manual for success in life. If we don't follow it, we will surely perish.

Are you known in your workplace and at home as a woman of integrity? If you don't feel whole and complete, go to the Bible and start basing your life on the Word of God. Do it today!

ARE YOU THE LIGHT IN YOUR WORLD?

Matthew 5:14-15 (Weymouth)

You are the light of the world; a town cannot be hid if built on a hilltop. Nor is a lamp lighted to be under the bushel measure, but on the lampstand; and then it gives light to all in the house.

Christians, the followers of Jesus Christ, are called "the light of the world." But are we really being the light to this dark world?

Are we really being noticed as the ones that bring light to situations, solutions to problems, and peace where there is war? Many times we just pray for those few who are out there taking the Gospel, the light, to the world, and we don't do anything to be a light ourselves.

We each are a light because we have been given the very life of God. He has also given us the oil to keep our lamps lit—the Holy Spirit. Our bodies are the lamps that illuminate the darkness around us. How do we not run out of oil for our lamps? We stay hungry and thirsty for God. The more time we spend with the Lord, the more oil or power He gives us to continue to be a light.

The last part of the verse says, "it gives light to all in the house." The light is for the people. The light is the good news of the Gospel that brings life. I encourage you to make a decision to be a light in your workplace. You may be the only lamp around. Keep your lamp full of oil by being filled with the Holy Spirit.

24

AVOID AND HATE BRIBES

Proverbs 15:27 (NLT)

Dishonest money brings grief to the whole family,
but those who hate bribes will live.

Once in a while during your career you may encounter a person who will offer you special gifts (or bribes) in exchange for something else you may want (a promotion, more sales referrals, better deals, etc.). Be careful in accepting those gifts. First of all, most companies have policies forbidding bribes and you can lose your job. You could also be prosecuted and sent to jail. The Bible says that taking gifts for something (quid pro quo) will bring grief to the whole family. We have clearly witnessed how this behavior destroys families just from watching the news and hearing about the white collar crime that is going on.

Even when you own a company and you are the boss, remember you still answer to God. Avoid and hate bribes and you will live. You will keep peace and joy in your household.

BE A PERSON OF INTEGRITY AND FIND HAPPINESS

Psalm 119:1-2 (NLT)

Happy are people of integrity, who follow the law of the Lord. Happy are those who obey his decrees and search for him with all their hearts.

Being a person of integrity is being someone who is honest, trustworthy, truthful, and has no hidden agenda. That is what we are when we seek God with all our hearts—just because we love Him. This pleases God. When we seek Him first and above all things He adds everything else to our lives. This includes His spiritual gifts as well as natural talents and gifts.

These two verses also say that people of integrity are those who follow the law of the Lord and obey His decrees and commandments. Nowadays it is hard to find people of integrity in the workplace. It is time to change that! Christians must, by our actions, demonstrate what a person of integrity is. Our reward is happiness in our lives. Happiness attracts people because it is the joy of the Lord reflected in us and through us.

David prayed to God in verse 5, "Oh, that my actions would consistently reflect your principles!" As David, this is to be our daily prayer.

BE A TRUSTWORTHY WOMAN

Proverbs 11:13 (NLT)

A gossip goes around revealing secrets, but those who are trustworthy can keep a confidence.

Are you the person people go to with personal problems or when they have the need to discuss something confidential? We all know people to talk to if we want the news to travel around. We also know individuals who will keep a secret and keep things confidential. God expects us to be trustworthy. If we can't be trusted with people's secrets, how can He trust us with His? God has secrets He is willing to reveal to those who love Him. However, He won't reveal them to someone who is not mature enough to handle them.

We should be like a vault! When someone confides personal information to you, respect that person and keep the information confidential. Be trustworthy. For example, when management discusses confidential matters about the company to you, don't be the one who leaks the information to the rest of the staff or the public.

When you are a trustworthy woman, people will hold you in high esteem and God will reward you with His secrets.

BE A WOMAN OF YOUR WORD

Numbers 30:2 (KJV)

If a man vow a vow unto the Lord, or swear an oath to bind his soul with a bond; he shall not break his word, he shall do according to all that proceedeth out of his mouth.

God expects us to be women of commitment. God is a God of commitment, is faithful to His Word, and always delivers what He promises. In our culture, we have become used to making promises and not keeping them. We have learned to treat our word casually and lack of follow-through has become normal. If we, as Christians, are to imitate Jesus in all we do, fulfilling our commitments and promises is essential to our success.

Fulfill your promises—every one of them—and follow through in all your commitments. Be a woman of your word. This is a serious matter to God, and you must make the necessary changes to follow His example. Being a person of your word may be the only witness of Jesus some people will ever see.

BE HONEST AND FRANK BUT LOVING

Proverbs 28:23 (NLT)

In the end, people appreciate frankness more than flattery.

Often people ask our opinion about various things. Are you honest on your answer, or are you afraid of hurting their feelings and hide your true opinion? We need to be honest when people ask us our opinion or feedback about something. There is a way to communicate honestly without being rude or unprofessional. We need to discern the situation and take into consideration who is around at the time we are asked, if it's a personal or professional matter, and who the person asking us is. If it is your best friend and they are seeking your opinion, feedback, or advice, tell them the truth as you see it in a loving way. If it is a co-worker who needs your opinion on a work related matter, give your opinion in an objective, professional way. Sometimes you may need to clarify and tell them up front to not take what you say personally.

If your spouse or child asks you for feedback, you need to tell them the truth, always in a loving way. You have the power to destroy or build your family members with your words. Therefore, use those opportunities to build them up. You can correct them in a loving way while being frank and honest. In the end, everybody appreciates the truth, whether they admit it or not.

BE HUMBLE, GENTLE, AND PATIENT

Ephesians 4:1-2 (NLT)

Therefore I, a prisoner for serving the Lord, beg you to lead a life worthy of your calling, for you have been called by God. Be humble and gentle. Be patient with each other, making allowance for each other's faults because of your love.

In this verse Paul is writing to the church of Ephesus, and he is begging them to live a life worthy of their calling. We are all called to serve Him in a special way. But in order for us to walk in the will of God, in our calling, we must be humble, gentle, and patient with one another. These are rare character traits in the business community and the workplace. God cannot use us if we are proud because in our pride we become deceived, rude, and impatient. Gentleness is another rarity these days. People don't treat each other gently, but abruptly. Our lives have become so busy we don't have patience to wait for anything, help somebody in need, or just love people.

Have you realized that you have been called by God? I encourage you to strive to be a humble, gentle, and patient woman so God can use you to the fullest.

BEING A LEADER IS A SERIOUS RESPONSIBILITY

Romans 12:6-8 (NLT)

God has given each of us the ability to do certain things well... If God has given you leadership ability, take the responsibility seriously.

If you read verses 6 through 8 of Romans 12, you will see a variety of gifts the Lord can give people. Part of being successful is to know yourself well and know what gifts and talents you have been given. If you know you have the gift of leadership, take the responsibility of the gift seriously because you will be leading people. When you are a manager, supervisor, business owner, team leader, church lay leader, or community leader, you have a big duty. It doesn't matter what your role is; what matters is that you do it from your heart and follow the example of Jesus as a leader in every way.

Don't get impatient with God when He gives you small leadership roles. These serve as preparation for future bigger roles.

31

BUILD A GOOD REPUTATION

Ecclesiastes 7:1 (NLT)

*A good reputation is more valuable than
the most expensive perfume.*

What is reputation? It is the general estimation in which a person is held. It is how a person is thought of by others and when a person is held in high esteem. Reputation is a specific characteristic or trait ascribed (attributed, credited) to a person or thing (paraphrasing from *The American Heritage Dictionary*).

Reputation can be good or bad. It is the product of your actions, a reflection of your character, a trait you develop over time ascribed to you. You and your reputation go together. Fortunately or unfortunately, reputation travels before you. Once created, people talk about you as a person of good or bad reputation. Furthermore, once a bad reputation is formed about you, it is very difficult to reverse it.

How do you create and keep a good reputation? Consistency is the key. It is by consistently being a person of character, honesty, and truthfulness, and by having an unchangeable core belief system founded on the Rock (Jesus). It is by being *you* in all circumstances. It is by acting the same at home, at work, or in a public place, with friends and strangers. It is by treating people with respect and dignity when you are alone with them and when you are in public. It is by being transparent and not having a hidden agenda. It is by not compromising your beliefs and your personal ethical standards.

When you base your life on the Word of God, believe what it says, and do the Word, you create a good reputation for yourself. As a Christian, you also have the responsibility to represent Jesus and give Christianity a good reputation. As His representative, you are accountable to God to bring people to Him because of your life example.

32

CHANGE FROM YOUR HEART AND PRODUCE GOOD FRUIT

Matthew 3:8

Let your lives then prove your change of heart (Weymouth).

Prove by the way you live that you have really turned from your sins and turned to God (NLT).

John the Baptist said those words to the Pharisees and Sadducees when they came to him to be baptized because they were doing the baptism as a religious act instead of being baptized with a repentant heart.

God knows our hearts and motives. When we accept Christ in our lives, we shouldn't have to say anything for others to notice we have changed. Our lives should reflect our change of heart. Our friends and relatives should see a change in how we behave in every area of our lives. It doesn't matter what we say; in the end they won't believe us until they see a change in our lifestyle.

As followers of Jesus Christ, we are to produce not just any fruit or bad fruit but *good* fruit. Producing good fruit is our responsibility. Verse 10 states, "already the ax is lying at the root of the trees, so that every tree which does not yield good fruit is hewn down and thrown into the fire." If we don't produce good fruit then, like those trees, we will be cut off and thrown into the fire. If we are not producing good fruit, it means we really didn't make the decision to follow Christ from our hearts to begin with. Therefore, let's change from the heart and produce good fruit.

CHOOSE THE NARROW GATE

Matthew 7:13-14 (NKJV)

Enter by the narrow gate; for wide is the gate and broad is the way that leads to destruction, and there are many who go in by it. Because narrow is the gate and difficult is the way which leads to life, and there are few who find it.

There are three important points in these verses. First of all, it is our choice to go through the narrow gate or the wide gate during our earthly lives. It is a daily decision we have to make that starts the day we are born again—the day we chose to follow Christ.

Secondly, there are many ways to choose on the broad gate, and all of those ways lead to destruction (the highway to hell). On the other hand, when we choose Christ, there is only one way—the narrow gate—Jesus. He is the only way that will lead us to life. When we choose to follow Him and live our lives His way, we are walking on the narrow road and through the narrow gate.

The third point is that not everybody finds the narrow gate. We have to seek it diligently and from our hearts. God promises that if we seek, we shall find. Therefore, if we seek the narrow gate, we will find Jesus, and He will lead us through it. It is narrow, meaning there is no room for sin, and it is difficult because our flesh wants to go through the wide gate. But with Jesus by our side and as our leader, we will walk the narrow path until we reach our destination of eternal life with Him.

CONTROL YOUR TONGUE AND LIVE A LONG LIFE

Proverbs 13:3 (NLT)

Those who control their tongue will have a long life; a quick report can ruin everything.

The Bible warns us in many places to control our tongue and what we say. The tongue is a very small organ but it is extremely powerful. It can build or destroy other people or even ourselves. Proverbs 11:9 (NLT) says, "Evil words destroy one's friends; wise discernment rescues the godly." It is wise to control our tongue. It is foolish not to. We may have experienced situations where we were wise and kept silent about an issue, then found out we were wrong in our thinking and would have made a mistake by speaking too soon. Other times, we may have spoken too soon and ruined relationships, only to find out later we were wrong or had wrong information. It is hard to repair relationships once they have been broken by evil, hurtful words.

Let's hang on to the promise of having long life by learning to control our tongue. One way we can achieve that is by learning to control our temper. Usually these two go hand-in-hand. People with a quick, uncontrolled temper are the ones who are quick to judge and speak out hurtful words.

If this is a weak area in your life, ask God to help you gain control of your temper and your tongue. Ask Him to help you find opportunities to use your tongue to build people up instead of to destroy them. I can assure you He will give you those opportunities right away—your workplace may be the first. Beware, however, of the enemy's ways. The moment he knows you want to turn around and make a change for the good, he will send you opportunities to fail—the workplace again is the perfect place to fail in this area. But don't be discouraged because once you ask God to help you, He will give you the wisdom to discern situations and the strength to do the right thing to control your mouth.

35

DEVELOP A GODLY CHARACTER

Psalm 89:8, 14 (NLT)

...Faithfulness is your very character...Your throne is founded on two strong pillars—righteousness and justice. Unfailing love and truth walk before you as attendants.

This psalm describes the character of God. We, as His children, are to imitate Him and develop these vital character traits in our lives: faithfulness, righteousness, justice, love, and truth. We must remember He is all of these virtues. Each one is the very person of God and, at the same time, He is each one of those toward us.

We are to be known for our godly character. The only way to develop those character traits is by spending time with God. The more we seek Him, the more we get to know His person and character. The more we know Him, the more we will want to imitate His character.

If you find yourself in a situation at work or home where you think there is no way out, remember to seek God for who He is first and everything you need—including His character traits and virtues—will be given to you. He loves you and will always be faithful to you.

DISHONESTY IS DETESTABLE TO THE LORD

Deuteronomy 25:13-14 (NLT)

You must use accurate scales when you weigh out merchandise, and you must use full and honest measures.

God gave the command above to the Israelites through Moses. But this also applies to our business conduct today. Honesty is a rare character trait these days and, unfortunately, even Christians have the reputation of not being honest. We, as representatives of Christ on earth, have the responsibility to conduct business in an honest way. It doesn't matter if we are in the retail business, wholesale, services, health care, restaurant, or any other type of business. Verse 15 states, "Yes, use honest weights and measures, so that you will enjoy a long life in the land the Lord your God is giving you." It is extremely important to the Lord we obey in this area as "those who cheat with dishonest weights and measures are detestable to the Lord your God" (v. 16).

Purpose to be honest in everything you do. For example, if you are filling out your time card and write eight hours worked when you only worked seven, that is dishonesty. It is also important to fulfill your commitments with everybody—including Christian brothers and sisters. If they work for you, pay them what you agreed. If you work for them, deliver what you agreed on.

You will have opportunities daily to be, or do, something dishonest. Don't fall in that trap so you can obtain the promise of long life.

Do a Good Job While You Are Here

Ecclesiastes 9:10 (NLT)

Whatever you do, do well. For when you go to the grave, there will be no work or planning or knowledge or wisdom.

God has blessed each one of us with different and unique gifts and talents. It is our responsibility to develop and use those gifts and talents to the best of our ability. Therefore, we must educate ourselves, expand our knowledge, and improve those gifts to become skilled individuals.

Whatever you do, do it with excellence and from your heart. Become a diligent, honest, hard working woman, and you will be successful. Remember, your time on earth is short and is preparation for your eternal calling. Therefore, do a good job while you're here. When you do your part and trust God with your life, He will do the rest and bless you by using you for His purposes.

Do People View You as a Godly Leader?

Proverbs 29:2 (NLT)

When the godly are in authority, the people rejoice. But when the wicked are in power, they groan.

If you are in any type of leadership position, either at work, at church, or any other volunteer position, do people rejoice when they know you are in authority? Does your character reflect that you are a godly leader?

The people in authority over you have a tremendous influence in your life. The same way, when you are the leader, you influence those under you and have great power over their lives. What are you imparting to the employees or volunteers who are under your leadership? Are you exercising your authority in a godly way?

When you are a godly leader, you can build a godly team of people because you will impart in them your character. A godly team can accomplish much when they work together, but it all starts with you as the person in authority.

DO WHAT'S RIGHT AND YOU WILL SEE HIS FACE

Psalm 11:7 (NLT)

For the Lord is righteous, and he loves justice. Those who do what is right will see his face.

In the business world you will often witness injustice. You may experience injustice towards you or witness injustice towards others. You can't control what others do, but you can control what you do and the decisions you make. Always do what is right, regardless of the outcome. God is a just God and you are to follow His example. It is His promise that if you do what's right, you will see His face. What an awesome promise that is! When you are faced with a difficult decision, ask God for wisdom. He will give you the "just" answer, and you will know the right thing to do.

Do You Possess the Qualities of Discretion and Prudence?

Proverbs 11:22 (NLT)

A woman who is beautiful but lacks discretion is like a gold ring in a pig's snout.

Proverbs 5:1-2 (NLT)

My son, pay attention to my wisdom; listen carefully to my wise counsel. Then you will learn to be discreet and will store up knowledge.

Have you ever wondered why some women who look, on the outside, all put together, are beautiful and work hard, yet are not successful? One reason is that they lack discretion. Discretion, according to *The American Heritage Dictionary*, means being discreet and prudent, having good judgment and common sense, and being cautions.

Wow! When I researched what the word discretion meant, that is what I found out. God's words are precise and rich in meaning. Do you know how to become a discreet, prudent woman? By getting God's wisdom. When you acquire His wisdom, you learn to discern every situation you encounter and act discreetly and with prudence.

Also notice this verse says a woman who has discretion is like a gold ring. I believe this means you can become very valuable as a person when you have discretion and prudence. Therefore, ask God for wisdom so you can acquire these two precious qualities.

DON'T BE OF A DOUBTFUL MIND

James 1:6 (NLT)

But when you ask him, be sure that you really expect him to answer, for a doubtful mind is as unsettled as a wave of the sea that is driven and tossed by the wind.

The verse above tells us we have to ask in faith and really believe and expect God to respond. Once we hear His answer, we then trust it is what He wants us to do.

An indecisive person creates frustration to those around them. If you are a manager, you will be faced with many decisions to make on a daily basis. You must learn to make quick decisions with the information you have at that moment. Once you make your decision you must feel comfortable with it and take responsibility for the consequences—good or bad.

Always do what's right when making decisions. When you have the peace of God, you can be sure you've made the right one.

DON'T CRITICIZE EACH OTHER

James 4:11 (NLT)

Don't speak evil against each other, my dear brothers and sisters. If you criticize each other and condemn each other, then you are criticizing and condemning God's law. But you are not a judge who can decide whether the law is right or wrong. Your job is to obey it.

The office environment is the perfect field to criticize other people. You will find countless things to criticize about your boss, company owners, co-workers, and employees, and if you don't watch it, your mouth will get out of control.

When we criticize other people, we are judging them. The Bible says that when we criticize and judge others, we are condemning God's law and only He has the right to do that. Condemning God's law means that only He can judge people's actions because He knows their hearts and whether the law is right or wrong. Our job is to obey God's law and not judge others. If you want to be a positive influence in your office, stay away from criticism.

DON'T FORGET TO GIVE A GENTLE ANSWER

Proverbs 15:1 (NLT)

A gentle answer turns away wrath, but harsh words stir up anger.

Proverbs 16:24 (NLT)

Kind words are like honey—sweet to the soul and healthy for the body.

With all of the daily pressures and stresses of the workplace, circumstances arise when it is very easy to get upset or lose our temper with co-workers, customers, supervisors, or vendors. Nevertheless, we can use those situations as great opportunities to exercise our love walk and practice a Christ-like attitude. There are things we can do to control our temper and avoid saying things we will later regret. We can try counting to ten (or one hundred if we need to). We can also leave the room for a moment to gather our thoughts. Finally, let's not forget to use the advice God gives us in His Word.

The next time someone upsets you at work remember this passage from Proverbs. It works. A gentle answer from you destroys the enemy's weapon of anger, strive, and division. The Word of God is your manual for success. This includes success in the workplace.

DON'T PLAY FAVORITES

James 2:1 (NLT)

My dear brothers and sisters, how can you claim that you have faith in our glorious Lord Jesus Christ if you favor some people more than others?

Favoritism is something that always creates anger, jealousy, and resentment amongst employees in the workplace. When you are the one being favored, you initially feel flattered, but then you start feeling guilty and alone. You can lose friendships and eventually your co-workers' trust because of the unfair treatment. They may end up thinking you got where you are only because it (the job, position, title, etc.) was handed off to you. They don't trust your capabilities anymore.

When someone else is being favored over you, you can start feeling jealous or feel resentment toward that other person. This attitude can then start affecting your own performance. If you are the boss favoring a particular person, you will eventually self-destruct your own team.

Treat all your clients the same way no matter how much business they bring to your company. Treat all your employees and co-workers the same no matter what their positions are or what they do for you or the company. At home, if you have children, treat them all the same so they grow up loving each other, creating great memories, and respecting you as a fair mother.

Favoritism brings negative results any way we look at it because it hurts people. We are to treat everybody the same. God is the only one who can play favorites because He has the ability to make each one of us feel like His favorite child—all the time.

45

DON'T PRETEND TO BE GOOD... JUST BE

1 Peter 2:1 (NLT)

So get rid of all malicious behavior and deceit.
Don't just pretend to be good! Be done with hypocrisy and jealousy
and backstabbing.

Hypocrisy, jealousy, and backstabbing are common in the workplace. You need to guard your heart against those behaviors as they are signs of spiritual immaturity. You are to strive to be honest, sincere, truthful, and of a pure heart. For example, instead of pretending to like a co-worker and then backstabbing him or her, make the effort to really get to know that person. Then you can avoid hypocrisy from entering into your heart. The same way, it is hypocritical to pretend to embrace what the leadership of your company is doing and then criticize everything they say or do.

Instead of getting jealous of what other people have, thank God for what you have and for what He's done for you. When you focus on Him, you will have a grateful heart. When you spend time with the Lord, you become more like Him—genuine, transparent, and honest. There will be no room in your heart for hypocrisy, jealousy, or backstabbing.

DON'T BE A LAZY EMPLOYEE

Proverbs 10:26 (NLT)

Lazy people are a pain to their employer. They are like smoke in the eyes or vinegar that sets the teeth on edge.

Companies look for hard-working employees. They look for people who take the initiative to create change, improve processes, and are not afraid of learning new things. Unfortunately, many Christian employees don't rise up to the challenge all the time. There are many non-Christian workers that have more initiative and a much better attitude toward innovation and change than Christians do.

Jesus is our example of how we are to behave in every area, including as employees or workers. If we are God's workers here on earth and we are to do our jobs as unto the Lord, then we must follow Jesus' example of being a person of initiative, hard work, and creator of change. Jesus changed everything during His years on earth and changed the destiny of mankind forever.

As a manager, having lazy employees is a pain. It feels like having a thorn on your side that you don't know how to take out. Lazy people are usually nice, but they are unmotivated to improve. They don't want to rock the boat, create any waves, or make things difficult because that would take them out of their comfort zone. Even though this verse refers to lazy employees, laziness is also reflected in other areas of a person's life. If we are lazy in the spirit, we will never grow spiritually. If we are lazy in the flesh, we will not be healthy and it's going to show in our bodies, our temples. If we are lazy as a housekeeper, our homes will be a disaster.

Just as companies look for non-lazy, hard-working people, so does God. He needs people to work hard and help Him get the Gospel to the world so His plan can be accomplished.

Don't Be a People Pleaser

Galatians 1:10 (NLT)

Obviously, I'm not trying to be a people pleaser! No, I am trying to please God. If I were still trying to please people, I would not be Christ's servant.

We cannot be people pleasers and be Christ's servants at the same time. We will continually be in conflict between what the world says and what is right and true. The Apostle Paul warns us of preachers who twist the Gospel just to please people and grow their churches when he says to the Galatians "you are being fooled by those who twist and change the truth concerning Christ" (v. 7). As Christians, it is our responsibility to know the scriptures for ourselves. We need to read and study the Word on our own.

In the workplace, we have many opportunities to be people pleasers. For example, investors want to hear your company is doing great and the stock price is going up. Well, if that's not the case, don't cook the books. Tell the truth.

Many companies could have been saved and many people would not have gone to jail or lost their jobs if company leaders would have told the truth. If you know something is not right at work, you need to tell the truth. Nowadays, even though senior management and board members are ultimately responsible, anybody who has any knowledge of anything illegal may be held personally responsible as well. When you tell the truth and don't compromise your integrity, God promises He will vindicate you and protect your reputation. Therefore, don't be a people pleaser and please God only.

48

DON'T BE AFRAID TO TELL THE TRUTH

Proverbs 17:7 (NLT)

Eloquent speech is not fitting for a fool;
even less are lies fitting for a ruler.

When we are wise, our speech is eloquent, our thoughts are well prepared, and we make an impression on people. The Bible tells us this is not a characteristic of fools. But more importantly is the second part of that verse, "even less are lies fitting for a ruler." Just as incompatible as eloquent speech and a fool are, telling lies is worse for a leader.

It is imperative that leaders in business do not tell lies. They must stick to the truth always and do what is right. This is the very reason so many companies in America are falling apart—because somebody lied. It is *not* okay to exaggerate sales reports, total revenues, or hide important information from customers, shareholders, or employees. In the end, the truth invariably comes out to the surface, and then it's too late to stop the damage done to other people.

Many companies are under investigation these days. If you are ever questioned, tell the truth. Proverbs 12:17 (NLT) says, "An honest witness tells the truth; a false witness tells lies." Proverbs 13:5 (NLT) tells us "those who are godly hate lies; the wicked come to shame and disgrace."

No matter what position you hold at a company, it is important for you to always tell the truth, no matter the outcome. If you are in any leadership position, you must realize that your decisions (and lies) will have a tremendous effect on the people that work for you, your company, and ultimately you and your family.

Don't be afraid to tell the truth because God will always be with you and protect you.

DON'T BELIEVE EVERY STORY YOU HEAR

Proverbs 18:17 (NLT)

Any story sounds true until someone sets the record straight.

In the office we hear stories all the time; some are good and some are bad. But how do we determine which ones are true and which ones are a lie? There are individuals whose specialty in the office is to spread news—all the news (good, bad, true, or lies). They like to be known as the one who is in the know, in the loop of things.

Be careful not to become that person yourself. And beware of those people. Stay away as much as possible, and never disclose something personal you don't want everybody else to know about. The first step in discerning the truthfulness of a story is to consider the source. If it is the type of person described above, question the story and disregard it. There are other stories that are true but are about somebody else's personal life. That is gossip. Stay away from gossip. It will destroy the person who is being talked about, the one sharing it, and ultimately you, the listener.

You may choose to challenge that individual by saying that those are personal things or issues that should not be discussed in the office, or you may choose to simply not participate in the grapevine. Soon, people will notice your lack of participation in that destructive behavior and will respect you more. There will be others, however, that will reject you for that very reason. That is okay. You don't need that relationship. Proverbs 20:19 (NLT) says, "A gossip tells secrets, so don't hang around with someone who talks too much."

As a Christian woman in the workplace, you need to be bold and set the record straight. It takes a lot of courage to stand up for what is right, but God will be with you every step of the way.

DON'T COMPROMISE WITH THE WORLD

Proverbs 25:26 (NLT)

*If the godly compromise with the wicked, it is like polluting a
fountain or muddying a spring.*

If you have accepted Christ in your heart, you are a godly person. Of course, becoming more and more like Jesus is a lifetime process. We have His example on how to live a godly life. Being godly is simply separating ourselves from the world. We are either worldly or godly. We can't be both. We usually start worldly and little by little become godly as we follow Christ. Unfortunately, we can go backwards in our walk with God as well. When we distance ourselves from Him by choosing worldly things and making worldly decisions, we are compromising our godly standards.

The Bible tells us that every time we compromise with the wicked, we are polluting the clean water that should flow out of us. When we compromise our beliefs with the world, our water becomes dirty and that is what will flow out of us unto others. God cleanses us. The world pollutes us. We are to be like a river with flowing water. But we have to choose to have clean water by aligning our lives with the Word of God. Then His Word flows like a mighty river through us. The life of God is in us. This water flows from our hearts, the inner part of our being, and its purpose is to bring life to all of those around us.

How do you keep yourself, your heart, clean and unpolluted? Simple—don't compromise with the world's system. In the workplace, you will need to make the choice almost on a daily basis—do you compromise or not? Learn and believe the Word of God, and then stand firm on it and don't compromise.

DON'T RUSH TO BE THE FIRST!

Mark 9:35 (NLT)

He sat down and called the twelve disciples over to him. Then he said, "Anyone who wants to be the first must take last place and be the servant of everyone else."

The disciples were arguing amongst themselves about which of them was the greatest. When Jesus asked what they were talking about, they did not answer. Then Jesus explained to them that in the Kingdom of God it is different than the world. When we are first and the greatest here on earth, the world gives us instant gratification, recognition, and fame. The world also expects people to serve all of those in high earthly places. In the Kingdom of God, it is the opposite—the higher you are in leadership, the more you have to serve others. The best example we have, of course, is Jesus Himself. He, who is the Son of God and King of kings, came here to serve us. The ultimate act of service He did for us was to die on the cross for our sins so we can be forgiven and restored to the Father.

Remember how Jesus served the people whenever you are promoted to higher positions of leadership. Yes, you can be a successful leader in an organization and have people serve you in the office. Yet you can still be a servant to all of those under you by genuinely caring for them. How do you serve them? By praying for them, treating them with dignity and respect, and giving everybody a chance to succeed.

Our goal should be to follow Jesus' example of leadership and service so we can get our reward when we get to heaven.

FOLLOW THE PEACE FROM YOUR HEART

Colossians 3:15 (NLT)

And let the peace that comes from Christ rule in your hearts.

Whenever you have to make a big decision in life, first ask God for wisdom and discernment, and then follow what gives you peace in your heart. You can follow this pattern both at work and at home. It always works because God is a God of peace.

If you have children and one of them asks you to do something you don't have peace about, simply say no and tell them why. If a decision is about to be made at work that will affect other people (employees or customers) and you don't have peace about it, state your concerns to the appropriate parties (your manager or project team, for example) and reasons why you disagree. Of course, in a work situation, you will have to do your homework and research before just saying, "I don't have peace" about something. Many times the Holy Spirit communicates in subtle ways and lack of peace about a particular situation is one of them.

Follow the peace in your heart and also be at peace with the people around you. The rest of this verse says, "For as members of one body you are called to live in peace. And always be thankful." When you have peace in your heart, it will be easy to be at peace with others.

GIVE GOD CONTROL OF YOUR MOUTH

Psalm 141:3

Take control of what I say, O Lord, and keep my lips sealed (NLT).

Set a guard, O Lord, over my mouth; keep watch over the door of my lips (NKJV).

The mouth is a small part of the body, yet it has the power to build or destroy other people as well as our own lives. We need to be aware of what we say about ourselves, about circumstances, and about God. Many times we offend God, and He hurts. Every time we speak doubt in any area of our lives, we hurt Him. With our doubts, fear, and lack of faith, we are sending Him the message that what Jesus did was not enough. Every time we reject His gifts of salvation, healing, grace, favor, peace, etc. we are telling Him that Jesus went to the cross for nothing.

The workplace is an environment where it is easy to lose control of your mouth because there are so many opportunities to offend others and get offended. Therefore, be aware of what you say at all times, and give God control of your mouth.

GOD CARES FOR THE HUMBLE

Psalm 138:6 (NLT)

Though the Lord is great, he cares for the humble, but he keeps his distance from the proud.

Repeatedly in the Bible, we read that God rebukes the proud and always cares for the humble. He stays away from proud people because His very nature rebukes it. Pride in our hearts is the one thing God will not work with. "Pride leads to disgrace, but with humility comes wisdom" (Proverbs 11:2 NLT). When we have a humble heart, the Lord will entrust us not only with natural riches but with His true treasures from heaven—such as wisdom. When we are humble, He can pour out His wisdom in us because He knows we will not abuse it. When we use both material and spiritual riches for His purposes, He blesses us even more.

Whatever you do in your working life, always guard your heart from pride. Purpose to stay humble by continually remembering what He did for you and by always thanking Him for everything you have and are. Remember, God cares for the humble.

55

GOD DELIGHTS IN THOSE WHO HAVE INTEGRITY

Proverbs 11:20 (NLT)

The Lord hates people with twisted hearts, but he delights in those who have integrity.

God is looking for people with a pure heart, with no hidden agendas, just a humble heart that loves Him. Yet people with twisted hearts are what we find most these days. They not only have a hidden motive with their relationships with other people, but with God as well. There are many churches that are, unfortunately, teaching people to give to God with the main motive to get back His blessings and benefits. This is not true love for God. True love is how He loves us, unconditionally and without expecting anything in return. He only expects us to love Him back, yet even then we have the choice. We are to love God for who He is, not for what He can do for us and definitely not for all the material blessings He can provide.

Our motives to give to His Kingdom should be simple—just give from the heart. First of all, we should give Him our hearts, then give out of our material resources, our time, our labor, and our gifts.

A person of integrity cannot have a twisted heart because integrity goes against lying, dishonesty, and untruthfulness—traits that are becoming rare in the workplace. God delights in those with integrity. He takes pleasure in them because it brings Him honor and glory. Then, as our good Father, He blesses us.

When we seek God first, our hearts become pure and whole. Our goal should be to become women of integrity so God can delight in us and we can be an example to other women in the workplace. Only then will we experience His true blessings.

GOD HAS CALLED US TO BE HOLY

I Thessalonians 4:7 (NLT)

God has called us to be holy, not to live impure lives.

We are to live our lives in a way that pleases God and, therefore, need to guard our hearts from impurity.

In the workplace, it is common to have improper relationships. If you are married, you must be careful to always protect your marriage and take proper precautions. You are human and sometimes there will be other men you may be attracted to. You must keep your distance and not develop close relationships with them. Affairs can happen to anybody if you allow thoughts and circumstances to take place. Avoid temptation and the wrong appearance by not going out alone on social events with other men.

If you are a single woman, you are to avoid having sexual relationships before you are married. This behavior will open a door for the enemy to come and destroy your life. "God wants you to be holy, so you should keep clear of all sexual sin. Then each of you will control your body and live in holiness and honor—not in lustful passion as the pagans do, in their ignorance of God and his ways" (I Thessalonians 4:3-5 NLT).

Don't forget God has called us to be holy, and this is a daily fight we can only win with His help.

GOD WANTS US TO SPEAK THE TRUTH— ALWAYS

Psalm 15:1-2 (NLT)

Who may worship in your sanctuary, Lord?
Who may enter your presence on your holy hill?

Those who lead blameless lives and do what is right,
speaking the truth from sincere hearts.

In today's business world telling lies is an everyday occurrence— from the advertisements that promise things about products that are not true to businesses exaggerating the truth about their revenues and product sales.

Part of doing what is always right is telling the truth always— not only when it's convenient, but also when it's difficult. We all have opportunities to tell the truth or to tell a lie. We must be careful to not shade the truth or exaggerate it. This is the same as lying. The Bible says, "The truth will set you free" (John 8:32 NLT). We must not be afraid of telling the truth, for it is a promise of God that if we do what is right and speak the truth from sincere hearts, we will worship in His sanctuary and be in His presence.

Remember this promise the next time you are faced with telling the truth or not.

GOD'S WILL FOR YOU IS NOT THE WORLD'S

Romans 12:2 (NLT)

Don't copy the behavior and customs of this world, but let God transform you into a new person by changing the way you think. Then you will know what God wants you to do, and you will know how good and pleasing and perfect his will really is.

Part of doing what's right consistently is to not follow what the world does and to not do what everybody else does. Copying the behavior of the world is a trap of the enemy to make you compromise.

In the workplace, it is easy to go with the flow and not stand up for what you believe is right. Allow God to change you from the inside out. Let Him change your mind and your heart. People will notice you are a person of character—confident and solid. When He renews your mind, you will know what He wants you to do in every situation. He has a perfect will for your life. He will reveal it to you when you allow Him to change you. How does He change you? By spending time with Him in His presence and reading and meditating on His Word daily.

GUARD YOUR HEART AND YOUR MOUTH

Proverbs 4:23-24 (NLT)

*Above all else, guard your heart, for it affects everything you do.
Avoid all perverse talk; stay away from corrupt speech.*

Proverbs 2:12 (NLT)

*Wisdom will save you from evil people,
from those whose speech is corrupt.*

Proverbs 16:28 (NLT)

*A troublemaker plants seeds of strife; gossip separates
the best of friends.*

When working with others, regardless of the company or type of work you do, you will encounter numerous opportunities to gossip. Gossip can be as dangerous as spreading rumors about others, or as seemingly innocent as talking about another person behind her back (even if the information is true).

Turn and run from this trap. Gossip is destructive, and it will open a door to the enemy in your life. Even if you only listen to gossip, you are still enabling this negative influence to affect your heart. Eventually, what's in your heart will come out of your mouth. So instead, speak and believe the best of all people, avoid gossip, and walk in love.

HAVE A GENEROUS HEART

Philemon 1:6 (NLT)

You are generous because of your faith. And I am praying that you will really put your generosity to work, for in so doing you will come to an understanding of all the good things we can do for Christ.

In this letter, Paul was asking Philemon to receive back a slave who had stolen from him and left. The slave then went to prison, got saved, and now was sent back by Paul.

When we become a Christian, we become generous. In order to serve God we must be generous with others, for it is through generosity they can see God. Generosity covers every area of our lives. Usually we associate generosity with finances, but we must also be generous with our time and our deeds. We are generous when we help our friends, help others succeed at their work, encourage people to better themselves, and when we pray for others. These are examples of how we can show generosity toward others.

When we have an understanding of how much we can do for Christ, we will want to be generous all the time, toward everybody, and in every way we can.

HONESTY IN BUSINESS IS CRUCIAL

Matthew 5:37 (NLT)

Just say a simple, "Yes, I will," or "No, I won't." Your word is enough. To strengthen your promise with a vow shows that something is wrong.

Psalm 51:6 (NLT)

But you desire honesty from the heart, so you can teach me to be wise in my inmost being.

Christians should be known by their honesty. Not only is honesty a character trait of Jesus, it is a universal value we are commanded by God to possess and uphold. Therefore, we must seek to be honest from our hearts, not just our lips.

When doing business, whether you are a manager, a vendor, or someone's customer, you must always exercise honesty. Your colleagues and customers should never have to question your word or your commitment.

The best way to establish clear and honest communication is to say what you mean. Make a decision or a commitment, then follow through no matter what. In other words, stick with what you say and say what you mean—always. Be *consistently* honest in everything you do. This helps you become a better witness for Christ, and you may be the only witness of Jesus some of your colleagues ever see.

62

HOW DO WE BECOME HUMBLE?

Matthew 18:4 (NLT)

Therefore, anyone who becomes as humble as this little child is the greatest in the Kingdom of Heaven.

That is what Jesus told His disciples when they asked Him which one of them would be the greatest in His Kingdom. Because of our human tendency to compete with others in everything, we have to watch and guard our hearts at all times.

Many Christians compete with one another to see who is more spiritual. They compare how involved they are with their church or ministry or how many times they attend services versus other people. This behavior makes their Christian life become a works program instead of being an example of Christianity.

In the workplace, no matter what position you hold at a company, you need to be humble and recognize God gave you that position to begin with. He is looking for humble hearts willing to do His will. You can influence more people when you are humble instead of proud. Pride repels God and the people around you.

The main thing we have to recognize is that alone we can do nothing, but with God we can do all things.

63

HUMBLE YOURSELF BEFORE GOD

James 4:6-7 (NLT)

"God sets himself against the proud, but he shows favor to the humble." So humble yourselves before God. Resist the Devil, and he will flee from you.

When we humble ourselves before God, we are recognizing our sinful nature and that we can do nothing without Him. He cannot work with pride because pride takes you away from Him. Humility, on the other hand, brings us closer to God. Therefore, we must be humble and seek God with all our might. Verse 8 says, "Draw close to God, and God will draw close to you."

We are also to resist the Devil and he will flee from us. God gives us grace to fight and resist the Devil. This includes fighting and resisting him so pride doesn't enter our hearts. How do we stay humble? "When you bow down before the Lord and admit your dependence on him, he will lift you up and give you honor" (v. 10).

No matter what position you hold at your work, don't let pride enter into your heart. Stay humble so God can always use you.

INTEGRITY—THE KEY TO REMAIN IN THE LAND

Proverbs 2:20-21 (NLT)

Follow the steps of good men instead, and stay on the path of the righteous. For only the upright will live in the land, and those who have integrity will remain in it.

In our lives, we know some individuals we admire and some we hope we never turn out to be like them. The Bible instructs us to follow the steps of good men, to use them as our example. If you don't have such a person in your life right now, ask God to send you one, someone you can trust and follow his or her steps.

The Bible also tells us to stay on the path of the righteous because only they will live in the land. The land represents the place God has promised us, the Promised Land we get to enjoy here on earth when we obey Him.

Notice also that only those who have integrity will remain in the land. Some people will see the land but won't enter it, like Moses. Others will visit the land but won't be able to stay. Only a few will stay and remain in the land—those who have integrity.

Being a person of integrity these days is uncommon. Men and women compromise their beliefs frequently for fear of being rejected. Not compromising, but rather standing for what you know is right, is part of carrying your cross and being a Christian. If you are consistent and don't give in to the world, you will be noticed and your reputation will be that of a person of integrity. People will respect you, and you will become a good woman whose steps others will want to follow.

Be a person of integrity always, in every situation, and in every area of your life so you can be an example to others.

IT IS WORTH IT TO BE A PERSON OF INTEGRITY

Psalm 18:25-26 (NLT)

To the faithful you show yourself faithful; to those with integrity you show integrity. To the pure you show yourself pure, but to the wicked you show yourself hostile.

Sometimes we wonder if it's worth it to be faithful to God, to be people of integrity, and to have a pure heart. We see the wicked obtain victory after victory and enjoy all the benefits this world has to offer. We see corrupted people become successful in the corporate world. We see people who don't love God become influential and powerful. We almost envy them and want to give up our sacrificial lifestyle. But we must not give up.

It is a promise of God that He is faithful to those who are faithful to Him and are committed to living a godly life. Being a person of integrity does pay off in the long run—even here in the world. The truth always comes out in the end, and all those people who don't have morals or integrity in business eventually fall. It is only a matter of time. They will only get to enjoy their worldly success and fame for a short season. Besides, what is this life compared to eternity? It's nothing but a vapor! It is just a brief moment in our eternal existence.

The wicked are the ones that reject God and His Son Jesus. They have a destiny too and it is not heaven; it is hell—eternal damnation and separation from God.

How you live this life and the decisions you make here will determine your eternal destiny. There is one major decision that I hope you will make in your life time. That decision is to become a follower of Jesus Christ—the one and only that will take you to the Father. Giving your life to Him will ensure your salvation and your eternal destiny with Him.

Keep a Quiet Spirit

Ecclesiastes 10:4 (NLT)

If your boss is angry with you, don't quit! A quiet spirit can overcome even great mistakes.

During your working life you will probably make mistakes along the way. Some of those mistakes will make your boss become angry with you. He or she may correct you and give you a list of consequences for your mistake. Everything you do has consequences, and without correction you cannot improve your performance.

However, there is an appropriate way of giving and receiving correction. If you have a boss that respects you as a person and treats you with dignity, when he or she corrects you for your mistakes, don't quit. He or she deserves you to continue trying to do your best to improve your performance. Give him/her a chance to teach you and coach you. Don't get offended; listen to the correction, learn from the mistake, and move on.

Learn also to forgive yourself from your own mistakes. Forget about the embarrassing incident and don't do it again. Continued mistakes in the same area will affect your performance and could eventually cost you your job.

On the other hand, if you have a boss who humiliates you and corrects you in public, mocks you, and treats you with disrespect, he or she does not deserve your loyalty as an employee. You probably need to look for another job. Nobody deserves to be treated disrespectfully, and if you stay in such an environment, you are allowing them to treat you like that and are condoning the behavior.

In either case, the Bible tells us to keep our peace because a quiet spirit can overcome even great mistakes.

KEEP YOUR WORD

Proverbs 12:22 (NLT)

*The Lord hates those who don't keep their word,
but he delights in those who do.*

God is a God of His Word. In fact, He is His Word. Jesus is God's Word made flesh. He and God are one. He made us in His image, therefore, He expects us to behave like Him.

God promised in His Word through prophesies that He would send Jesus (so we could learn from His example and to restore our relationship with Him), and He did. God gave us Jesus and His written Word so we can get to know Him through them. Then when Jesus left earth, God sent us His Holy Spirit so He could dwell in every one of us. He did that so each person can know Him personally and to give us specific, personal direction in our lives.

The Bible says God hates those who don't keep their word because they are the opposite of who He is—a person of His Word. But He delights in those who do keep their word. This includes your word toward God and toward people. He wants us to treat others as we want to be treated, and we all want people to keep their word and promises to us.

In the workplace, being a person of your word means you do what you said you would do. It means that if you are working on a project, you deliver the expected results on the promised date. If you are working in a team, you do your part and help the team be successful.

At home it means you do what you promised your friends, spouse, or kids you would do. You show up to their games or take them to places if you promised them. Of course, there will be outside circumstances when we won't be able to fulfill our promise, but let those be the exception, not the rule. Otherwise, always keep your word.

LOOK AT THOSE WHO ARE HONEST
AND GOOD

Psalm 37:37 (NLT)

*Look at those who are honest and good, for a wonderful future lies
before those who love peace.*

God tells us many times in His Word to look at those who are
honest and good. He knows the people around us influence us
and, therefore, encourages us to choose our friendships wisely.
The relationships we choose are vital to our success in life. Since
the beginning of our social life, usually by the time we start going
to school, we begin choosing our friendships.

The Bible specifically tells us what kind of people God wants
us to be around. Choose those who are good, honest, godly, with
a pure heart, and that love God. These are the friends we are to
fellowship with. If you wonder then, what happens to the rest of
the people? Are we not to love them? Notice the Bible doesn't say
to not *love* them. We are simply not to *fellowship* with them. Fellowship is a sharing of the heart.

In business, it is important to network with people, but don't
waste your time networking with dishonest people, gossipers, or
trouble makers. Follow God's advice to look at those who are honest, good, and love peace, so you can expect a wonderful future as
well. Ask God to connect you and grow your network with these
kinds of people, and you will succeed.

PURPOSE IN YOUR HEART TO PLEASE GOD

I Thessalonians 2:4 (NLT)

...Our purpose is to please God, not people. He is the one who examines the motives of our hearts.

We all know individuals who are people pleasers. They are also usually very unhappy. As Christians, we cannot be concerned about pleasing people. We are to please God only. He is the only one who knows our hearts and our motives. When we please God, we have peace and joy. We are walking in His will for our lives.

In the workplace, you find people who, in order to please others, compromise their beliefs instead of doing what's right. There are others who always have a hidden agenda. They work hard at pleasing other people, yet they resent it and become unhappy and complain.

Always follow your heart. Work hard at pleasing God, not people. When God sees your heart and your pure motives, He will bless you.

REFUSE TO GET OFFENDED; RECEIVE THE MESSAGE

Matthew 13:57 (NLT)

And they were deeply offended and refused to believe in him. Then Jesus told them, "A prophet is honored everywhere except in his own hometown and among his own family."

When Jesus returned to His hometown of Nazareth and started teaching to the people there, they were offended because of who Jesus was. In their eyes, He was just the son of a carpenter and all His brothers and sisters lived among them as regular people. They questioned His integrity and closed their hearts to the teachings. They chose to reject Him and did not believe in Him.

Sometimes we criticize the messenger, the person who delivers the message of the Gospel, and we miss out on the teaching. We focus on the outward appearance and reject the entire message. This is a device of the enemy to keep us from receiving the truth and from believing. God cannot perform where there is no faith. Verse 58 states, "And so he did only a few miracles there because of their unbelief."

Don't be like the unbelieving people in this story. Ask God to place you in the right church so you can receive the message of truth and believe it. Believe the Gospel of good news, and God will perform miracles in your life. Don't get offended by the messenger. Instead, receive the message.

In the workplace it is easy to get offended. And when your heart is offended, you don't allow the Lord to work in or through you. Therefore, choose to not take the offense, so He can do miracles in your life and you can be an example to others.

TAKE CONTROL OVER ANGER

Psalm 4:4 (NLT)

Don't sin by letting anger gain control over you.
Think about it overnight and remain silent.

For most people, it is easy to become angry. Most of us encounter situations on a daily basis, both at work and at home, that will provoke our anger. How do we deal with anger? Well, the Bible tells us one clue—to think about the situation overnight and remain silent. Anger usually cannot elevate to a point of destruction if one person remains silent. If we don't take control of our anger, it will control us and we will do things we will later regret. The things we say, things we do, and decisions we make while angry may be wrong and may have negative consequences in our lives. Why is it so hard to control our anger? Because we are humans and the enemy uses anger as a weapon to destroy us and those around us.

We can use anger to fight the enemy instead and redirect that energy toward him. We must recognize there will always be circumstances that provoke us. But we can, and must, take control of ourselves because we sin when we let anger control us.

Therefore, the next time you become angry because of a work related issue, try this method of thinking overnight and see what happens. I assure you there will be plenty of opportunities for anger to rise up against your boss, co-workers, or employees. Try God's approach to handle anger, and you will see the incredible results. Try it at home too. The next time your spouse, kids, parents, or a friend makes you angry, take control over the anger before it controls you. Don't answer. Think about the situation overnight and remain silent.

TAXES: SHOULD WE PAY THEM OR NOT?

Mark 12:14-15 (NKJV)

… "Is it lawful to pay taxes to Caesar, or not? Shall we pay, or shall we not pay?"

The Pharisees and supporters of Herod asked Jesus the question above to trick Him. Then Jesus asked them to bring a coin. When they brought it to Him, He asked whose image was imprinted on it and they said "Caesar's." Then Jesus replied, "Render to Caesar the things that are Caesar's, and to God the things that are God's" (v. 16). Everybody was amazed at His answer.

The key point we must see is that while we are here we all have to pay taxes in one way or another. Tax avoidance is one of the biggest white collar crimes in America. We, as Christians, have to be an example of obeying the laws of the land. Even Jesus paid taxes at the temple when He arrived with Peter at Capernaum (Matthew 17:24-27 NLT).

The next important point is that when we obey the laws of the land, God will make sure He provides for all our needs and paying taxes is one of them. Of course, we must also be wise and good stewards of our money. We can take advantage of the tax deduction opportunities allowed by the law.

God will bless you when you do the right thing consistently and don't compromise with the world. Be consistent in being ethical and choosing to do what's right despite what everybody else is doing.

THE GODLY WILL OVERCOME

Psalm 112:4 (NLT)

When darkness overtakes the godly, light will come bursting in.
They are generous, compassionate, and righteous.

In this verse, I want you to notice that it says "when" darkness "overtakes" *you*, the godly. Because we live in this world, we will be attacked with darkness and can be overtaken by it. Nevertheless, God promises to send the light bursting in to rescue us. The Greek version of this verse says, "The Lord is" gracious, compassionate, and righteous. We, as godly people, acquire those attributes from God, and that's why we can say confidently we, the godly, are gracious, compassionate, and righteous. The closer we walk with God, the more of His character and attributes we become.

The Bible says in verses 5 through 9 of the same chapter that all goes well for those who are generous and the righteous will be long remembered. They don't fear bad news because they trust the Lord will take care of them. What they do will not be forgotten, and they will have influence and honor. These are some of the many good things the Bible says about the godly.

Most importantly, as said in verse 6, "such people will not be overcome by evil circumstances." We will face darkness in the workplace, at home, and in the community we live in, but we can overcome—each one of those circumstances—with the power of God in our lives and by being godly.

THE GOLDEN RULE... ARE YOU DOING IT?

Matthew 7:1-2 (NLT)

Stop judging others, and you will not be judged. For others will treat you as you treat them.

Why is it so easy to judge others and forget our own faults? This is something we all need to work at on a daily basis. The well known golden rule of "do unto others what you would like them to do unto you" seems to be forgotten too often. Jesus tells us what to do. First, focus on getting your own log out of your eye, then you will be able to see well and "deal with the speck in your friend's eye" (v. 5).

If our vision is impaired because we have a log in our own eye, how can we see to help others? Truly, we are in no position to do so. We need to deal with our own issues first, then we can help other people. Jesus tells us to watch our own lives but, at the same time, He helps us remove the logs from our lives. Judging others is a serious matter for Jesus. In fact, He commands us not to do it.

The workplace offers an environment where it is easy to judge co-workers, customers, vendors, or the leadership of the company. Purpose to not judge the people you work with, and allow God to work in your own heart instead.

75

THE LORD SETS THE STANDARDS

Proverbs 20:10-11 (NLT)

The Lord despises double standards of every kind. Even children are known by the way they act, whether their conduct is pure and right.

Being a person of integrity, among other things, means we are to live our lives by one set of standards only. God sets the standards for our way of life in every area. He gave us His written Word and His Son Jesus to show us those standards. It is our responsibility to live a godly life with no hidden agenda or impure motives.

There are many people in the corporate world that live double lives. They are and act one way in public and another way (the real them) at home. The Lord despises double standards. *Despise* is a very strong word. God uses words carefully, and He means exactly what He says in every word. Therefore, we must be careful to not have double standards.

Take time to examine your heart. Are your motives pure? Do you have a different set of standards at the office than at home? Who are you trying to fool? God knows your heart, your motives, and everything about you, so you can't fool Him. The people you work with may be deceived for a while, but sooner or later the true character of people comes out. This will create great disappointment in those around you, and you could lose your friends and their trust because they don't truly know you.

Learn and follow the standards set by God for your life. This will bring blessings in your life and you will be an example to others.

76

THE LORD WATCHES OVER THOSE WHO DO RIGHT

Psalm 34:15 (NLT)

The eyes of the Lord watch over those who do right; his ears are open to their cries for help.

Psalm 38:20 (NLT)

They repay me evil for good and oppose me because I stand for the right.

During the course of our working life, we will get daily opportunities to stand for what's right or to compromise in order to not make any waves. We must not be afraid to always stand firm and do what's right. Why is it we are afraid of speaking the truth and standing firm for what we believe? The enemy puts doubt and fear in our minds so we compromise. It is a promise of God that He watches over those who do right. The Bible also tells us from David's example that there will be those who will dislike us, and even hate us, because we stand for what's right. But be of good cheer, Jesus overcame the world (John 16:33 NLT), and we are more than conquerors through Him that loved us (Romans 8:37 NLT). We will come out okay in the end.

Don't compromise. Stand for what's right, and God will come through for you every time.

TO BE HAPPY WE NEED TO BE JUST AND DO WHAT'S RIGHT

Psalm 106:3 (NLT)

Happy are those who deal justly with others and always do what is right.

God is just and fair. He is also no respecter of persons. If any person loves Him and accepts Jesus as Savior, that person will be saved no matter what color, race, or age he or she is, or what background he or she has. He also expects us to walk in love, and part of that is being just with others (all people). We cannot favor some people over others if we are to imitate Him.

Every person wants to be happy. Well, the Bible tells us right here how to be happy: be just with others and always do the right thing. Notice that it says *always*, not sometimes, and not to some people only. Doing what is right *always* is a lifestyle. It is a decision we make on a daily basis. We can only know what the right thing to do is all the time when we are in constant communication with God.

In the workplace, you will have daily opportunities to deal justly with others and always do what is right. If you are in management, be fair to all your employees. If you are in sales, be fair to all your customers—and always do what's right.

TRUTH STANDS THE TEST OF TIME

Proverbs 12:19 (NLT)

Truth stands the test of time; lies are soon exposed.

Have you ever witnessed how little kids tell a lie because they are afraid to tell the truth? Have you seen also how pretty soon they can't hold it anymore and spill all the truth out? I think we all have been there. A lie in our hearts is a burden. It's like a thorn in your heart that won't go away until it is removed. Even after it is taken out, it leaves a scar that must be healed. Occasionally we lie to purposely hurt somebody. Other times we lie to protect somebody or ourselves from the consequences of the truth. But in reality, we are hurting ourselves in every case. Lies are a weapon of the enemy to destroy us and other people.

Jesus never told a lie. God has never lied and never will. He and His Word are one and that's why His Word prevails and stands the test of time. God has fulfilled every promise and kept His Word with men throughout the times. We are the ones that have not kept our part of the deal. We see in the Bible example after example of how men and women didn't keep their word and covenant with God. We do the same now when we don't obey His Word and what He tells us to do.

In the workplace, it is easy to look the other way with things that are not right, or cover the truth to protect ourselves, a co-worker, or the company. You must never hide the truth or tell lies to protect anybody—including you. It will only be a matter of time when the lies will be exposed and the truth will come out. The Devil will always turn the situations around and accuse you later. So don't fall into the trap of lying and don't be afraid to tell the truth. Live an honest, truthful life and you will live in peace.

Unbelievers Are Watching Our Behavior

1 Peter 2:12 (NLT)

*Be careful how you live among your unbelieving neighbors.
Even if they accuse you of doing wrong, they will see your honorable
behavior, and they will believe and give honor to
God when he comes to judge the world.*

Unbelievers watch Christians' lives and behaviors all the time—at work and at home. They are looking for an excuse to accuse us of doing wrong and to say "why should I become a Christian when they are a failure?"

As representatives of Christ in the business arena, we must behave in an honorable way so we don't bring shame to Him. A few Christians who behave wrongly ruin the reputation of all Christians. The Bible says that if unbelievers see our honorable behavior they will believe and give honor to God when He comes to judge the world. Let's keep that in mind during the course of our daily lives.

Watch and Pray

Matthew 26:41 (NLT)

*Keep alert and pray. Otherwise temptation will overpower you. For
though the spirit is willing enough, the body is weak!*

Those were the words of Jesus to His disciples in the last hours He spent with them. When Jesus was getting ready to be crucified, He asked the Father to pass that suffering from Him, to make it go away *if* it was His will. But He knew He had to drink from the cup and go through crucifixion so He could fulfill His mission and calling on earth.

Jesus' high calling is the ultimate, most difficult high calling that any human being will ever be asked to do. In order to go through it, He had to be prepared. Part of that preparation was exactly what He told His disciples to do: keep alert (for the tactics and traps of the enemy) and pray (so you can fight the good fight and have the victory over every temptation).

The body is weak and lazy. It wants to do the easy thing, which is to follow the world's ways. Therefore, the spirit must be strong in order to lead the flesh and command it to follow Christ. We all have a special calling in our lives that only we are called to do. Only by watching and praying, will we be able to fulfill our highest calling.

Do you know what your high calling is? Is your current job helping you in any way to fulfill it? Ask the Lord to guide you and place you in positions that will help you prepare to do what He's called you to do. Pray, pray, pray so your spirit is strong!

81

WE ARE TO PRAY FOR OUR ENEMIES

Matthew 5:44, 47 (NLT)

But I say, love your enemies! Pray for those who persecute you!...
If you are kind only to your friends, how are you different from
anyone else? Even pagans do that.

Usually what Jesus tells us to do is contrary to what we *want* to do. During our working life we can create friendships that last forever. Unfortunately, sometimes we also create enemies that also last forever unless we make changes to stop the situation. The only way to stop enemies from hurting us, and to keep our hearts pure of unforgiveness, is by praying for them. It is hard if we try to pray and forgive on our own but God can help us pray for our enemies.

Many of us don't have big enemies, but there are people who don't like us as well as others, individuals whom we rub the wrong way, and others who simply don't like us for whatever reason.

During my working life, I have experienced what praying for those who have hurt me does. It first transforms my heart. I forgive that person and start seeing them through the eyes of Jesus, with His compassion. Then, even if their behavior continues, it doesn't bother me anymore. I have also experienced a change in me when I started praying for somebody I didn't like for whatever reason. The Lord put a special interest in me to get to know that person and whatever bothered me about them before disappears. That's when I know I have attained the victory over that situation.

We, as followers of Christ, have to differentiate ourselves from the world, the pagans. We also all have one enemy in common—Satan, the enemy of our soul. In that case, we don't pray *for* him. We pray *against* him and his devices. With prayer we obtain the victory against all his plots.

82

WE MUST BE FAIR WHEN DOING BUSINESS

Proverbs 16:11 (NLT)

The Lord demands fairness in every business deal; he sets the standard.

As a Christian, you have a responsibility to represent God in all you do—that includes your business activities as well. When you do business, you will deal with all kinds of people from various parts of the world. They will likely be from different cultures and backgrounds. In addition to that, their beliefs and values will most likely be different from yours. Nevertheless, as an ambassador of Christ, you must represent Him everywhere you go.

Your character must show consistency and fairness toward all people—all the time. It doesn't matter how they treat you, you must always act as a representative of Christ. This may be the only opportunity they have to see the love of Jesus.

God is a fair God. "He will make your innocence as clear as the dawn, and the justice of your cause will shine like the noonday sun" (Psalm 37:6 NLT).

83

WE MUST PROTECT OUR EMPLOYER'S INTEREST

Proverbs 27:18 (NLT)

Workers who tend a fig tree are allowed to eat its fruit. In the same way, workers who protect their employer's interests will be rewarded.

Most of us work for somebody else's company as an employee. Therefore, we may forget that some people worked very hard and dedicated their lives to make this company successful and to bring it to its current position. Part of being a person of integrity is to care for the company you work for as if it was your own. In fact, we have a responsibility to watch for and protect the company that pays us for our work. Part of protecting our employer is to watch our expenses, our processes, and to not waste any resources—including our time. Efficiency in every area should be our goal. By cutting expenses and increasing the sources of income, we will maximize the profits of the company. We should also pray for God's protection over the company's assets and for the leaders to have godly wisdom to lead the company.

It is honorable to tend and protect your employer's interests because you will be rewarded. This reward doesn't necessarily have to be monetary. It can be the peace and happiness you will have while working there. It can be visibility in the community or simply the satisfaction of knowing you contributed personally to the success of the company. God will honor your loyalty, faithfulness, and hard work whether the company recognizes you or not.

84

WE NEED TO BE HUMBLE TO FULFILL OUR MISSION

Philippians 2:4 (NLT)

Don't think only about your own affairs, but be interested in others, too, and what they are doing.

It is easy to get wrapped up in our own lives and forget what everybody else is doing. When we focus on ourselves only, we don't notice the needs of those around us and may miss opportunities to help and minister to them. But the moment we focus our attention on others, we recognize their needs and think of ways to help them. This help can be in any way such as helping a friend at work or a neighbor with her kids. It doesn't matter what it is, what matters is that we have a genuine interest in our hearts to help others.

God's help to people comes, most of the time, through other people. When we are willing to help others, we become available for God to use us. As He blesses other people through us, our need to be useful and to have a purpose is also met.

Our attitude should be like that of Jesus. "Though he was God, he did not demand and cling to his rights as God. He made himself nothing; he took the humble position of a slave and appeared in human form. And in human form he obediently humbled himself even further by dying a criminal's death on a cross" (vv. 6-8). Jesus accomplished His mission. He was humble and was only interested in others, so God rewarded Him with the highest reward—a special place in heaven, to the right hand of the Father.

The same way, we have a mission, and, in order to accomplish it, we must be humble like Jesus and focus on others. When we are done with our race, God will reward us too.

WE NEED TO CHANGE OUR BEHAVIOR

Colossians 3:8-9 (NLT)

But now is the time to get rid of anger, rage, malicious behavior, slander, and dirty language. Don't lie to each other, for you have stripped off your old evil nature and all its wicked deeds.

If you have accepted Christ into your life as your Lord, then it's time to put off the bad things you used to do when you were not saved. It's time to start over. God will give you the strength to get rid of every one of the things mentioned above. You will need patience with yourself since the change in behavior takes time as you grow and mature in the Lord.

Verses 12-14 of Colossians 3 say "you must clothe yourselves with tenderhearted mercy, kindness, humility, gentleness, and patience...forgive the person who offends you... And the most important piece of clothing you must wear is love." We, as Christian women in the workplace, must show these traits. Otherwise, how can we make a difference or be noticed?

When you have a change of heart and, consequently, of behavior, people will want to know why. That is your opportunity to share the Gospel. Sometimes, you won't have to say a word; just be your *new* self.

WHAT KIND OF FRUIT ARE YOU PRODUCING?

Matthew 7:17 (NLT)

A healthy tree produces good fruit, and an unhealthy tree produces bad fruit.

The Bible warns us about false prophets who look like sheep but are really wolves. It teaches us we will know and identify them by observing how they act—by their fruit.

Verse 20 tells us, "the way to identify a tree or a person is by the kind of fruit that is produced." Even though these verses refer to false prophets, we can also apply the same principle to our daily lives. The question today is: what kind of fruit are you producing in your life?

I examine myself often to see what kind of fruit I'm producing. I find the results very predictable. When I'm not spending enough time with the Lord and I allow the busyness of life to overtake me, my fruit is not good. In those times, I produce fruits of anger, short temper, impatience, irritability, and unhappiness, to name a few. On the other hand, when I spend time with the Lord, water my tree with His Word, mediate on Him, and obey what He asks me to do, I produce good fruit. Instead of anger and short temper, I have compassion. Instead of impatience, irritability, and unhappiness, there is grace, contentment, patience, and happiness. I also produce fruit of peace amongst the people I'm around.

Therefore, don't let the busyness of life with the work demands and family commitments rob you of spending time with the Lord. It is the only way you will produce good fruit and help those around you. Remember, the fruit you produce is for others to partake of.

WORK HARD AND ENTHUSIASTICALLY

Romans 12:11 (NLT)

Never be lazy in your work, but serve the Lord enthusiastically.

God expects you to work hard and as unto the Lord. No matter what you do, always work with enthusiasm. It is contagious and your work environment will change because of your attitude.

Enthusiastic people are always positive, exciting, and a joy to be around. They attract people because of their good attitude. If you work hard and bring enthusiasm to your work, you will not only enjoy work more, but you will be a witness to others of God's love.

88

YOUR MOUTH REFLECTS YOUR HEART

Matthew 15:11, 18 (NLT)

You are not defiled by what you eat; you are defiled by what you say and do... But evil words come from an evil heart and defile the person who says them.

The Pharisees criticized Jesus because His disciples didn't wash their hands before eating their meal. Jesus confronted the Pharisees by telling them that unwashed hands could never defile them but the words that come out of the mouth is what defiles them.

The Devil will always try to use our mouths to get us in trouble. But we must remember our mouths are ours, not the Devil's. Therefore, we have to control them and not allow him to use them on our behalf. We have to guard what we say constantly, for the mouth is a weapon that can destroy other people and ourselves. What we say and do reflects what we believe, who we are, and what's in our hearts.

Use your mouth to praise and worship the Lord instead. Use it to build people up, not to destroy them. Use it to proclaim the truth of the Gospel and to testify about the love of God. The workplace gives you a great opportunity to use your mouth to lift others, to encourage your co-workers, to say good things about your company, and to speak positive things into the lives of others.

In order for your mouth to speak the truth of the Word and build people up with God's love, your heart must be kept pure. How? By spending time with the Lord, reading, studying, and meditating on His Word. If that's what you put in you, that's what will come out of you.

ENCOURAGEMENT

Ask God with the Right Motives and You Will Receive

James 4:2-3 (NLT)

You want what you don't have, so you scheme and kill to get it. You are jealous for what others have, and you can't possess it, so you fight and quarrel to take it away from them. And yet the reason you don't have what you want is that you don't ask God for it. And even when you do ask, you don't get it because your whole motive is wrong — you want only what will give you pleasure.

There are many things we want in our lives. Notice I am talking about wants, not needs. Some wants are true desires of our hearts that the Lord has placed there. Other things we want just because our friends, neighbors, relatives, or co-workers have. We can then become jealous and start coveting other people's things.

First of all, if God has placed a desire in your heart, ask Him for that desire to manifest in your life with a pure heart, and He will grant it to you. An example could be if you have a desire to acquire a college degree. He knows your true heart motives. On the other hand, if you want something just because you are jealous or envious of what somebody else has, you will probably not get it. Why? Because even if you ask Him, He knows your heart motives are wrong.

Sometimes it is okay to ask God for something that somebody else has when your heart is right. However, you must first examine your heart motives and make sure you're going to use that gift, or whatever you desire, to glorify God. Then just ask God and trust He will give it to you.

For example, if you want a particular job right now, examine your heart motives. Let God give you the job He desires you to have and ask Him to change your motives to align with His will for your life.

BE DETERMINED TO DO HIS WILL

Isaiah 50:7 (NLT)

Because the Sovereign Lord helps me, I will not be dismayed.
Therefore, I have set my face like a stone, determined to do His will.
And I know that I will triumph.

We are all servants of the Lord and, as servants, we need to trust Him that He will help us when we are willing and determined to do His will. When we have that determination to set our face "like a stone" (as the verse above says), we mean business. Our decision to be persistent to do His will in our lives is a daily prayer. We can't do it alone. The first step, however, is to know His will for our lives. Do you know God's will for you? If not, ask Him to reveal His will to you for every area of your life—this includes your work and business life.

God wants to be involved in all the decisions we make concerning us. He wants to direct us in every area and in every detail. The key is to let Him. We need to recognize when we are following our own plan and when we are doing His will.

Once we have direction from the Lord, we must act by faith even when we disagree. He knows what's best for us always. But how do we know when we are in His will or not? Usually, one clue is peace, or lack of it, in our hearts. That is the best indicator He provides to us. When we are walking in His will, there is a peace that passes all understanding. When we have that peace, we also have the knowledge and assurance in our hearts that we will be triumphant. We will win.

If you are frustrated with your work situation or don't know for sure what your next step in your career is, ask God to clarify His will for you. Then trust Him and act by faith. Don't be dismayed. He will always be with you.

91

BE KIND TO THE POOR

Psalm 41:1-2 (NLT)

Oh, the joys of those who are kind to the poor. The Lord rescues them in times of trouble. The Lord protects them and keeps them alive. He gives them prosperity and rescues them from their enemies.

Jesus told His disciples that we will always have the poor amongst us. Why? Because we live in a fallen world that is not fair to all people.

There are two main ways we can help the poor. The first, and most important, is to preach the Gospel to them. Jesus commanded His disciples to do this when He was training them (Matthew 11:5 NLT). Jesus is the only hope of salvation for mankind. When the poor hear the good news of the Gospel and understand this life is only temporary, they accept Jesus. They receive the gift of hope and know that some day they will live in heaven eternally with God.

The second way we help the poor is to meet their physical needs of food, shelter, clothing, and other necessities. We do this by giving money and/or our time to organizations that provide these types of services.

Be kind to the poor, and God will bless you.

BECOME A MERCIFUL PERSON

James 2:13 (NLT)

For there will be no mercy for you if you have not been merciful to others. But if you have been merciful, then God's mercy toward you will win out over his judgment against you.

Mercy is a virtue not all of us possess. We need to develop and grow in mercy just as we do with patience. Mercy is very important to God because He is the God of mercy. There are some people who are naturally more merciful than others. This is something we can ask God to help us with. Whenever we ask Him to help us grow in areas like this one, He will present situations to us where we will have the opportunity to be merciful. We need to make sure we recognize those opportunities and pass the tests.

There are people in need everywhere. All you have to do is be more aware and willing to help on the spot. For example: if someone comes to you at work and they need help with a project, help them. Don't just send them away wishing them luck when you have tips that can help them. It is as simple as that. Notice I didn't say you have to do the project for them, just simply share your experience.

The Bible says that when we are merciful toward others, God will be merciful toward us. This is part of loving each other. Faith without works is dead. "We are made right with God by what we do, not by faith alone" (v. 24).

93

CALL, FEAR, AND LOVE THE LORD

Psalm 145:18 (NLT)

*The Lord is close to all who call on him, yes,
to all who call on him sincerely.*

Why is it that when we are overwhelmed with problems we feel God is far away? God is always there. He doesn't move. We are the ones who move closer or farther away from Him. His commitment to us is that He is close to those who call on Him. But we need to call on Him sincerely, from our hearts.

He also fulfills the desires of those who fear Him and protects those who love Him (vv. 19-20). The three significant words here are call, fear, and love Him. That is our part of the deal. His part is to draw close to us, fulfill our desires, and protect us.

We must do these three things with a pure and sincere heart. We can't fool God. He knows the most inner parts and secrets of our hearts. But how do we keep our heart motives right and pure? By always acknowledging everything He has done for us and by having a thankful heart.

If you are having problems at work or in your personal life, call upon the Lord. He will draw near to you and give you grace, wisdom, and direction.

94

DEALING WITH GRIEF AND DISTRESS

Psalm 31:9 (NLT)

Have mercy on me, Lord, for I am in distress. My sight is blurred because of my tears. My body and soul are withering away.

During the course of our lives, we experience times of great distress and situations when we feel we are withering away from grief. Losing our job can create great pain for us because our work is a major part of our lives. Yet the loss of a loved one could be much more impacting in our working life. When we lose someone to death like a child, our spouse, a parent, or a close friend, it creates a wound in our heart that only God can heal. Divorce, separation, or a child leaving home prematurely can also be as catastrophic.

These events change our lives forever, and it is in those moments that grief can settle into our hearts. It is normal to go through a grieving period, but we cannot stay there too long because it is deadly for us just as David said in verse 10, "I am dying from grief; my years are shortened by sadness. Misery has drained my strength; I am wasting away from within."

Even though we never forget tragic or sad events, we need to move on and let go of the grief and pain. We must continue the race God has set for each one of us and finish it. There are two things we need to do. First, just as David never gave up trusting God and kept running to Him for protection and comfort, we have to trust God that He will help us and lift us up. "So be strong and take courage, all you who put your hope in the Lord!" (v. 24). Secondly, we need to do what Paul did. He said to the people of Philippi, "No, dear brothers and sisters, I am still not all I should be, but I am focusing all my energies on this one thing: Forgetting the past and looking forward to what lies ahead. I strain to reach the end of the race and receive the prize for which God, through Christ Jesus, is calling us up to heaven" (Philippians 3:13-14 NLT).

DON'T GIVE UP. KEEP ASKING AND SEEKING.

Matthew 7:7-8 (NLT)

Keep on asking, and you will be given what you ask for. Keep on looking, and you will find. Keep on knocking, and the door will be opened. For everyone who asks, receives. Everyone who seeks, finds. And the door is opened to everyone who knocks.

Are you persistent with the things of God? Do you continue to seek God for the answer until you get it? Or do you give up after the first or second try and you don't get a response? The Devil is persistent in seeking your attention by pestering you and making you believe God is not listening. Don't give in. Don't give up, and don't stop asking God for what you need—whether it is a need of finances, a new job, a husband, healing in your body, a loved one to be saved, or anything else that is important to you. If it is important to you, it is important to God. It is His promise that He will give us what we ask for according to His will. He will be found and will open doors for us. We just have to be persistent.

Whatever your situation is, continue to seek the Lord about it until you receive an answer. This is crucial to your daily success in your walk with God.

96

ENDURE TEMPTATION AND RECEIVE THE CROWN OF LIFE

James 1:12-14 (KJV)

Blessed is the man that endureth temptation: for when he is tried, he shall receive the crown of life, which the Lord hath promised to them that love him. Let no man say when he is tempted, I am tempted of God: for God cannot be tempted with evil, neither tempteth he any man: But every man is tempted, when he is drawn away of his own lust, and enticed.

Our first tendency when we are going through trials or temptations is to think they came from God. Yet the Bible states God cannot be tempted or tempt anybody. Our sinful nature brings temptations and trials that come from the tempter and deceiver — Satan. We experience them because we live in a fallen world. God allows trials to happen in our lives to help us grow and mature.

The trials we experience at work sometimes can be (or seem) so big that we become overwhelmed. Our work represents a big part of our lives and we want to (and should) enjoy it. Therefore, we need to be patient and focus on the heavenly reward we will receive in the end. We must endure the trial with faith knowing God will help us. The Bible reminds us that if we endure temptation or testing, afterward we will receive the crown of life God has promised to those who love Him.

97

ENJOY EVERYTHING GOD GAVE YOU

Ecclesiastes 6:9 (NLT)

Enjoy what you have rather than desiring what you don't have.
Just dreaming about nice things is meaningless;
it is like chasing the wind.

Sometimes we get so preoccupied and focused on the next thing we want to acquire we don't enjoy what we currently have. It is very important to always thank God for what He gave us and not take anything for granted. This includes material things as well as natural and spiritual gifts. In the material realm, we often don't enjoy the present because we focus on the next house, car, boat, job, or whatever it is we want. While it is okay to press on and improve, we must learn to be content in whatsoever state we are as the Apostle Paul said in Philippians 4:11 (NLT).

We must also be content with our natural gifts and talents. We all have unique and different talents God gave us. Instead of desiring somebody else's gifts or just wanting different ones from what we have, we should develop the ones we do have and enjoy the process. Regarding spiritual gifts, the Bible says Jesus distributes His gifts "as He wills."

Therefore, discover and develop all the gifts (material, natural, and spiritual) God gave you and use them to give the glory to Him and enjoy the journey.

FORGET YOUR PAST. FINISH YOUR RACE.

Ecclesiastes 7:10 (NLT)

Don't long for the "the good old days," for you don't know whether they were any better than today.

We hear this phrase often. People yearn for the past. They wish things would go back to what they used to be. But the Bible says we must let go of the past. Whether it was good or bad, it doesn't matter. The past is a stronghold, a bondage that keeps us from moving forward in our lives. It slows down our walk with God. He cannot move us to our next stage of maturity and knowledge in Him until we let go of the past.

Paul tells us in Philippians 3:13 (NLT) even though he is not yet all that he should be, he is focusing all his energies on forgetting the past and looking forward to the future. It takes a lot of energy to focus on the past. We have to make the switch in focus so we can be successful in our future. There is nothing we can do about the past, but there is much we can do about our future with the Lord.

We each have a race to run and it takes all of our effort to run it. Carrying our past with us is like carrying a backpack full of rocks while trying to run a marathon. You will not make it or it will be unnecessarily difficult. We need to drop off the baggage at the feet of Jesus and move on.

If you yearn for a job you had years ago, it's time to move on and forget it! You need to enjoy your current job and start focusing on your future with your new company or situation. Use your previous experience to make your current job more successful instead. Be encouraged by Paul's words, "I press toward the goal for the prize of the upward call of God in Christ Jesus." (Philippians 3:14 NKJV). Therefore, forget your past and finish your race.

GIVE OF YOURSELF GENEROUSLY

Ecclesiastes 11:1-2 (NLT)

Give generously, for your gifts will return to you later. Divide your gifts among many, for you do not know what risks might lie ahead.

We usually interpret passages like this one to mean we should give money generously, but I believe it's referring to giving of ourselves. God gave gifts to all of us we can share with others. The Bible tells us to give and we will receive. How we treat others, we will be treated. Basically, we reap what we sow in every area of our lives.

In the workplace we have daily opportunities to give of ourselves to others. We can help our co-workers, our boss, or customers with our time, ideas, experience, knowledge, and our love. Sometimes we show people we care for them just by listening to them and treating them with respect and dignity.

This passage also tells us to divide our gifts among many. Our gifts are for us to share with everyone that crosses our path. I believe God puts people in our lives for a purpose. Some people are in our lives one time, and we have a one-time divine appointment. Other people, He puts in our paths for a long time or forever. He connects us with the people He knows we can help and we can receive help from them.

Therefore, treat the people He has given you with His love, and you will receive your reward right here in this life as well as in heaven.

100

GIVE YOUR BURDENS TO JESUS AND HE WILL GIVE YOU REST

Matthew 11:28 (NLT)

Then Jesus said, "Come to me, all of you who are weary and carry heavy burdens, and I will give you rest."

As working women, we may often feel weary. Sometimes our burdens are so heavy we can hardly make the next step. This is a scripture we need to get a hold of and personalize. Let's give our burdens to Jesus. He is there for us. He wants to take them. God is pleased when we give our burdens to Jesus because that act tells Him we trust Him and believe in Him fully.

Our rest starts in our spirit and soul. Jesus promises us that rest. When we have rest spiritually, we have peace, and that peace eliminates the stress of our burdens.

Praise God for your job and thank Him for the grace and strength He gives you to do all that He has called you to do on a daily basis. For those of you who are single working moms, don't despair. You are not alone, and Jesus wants to help you carry your burden. Jesus tells us in verses 29 and 30, "Take my yoke upon you. Let me teach you, because I am humble and gentle, and you will find rest for your souls. For my yoke fits perfectly, and the burden I give you is light."

101

GOD BENDS DOWN AND LISTENS AS WE PRAY

Psalm 17:6 (NLT)

I am praying to you because I know you will answer, O God.
Bend down and listen as I pray.

Do you know in your heart that God listens to your prayers? Do you believe that He answers? Or do you pray and say things just in case somebody is up there and maybe you'll get an answer?

The first step to know in our hearts that God listens is to have a friendship with Him, a relationship based on mutual trust. He trusts us with His gifts and expects us to do His will on earth. But it is our choice to trust Him back and to choose His will for us. When we choose to trust Him, we can expect Him to listen to our prayers and to answer them. Answered prayers are a reward for following His ways. David said it best in Psalm 18:20-21 (NLT), "The Lord rewarded me for doing right; he compensated me because of my innocence. For I have kept the ways of the Lord; I have not turned from my God to follow evil."

If we want God to hear and answer our prayers, we have to do our part, which is to do His will. He then places His desires for us in our hearts. When we ask Him in prayer for those desires, He listens and answers because they are His to begin with. This is a revelation we must receive in our hearts. It is a key to our success in our relationship with our Father.

Do you pray for God to help you with your job? Do you pray for your boss and leaders of your company? Do you pray for your company's success? Do you pray for your customers to be successful so they can continue to give you their business? Do you pray for your co-workers and employees so they are in good health and make good decisions? If not, today is your day to start. God will listen to your prayers and your workplace will be a better place to work.

102

GOD CHOSE YOU LONG AGO

1 Peter 1:2 (NLT)

God the Father chose you long ago, and the Spirit has made you holy. As a result, you have obeyed Jesus Christ and are cleansed by his blood.

If you don't have any other reason to feel special today, think of this one: God the Father chose *you* long ago! God himself chose you for His purposes and for you to live eternally with Him. In addition, His Spirit made you holy. You must strive to live a holy life on a daily basis. You accomplish this by obeying Jesus. His blood cleanses all your sins.

Live your life for God. Do everything you do as unto the Lord. Thank Him for everything He has given you and done for you. The God of the Universe, the Creator and Master of all has chosen *you*.

Let all your friends, family, and co-workers know that God is your God by choosing to live a holy life.

103

GOD GAVE US HIS PROMISE AND HIS OATH

Hebrews 6:17-18 (NLT)

God also bound himself with an oath, so that those who received the promise could be perfectly sure that he would never change his mind. So God has given us both his promise and his oath. These two things are unchangeable because it is impossible for God to lie.

God never changes. His promises and His Word don't either. The countless promises of God for us are all in the Bible, but if we don't know them, we'll never be able to receive them. The only way to learn about them is by spending time in His Word and by asking Him to reveal His promises to us. Then we must believe He will bring them to pass in our lives.

God cannot lie, and He gave us both His promises and His oath as His commitment to us. His promises are available for all of those who discover them and believe. Therefore, our commitment should be to believe and receive them. In addition to the promises we find in His Word for all believers, there are promises He gives us individually for our lives. We must do the same with those promises—believe and expect they will come true for us.

Don't give up believing and expecting for the things God has promised you—both for your work life as well as your family life.

104

GOD GAVE US THE NAME OF THE LORD

Proverbs 18:10 (NLT)

*The name of the Lord is a strong fortress;
the godly run to him and are safe.*

The name of the Lord is above all names. The name itself is powerful, like a strong fortress. The name itself represents what God is, His nature. He gave us the name of Jesus so we can use it not only as a weapon against the enemy but as our fortress and refuge. Jesus told us to ask the Father anything in His name because He knows the Father would grant it to us—because of Jesus.

When you are in fear, run to Him and say His name. The name of Jesus will give you comfort, peace that surpasses all understanding, and safety. The Bible tells us to not be afraid "for God has not given us a spirit of fear and timidity, but of power, love, and self-discipline" (2 Timothy 1:7 NLT).

Even though in the verse above Paul is referring to us sharing the gospel of the Lord, we can apply it to any area of our lives.

When we speak the name of the Lord, the enemy flees. We have the right to use His name given to us by God Himself. But how do we use the name of the Lord at work? Unfortunately, we probably can't say it out loud, but we can definitely say it in our minds. It doesn't matter. The name of the Lord is a gift to you. Therefore, use it and experience the peace and strength that it will give you.

105

GOD GIVES GIFTS TO ALL PEOPLE

1 Peter 4:10 (NLT)

God has given gifts to each of you from his great variety of spiritual gifts. Manage them well so that God's generosity can flow through you.

God has given us natural gifts as well as spiritual gifts. As good stewards, we are to discover, develop, use, and manage them so God can use us completely.

God is a generous God. When He sees we are using all the gifts He has given us, He blesses us with even more. He is looking for vessels where He can pour out His blessings and gifts.

The desires of your heart are connected to your high calling. Therefore, thank God for His generosity by managing all the gifts He gave you well. Look for jobs that align with the desires of your heart so your natural gifts can develop. You will be most successful in the areas where you have a natural gift. Volunteer at your church or community in an area where your spiritual gifts can develop as well.

Finally, as Christians, we share one common calling—to use every one of the gifts He gave us for His Kingdom. Every gift is designed to help and contribute to the big plan of God. Therefore, search your heart and ask God to reveal those gifts to you and start using them today.

106

GOD GIVES US STRENGTH

Philippians 4:13 (KJV)

I can do all things through Christ which strengtheneth me.

When we stop and think about all the things we have to do as working women, it can be overwhelming. Both single and married women are extremely busy these days because everybody pulls on them to help and volunteer with various activities. Some women also have to take care of children and/or parents in addition to having a career. This is when we need to remember two main things: 1) We must continually evaluate our priorities in life and put God first; and 2) God gives us the strength to do all the things He's called us to do through Christ.

We can't do all things at the same time, but, with His help, we will be able to focus on the most important ones for that day. We can count on the strength that comes from God.

107

GOD GIVES US THE GRACE TO ALWAYS DO WHAT IS RIGHT

Psalm 84:11-12 (NLT)

For the Lord our God is our light and protector. He gives us grace and glory. No good thing will the Lord withhold from those who do what is right. O Lord Almighty, happy are those who trust in you.

When we first come to Christ, we move from living in darkness to living in the light. As we grow in the knowledge of God, the Holy

Spirit teaches us all truth. As we become mature Christians and have a revelation of what is right and wrong, we have the responsibility to do what is right—always.

Doing what's right on a consistent basis and on our own strength is difficult, but we can do it with the help of the Holy Spirit. The Bible promises the Lord withholds "no good thing" from those who do what is right. In the workplace, we must make a decision to always do what's right regardless of the consequences—even if it includes losing our jobs. We have to trust God in every situation to give us the wisdom necessary to handle it correctly. We must trust Him to protect us and give us grace.

Our part is to not compromise our beliefs but rather to trust in God. His part is to protect us and be our light. He is our "sun and shield" (v. 11 KJV).

108

GOD HAS GIVEN US A FULL ARMOR TO FIGHT AND TO PROTECT OURSELVES

Psalm 91:4 (NLT)

He will shield you with his wings. He will shelter you with his feathers. His faithful promises are your armor and protection.

God the Father is our protector, our shield, our refuge, our cover. These and more are His promises of what He is to us. We have to appropriate these promises and personalize them, internalize them, and count on them as His final word. Armor is something we choose to wear. This means that without us choosing to put it on every day, we can be without His protection.

Choose to put the whole armor of God every day as soon as you wake up and before you go to work to face the world. Ephesians 6:11 and 13 (NLT) say, "Put on all of God's armor so that you will be able to stand firm against all strategies and tricks of the Devil…Use every piece of God's armor to resist the enemy in the time of evil, so that after the battle you will still be standing firm."

Ephesians 6:14-17 (NLT) tell us what those armor pieces are: the belt of truth; the body armor of God's righteousness; the peace of good news for shoes; faith as our shield; the helmet of salvation, and the sword of the Spirit, which is the Word of God. We are also to pray at all times in the power of the Holy Spirit for His protection.

The world is a battle field. We must fight against the enemy of our soul every day of our lives. God has given us an entire armor and the weapons we need to fight back and protect ourselves from the enemy. Therefore, choose to wear *your* armor starting today and always.

109

GOD HAS GOOD PLANS FOR YOU

Jeremiah 29:11-12 (NLT)

"…For I know the plans I have for you," says the Lord. "They are plans for good and not for disaster, to give you a future and a hope. In those days when you pray, I will listen."

God has a plan for each person. They are good plans meant for our well-being, to give us a future and a hope. We can make all the plans we want, but without asking God what His will is for us, those plans may not be worth pursuing. When we ask God what He wants us to desire, He will plant desires in our hearts. Then when we plan based on those desires, He will be involved and our plans will succeed. He will open doors of opportunity that no man can shut. He will give us the grace to live out His plan for our lives.

It is a promise that when we pray, He will listen. Ask God to reveal His plan for your life to you. His plan involves the various areas of your life—and they are good plans.

110

GOD HAS NOT GIVEN US THE SPIRIT OF FEAR

2 Timothy 1:7 (KJV)

For God hath not given us the spirit of fear; but of power,
and of love, and of a sound mind.

What Paul is telling Timothy in his second letter applies to us to-day. The enemy will attack us with fearful thoughts every day. Every time we encounter fear, we must fight it back and rebuke it standing on this passage. This is a great promise we must not forget. The power we have been entrusted with is the same one that raised Jesus from the dead, no less. Ephesians 1:19-20 (KJV) says, "And what is the exceeding greatness of his power to us-ward who believe, according to the working of his mighty power, which he wrought in Christ, when he raised him from the dead, and set him at his own right hand in the heavenly places."

The love we have been given is the very love of God—the love that can do all things. The self-discipline (a sound mind) is what we need to follow Jesus every day, to say no to our flesh and yes to our spirit. Our spirit responds to God's Spirit, our flesh doesn't until we make it. Remember this truth the next time you are in fear.

GOD IS OUR INHERITANCE

Psalm 16:5 (NLT)

Lord, you alone are my inheritance, my cup of blessing. You guard all that is mine.

When we think of inheritance, we immediately think of millions of dollars a distant relative left us. In reality, very few people leave a substantial inheritance to their families. Some parents, unfortunately, only leave debt and problems to their children.

One of God's promises to us is that He will bless us enough to leave an inheritance to our children's children. But in this verse, David wasn't talking about a worldly inheritance. He is referring to God Himself being David's inheritance.

God, as our inheritance, is all we need because He *is* and *has* everything we could ever need in this life and in eternity with Him. He is our source of refreshing and fulfillment. His cup is where we go to get ours filled up. He guards all He gives us, including our lives.

Therefore, receive God as your inheritance and you will never need or want anybody else's.

GOD IS OUR PLACE OF SAFETY

Psalm 59:9 (NLT)

You are my strength; I wait for you to rescue me, for you, O God, are my place of safety.

When you feel distressed and tired by the trials of your everyday life, remember this verse. God is your source of strength always.

He is your only place of safety where you can go and have rest and peace in the midst of the battle.

Life is an everyday fight. Even when we don't have major events or tragedies going on in our lives, we have to fight to be holy. We have to continually fight our fleshly desires and struggle to stay obedient and faithful to God.

Sometimes work can, and will, drain your energy to a point where there is nothing left to give. Take a break and go to God. Spend time with Him, for He will give you rest and restore your strength and energy. He will refuel your spirit. Verse 16 of the same chapter says, "But as for me, I will sing about your power. I will shout with joy each morning because of your unfailing love. For you have been my refuge, a place of safety in the day of distress."

113

GOD IS OUR REFUGE, OUR DUMPING PLACE

Psalm 142:2-3 (NLT)

I pour out my complaints before him and tell him all my troubles. For I am overwhelmed, and you alone know the way I should turn.

It is normal for women to feel low once in a while. Sometimes circumstances, stress, busyness, or simply the time of the month will make us feel overwhelmed and depressed. I want to focus on what to do during those times and how to get out of that state of being.

Even though the workplace seems to be the dumping place for our complaints and troubles, that is not appropriate. The workplace is just for that—to work. Though it is okay to once in a while share personal things with friends at work, we cannot abuse those relationships. Our dumping place is God. He is open to receive us, so we can pour out our hearts with all the complaints and troubles we may be having at any time. He can handle it. He asks us to do it because He knows what we need to do. God gives us examples of people, like David, who chose to go to Him for refuge and help. David said, "Hear my cry, for I am very low" (Psalm 142:6 NLT). "I am losing all hope; I am paralyzed with fear" (Psalm 143:4 NLT). "Come quickly, Lord, and answer me, for my depression deepens" (Psalm 143:7 NLT).

The Lord will listen to your prayers, just as He did with David, who said to Him later, "You are the one who rescued your servant David" (Psalm 144:10 NLT). Remember, "The Lord helps the fallen and lifts up those bent beneath their loads" (Psalm 145:14 NLT).

114

GOD SHALL SUPPLY ALL YOUR NEEDS

Philippians 4:19 (NLT)

And this same God who takes care of me will supply all your needs from his glorious riches, which have been given to us in Christ Jesus.

In this verse, Paul thanks the Philippians for helping him during his time of need. He assures them that the same God who takes care of him will also take care of them. God knows our needs, but He wants us to ask Him to meet those needs. When we ask Him, we allow Him to meet every one of our needs according to His riches in glory (abundant supply) given to us and made available to us because of what Jesus did for us.

We have many needs in our lives and on a daily basis. But we usually only ask Him for the big things such as finances, a house, a car, or a job. We forget the other things like rest, peace, joy, or wisdom, among others. What we consider smaller things, or not as important, are indeed needed for our success in life.

If you are tired, ask God to give you rest. If you are worried, ask Him for peace. If you are sad, ask Him for joy. If you don't know what to do in a certain situation, ask Him for wisdom. God is rich in every way, and He is waiting for you to ask Him so He can give you what you need. Ask Him in faith believing in your heart that He will come through for you. Because He will.

115

GOD SURROUNDS US WITH HIS LOVE

Psalm 5:12 (NLT)

For you bless the godly, O Lord, surrounding them with your shield of love.

All Christians have one thing in common that we must try to accomplish. That is to become more and more like Jesus, to be godly people. It is a daily fight with the flesh and the worldly influences. It is making a choice every day to follow Christ and to do God's will for our lives.

God blesses the godly. He gives them all of His benefits to enjoy here on earth as well as when we go to heaven. He shields us with His love from the enemy. This doesn't mean bad things won't happen to godly people. It means He surrounds us and covers us with His love so when the storms of life come our way, we are able to withstand and survive.

Some people think God's benefits are only financial, but the Bible says God will meet all our needs (including physical, emotional, and spiritual). We must not judge people based on the outward appearance. Having material possessions, living in luxury, or being at the top of the corporate ladder is not a sign of how godly a person is or how blessed they are. On the other hand, when someone is fighting an illness or has lost their job, for example, it is not an indication of how ungodly they are or that their suffering is a consequence of sin. No, we live in this world where we will be attacked in different areas of our lives. We must pray for our brothers and sisters and believe with them for their victory without judging them. That is being godly—when our hearts are pure toward God and toward people.

God's love shields us from the enemy. He surrounds us all with His love. "God is my shield, saving those whose hearts are true and right" (Psalm 7:10 NLT).

GOD WANTS TO BLESS US

Proverbs 10:22 (NLT)

The blessing of the Lord makes a person rich, and he adds no sorrow with it.

Proverbs 12:11 (NLT)

Hard work means prosperity; only fools idle away their time.

God wants to bless us and His blessing makes us rich (prosperous) in every area of our lives. One of those blessings is our job. When we work hard and unto the Lord, we prosper. Therefore, if we want to prosper in our job, we have to work hard and smart. That doesn't mean we have to work long hours every day, rather it means we prioritize our work, delegate, and learn to do our job more effectively and efficiently. In addition to working hard and smart, we have to be women of integrity with honesty and truthfulness being some of our main traits.

Time is another blessing the Lord has given us all. How we use our God-given time determines how much we prosper. We must use our time to do things that bring glory to God. He wants to bless our work, finances, home, health, and our relationships. But there is no sorrow in His blessings.

GOD WANTS TO MEET OUR NEEDS

Philippians 4:19 (KJV)

But my God shall supply all your need according to his riches in glory by Christ Jesus.

We all have natural and spiritual needs. God promises us He will meet all of our needs according to His riches in glory, not according to anything else. Besides the financial need, which is one main reason women work, we have other needs such as recognition, the need to be valued and feel important, and the need for relationships. In addition, we have spiritual needs such as feeling important in His Kingdom and feeling loved and accepted by Him. God is interested in every detail in our lives and in meeting each one of those needs. But we also have to do our part by seeking Him, thanking Him, giving to His Kingdom, and asking Him for what we need.

God gives us recognition for who we are. Many of us seek approval from others when all we need is His approval. He approves of us because He created us. God knows we are important, not only to Him but to others as well. He also knows how crucial it is for us to develop relationships so He helps us by putting people on our path. He *wants* to meet each of those needs. Even though He knows what we need, He wants us to ask Him in faith, knowing in our hearts that He will meet our needs.

GOD WILL REWARD YOUR GOOD DEEDS

Matthew 6:1, 4 (NLT)

Take care! Don't do your good deeds publicly, to be admired, because then you will lose the reward from your Father in heaven…
Give your gifts in secret, and your Father, who knows all secrets, will reward you.

During our working life, we have daily opportunities to help our co-workers with small and big things. Jesus tells us to be careful not to broadcast it when we help somebody because that's all the reward we will receive. Instead, we are to help others and keep it a secret. Then, our Father, who sees all things and knows all secrets, will reward us.

Sometimes, nobody will ever know what you did for somebody else to help them get a new job, to complete a task successfully, or to finish a project on time. It doesn't matter what it is. God knows. Other times, God Himself will make it public to the right people, at the right time. Let God surprise you with His reward, whether it's here on earth or in heaven. He will always reward you when you help others from your heart, with pure motives.

The same way we are to do our good deeds in secret, Jesus tells us to pray and fast in secret (Matthew 6:5 NLT). That way, only God knows, and He will reward us.

GOD'S THOUGHTS AND WAYS ARE HIGHER THAN OURS

Isaiah 55:8-9 (KJV)

For my thoughts are not your thoughts, neither are your ways my ways, saith the Lord. For as the heavens are higher than the earth, so are my ways higher than your ways, and my thoughts than your thoughts.

We will never be able to understand God with our natural minds. But that's okay. We, as believers, walk by faith having the revelation that He loves us. God's thoughts and His ways are so much higher than ours, so much bigger and different than we could ever imagine. How can we ever think our ideas are better than His? He already thought it all out, from the beginning to the end, from the moment we were born until our last breath here on earth and then in eternity.

Purpose to live your life God's way and not your way. Follow His plan, not your plan. Get to know Him by spending time with Him. Ask yourself these questions: Are your work and career plans aligned with God's will for your life? Are God's thoughts and ways reflected in your life?

120

GOD'S WORD PREPARES AND EQUIPS US

2 Timothy 3:16-17 (NLT)

All Scripture is inspired by God and is useful to teach us what is true and to make us realize what is wrong in our lives. It straightens us out and teaches us to do what is right. It is God's way of preparing us in every way, fully equipped for every good thing God wants us to do.

God wants each one of us to do something. He has a plan and a purpose for every person. But He doesn't expect us to go figure it out on our own. He provided us with a manual full of instructions, wisdom, and revelation to prepare us and equip us. He gave us the Word to use on a daily basis as our guide.

The Bible provides us direction for every area of our lives, including business. It teaches us what's right and wrong and how God expects us to behave and perform in the business world. Let's use it, spend time in it, and meditate on it day and night. We need it, and God knew it.

121

GOD'S PROMISES ARE PURE

Psalm 12:6 (NLT)

The Lord's promises are pure, like silver refined in a furnace,
purified seven times over.

The Bible is full of God's promises for our lives. Yet it is sad to see that humanity in general doesn't enjoy the full blessings of God. It all starts with us accepting Jesus in our hearts as our Savior. Then God can start working in us for the rest of our lives until we meet Him in heaven. As He works in us, His promises manifest in our lives. God is looking for pure hearts, for men and women who want to love Him back just because His is God, our Father, and our Creator. Our hearts should be like His heart and like His promises—pure like silver refined in a furnace and purified seven times.

When we want something in life, the first step is to examine our hearts and the motive. Why do we want success in any area of our lives? Is it to satisfy our own desires? Or are we including God in our plans of success? God's promise to us is that if we take delight in the Lord, He will give us the desires of our hearts. If we commit everything we do to the Lord and trust Him, He will help us (Psalm 37:4-5 NLT).

God gives us many promises. Some of my favorites are in Psalm 103:3-5 (NLT), "He forgives all my sins and heals all my diseases. He ransoms me from death and surrounds me with love and tender mercies. He fills my life with good things. My youth is renewed like the eagle's!" We must believe in God's promises—all of them—because they are pure and real.

122

GOD'S WAY IS PERFECT

Psalm 18:30 (NLT)

As for God, his way is perfect. All the Lord's promises prove true. He is a shield for all who look to him for protection.

Everything we need to live a successful life we can find in the Bible. God gave us instructions and commandments to help us follow Him. His way is perfect. The Bible also contains God's promises for our lives and proof that He fulfills each promise. In addition, as our shield and protector, He is always waiting for us to run to Him and seek His protection. Interaction plays an important part in our walk with God. Therefore, just as He does His part in being our shield, we have to do our part in running to Him. That's why when Jesus left the earth, He left His Holy Spirit so we could communicate with God.

The Holy Spirit has all the qualities of God. Through His Spirit, God tells us how much He loves us and also reveals His plan for our lives. The promises God gives to us personally can come true if we obey Him. Even though God has a plan for our lives, we still have to choose to do His plan and obey each step He asks us to do. Without obedience, His plan in our lives cannot happen.

Always keep the Lord involved in your everyday life. Sometimes you may not involve God when you need help in business because you think it's not a spiritual matter. However, God is the master of business, and you should involve Him. He is the one who gives you the business ideas to begin with. So, ask God for advice in your job and in your business endeavors. His way is perfect in every area.

HOW DO WE LOVE OTHERS?

Matthew 22:39 (NLT)

A second is equally important: 'Love your neighbor as yourself.'

The first commandment Jesus gave us is to love God with all our heart, soul, and mind. Then He said it is equally important to love others as ourselves. How do we accomplish this when there are so many unlovable, unlikable people in the world? By loving people as Jesus did, with the love of God in us. It is not possible to love all the people with human love, but it is possible to love every human being with the love of God.

How do we obtain the love of God in our hearts and the ability to love people with *His* kind of love? By asking Him to put that love in our hearts. "If you believe, you will receive whatever you ask for in prayer" (Matthew 21:22 NLT). Because it is definitely in the will of God that we love others, He will give us His love to love people.

How do we show godly love for people? The workplace gives us great opportunities to demonstrate it. Some ways are by praying for those in leadership and authority at our companies, by praying for our employees if we are in management, or by praying for co-workers when they have needs. We also show godly love when we don't gossip about others, when we respect our leaders, help another team on a special project, and show interest in our co-workers' families.

As you can see, there are many ways to show godly love at work. Ask God for opportunities to show His love through you.

124

I Will Not Be Shaken!

Psalm 16:8 (NLT)

I know the Lord is always with me. I will not be shaken, for he is right beside me.

When you know in your heart that the Lord is with you, you have a peace that surpasses all understanding. It is the peace of God working in you so you are not shaken.

There are certain life events that can shake you, such as the death of a loved one, the loss of your job, divorce, or living through a natural disaster. If you find yourself living through any of the above situations, know that God is with you. He is right beside you, walking through it with you. He is holding your hand and lighting the way when it's dark all around you. He is your comforter, your helper, your hope, and the one who loves you more than anyone on this earth.

The Lord Jesus is your Rock. Building your house on the Rock means you build your life based only on the truth of God's Word. It is doing always what's right and knowing the foundation is the love of God. Everything He does in your life is founded on His amazing love. In fact, the whole plan of salvation is based on His eternal love for *you* and desire to be with you forever.

When you build your life, your house, on Him, you will not be shaken when the storms of life come. Your house will stand. When the storm is over, you will still be standing on Him and His Word. It doesn't matter what it looks like on the outside or around you. You will know where you stand because of what you believe.

Remember these words when you go through a storm in your life. Hang on to the Lord, and you will not be shaken.

125

JESUS DID IT ALL

Isaiah 53:3 (NLT)

He was despised and rejected—a man of sorrows, acquainted with bitterest grief. We turned our backs on him and looked the other way when he went by. He was despised, and we did not care.

Do you know the man the prophet Isaiah is talking about? His name is Jesus Christ, our Lord and Savior.

Since we humans messed up and gave Satan control over this earth, God came up with a plan to bring us back to Him. It is the plan of salvation God gave to Jesus to fulfill when He was on this earth. It is a simple plan that humans complicated. God sent His only begotten Son to save us and for all who believe to have everlasting life. When we accept Jesus as our Lord and Savior, we accept salvation. We restore our fellowship with God the Father.

The following verses complete the story. "Yet it was our weaknesses he carried; it was our sorrows that weighed him down. And we thought his troubles were a punishment from God for his own sins! But he was wounded and crushed for our sins. He was beaten that we may have peace. He was whipped, and we were healed! All of us have strayed away like sheep. We have left God's paths to follow our own. Yet the Lord laid on him the guilt and sins of us all. He was oppressed and treated harshly, yet he never said a word. He was led as a lamb to the slaughter. And as a sheep is silent before the shearers, he did not open his mouth. From prison and trial they lead him away to his death…But it was the Lord's good plan to crush him and fill him with grief… He will enjoy a long life, and the Lord's plan will prosper in his hands. When he sees all that is accomplished by his anguish, he will be satisfied. And because of what he has experienced, my righteous servant will make it possible for many to be counted righteous, for he will bear all their sins" (vv. 4-11). If you haven't given your life to Jesus yet, it is never too late. Today is *your* day!

KNOW YOUR BENEFITS

Psalm 103:1-5 (NKJV)

*Bless the Lord, O my soul; And all that is within me,
bless His holy name! Bless the Lord, O my soul, And forget not all
His benefits:
Who forgives all your iniquities, Who heals all your diseases,
Who redeems your life from destruction,
Who crowns you with lovingkindness and tender mercies,
Who satisfies your mouth with good things,
So that your youth is renewed like the eagle's.*

Nowadays, companies strive to offer great benefits to their employees. Yet nothing compares to the benefits we have for being children of God. Psalm 103 gives us examples of those benefits. But how do we obtain them?

We seek God first—above all things (Matthew 6:33 NLT).

We accept Jesus as our Lord and Savior (John 3:16, Romans 10:10 NLT).

We believe and accept all of His promises. We appropriate them by faith and we live by faith (2 Corinthians 5:7 NLT).

Knowing who we are in Christ and that we are God's precious children is a revelation that we must obtain. Once we have that revelation in our hearts we can be successful in every area of our lives—both at work and at home. Therefore, know your benefits and thank God for them.

127

LET'S BE PATIENT WITH GOD

Psalm 37:7 (NLT)

Be still in the presence of the Lord, and wait patiently for him to act.

Our human nature is impatient. Our society today reflects our impatience as we expect faster results, quicker turn around with business deals, and adopt the fast food mentality. Everything we do now has to be quick; otherwise, we don't meet our client's expectations. The same way, when we are the client, we expect the same—speed.

The now mentality, along with improved technology, has worked against us in many ways. Employers expect employees to do more work in less time than before we had technology. We are expected to produce, produce, produce like machines.

The lack of patience leads us to treat people rudely and disrespectfully. We have become impatient even with our own kids. We expect them to learn sports, read, write, and ride their bikes all before they start kindergarten! We encourage and push them to grow up faster than they should.

Impatience also creates stress and disappointment due to unmet expectations. Our relationship with the Lord reflects this behavior. We ask Him for something, in a hurry of course, and expect to receive it instantly—or at least by the time we get home from work. God doesn't work that way. He is a God of time. He is eternal and therefore, never in a hurry. He is never late or early, always on time.

We must also realize that sometimes we are not ready to receive what we asked God for. We may have to change in some areas, and that takes time. Once we ask God for something, we must trust Him that He will bring it to pass at the right time and in His own way. Therefore, be patient with God.

128

LOVE GOD WITH ALL OF YOUR BEING

Matthew 22:37-38 (NLT)

*"'You must love the Lord your God with all your heart, all your soul,
and all your mind.'
This is the first and greatest commandment."*

Jesus gave us the principles to live our Christian life. The first one is to love God above all. The second one is to love others as we love ourselves. Why is this so difficult to do? Simply, because we live in this world and because we are human. It is hard and it is our daily fight, yet it is not impossible when we allow God, through His Holy Spirit working on our hearts, to help us love Him and others.

How do we *love* God? When we rededicate our lives to Him on a daily basis, when we acknowledge Him as our God and Father, when we accept Jesus as our Lord and Savior, when we have a humble and thankful heart, we *love* Him. When we ask Him to show us His love and to give us that love and compassion for others, we *love* Him with all our heart and soul. When we meditate day and night on His Word we *love* Him with all our mind. When we are faithful and loyal to Him, no matter what we experience in this life, we *love* Him with all our hearts.

The fact that we have problems and tribulations doesn't mean He doesn't care or doesn't love us. Tribulation is simply a consequence of living in a sinful world. We shouldn't let this be an excuse to not love Him back. He already loved us first by sending His only Son, Jesus, to die for us so we can be saved and live with Him eternally in heaven.

129

ONLY GOD IS OUR SOURCE OF STRENGTH

Philippians 4:13 (KJV)

I can do all things through Christ which strengtheneth me.

God is our source of strength; nothing, or nobody else, can give us that—only Him. These days we have so much to do, so many priorities, that some days we don't know where to start. That's when we run to our source, the Lord. First, we ask Him to refocus us and realign our true priorities. Once we are on track again, we ask for the grace and the strength to do what He has called us to do.

God has a big plan for each of us; however, He doesn't expect us to do it all at once. He takes us one step at a time—from the big picture to the daily tasks—to accomplish His vision for us. We can do all the things He has called us to do through Christ because He gives us the strength we need on a daily basis.

130

ONLY JESUS NEVER SINNED

Ecclesiastes 7:20 (NLT)

There is not a single person in all the earth who is always good and never sins.

We are all sinners because we are human. But there is hope. God sent Jesus to forgive our sins and save us from eternal damnation. All we have to do is accept Jesus into our hearts as our Lord and Savior. That is the first step. Then we are to live our lives following Jesus' example. His life recorded in the Bible represents all the guidelines and expectations of a Christian.

Our Christian life is a daily walk where we have to repent daily of our sins. We cannot always do good or stop sinning once we get saved. But God forgives us when we repent from the heart and when we forgive others. The Bible says if we don't forgive others, then God will not forgive us.

Jesus was the only human being who walked on the earth and never sinned. He loved God, His Father, above all. He obeyed all of His commands and always walked in His will. Jesus is our example of the ultimate Christian life.

God doesn't expect us to be perfect because He knows we live in an imperfect world with evil all around us. He expects us, however, to follow Jesus' example, to love Him above all, and to obey His commands. As we strive to live a sinless life, He sees our hearts and helps us. He cleanses us from our sins, changes us, and gives us a fresh start daily.

131

OUR GOD IS A GOD OF MIRACLES AND WONDERS

Psalm 77:13-14 (NLT)

O God, your ways are holy. Is there any god as mighty as you? You are the God of miracles and wonders! You demonstrate your awesome power among the nations.

This is a psalm of Asaph praising God for His mighty power and asking Him for help. If you are in need of a miracle right now in your life, stand on this verse and believe you serve a God of miracles and wonders. He is able to do and perform beyond what you ask or think. The God of this universe is your Father and He loves you. He is willing and able to perform miracles in your life.

Don't give up. Keep on fighting and praying in faith, believing the Lord will come through for you. No situation is impossible for God. Everything is possible for those who believe. Matthew 19:26 (KJV) says, "With men this is impossible; but with God all things are possible."

There is no situation at work or home God cannot resolve.

PATIENCE, ENDURANCE, JOY, THANKFULNESS

Colossians 1:11-12 (NLT)

We also pray that you will be strengthened with his glorious power so that you will have all the patience and endurance you need. May you be filled with joy, always thanking the Father, who has enabled you to share the inheritance that belongs to God's holy people, who live in the light.

As Christian working women we need four major ingredients to be successful in every area of our lives. They are: a thankful heart, patience, endurance, and joy. We must be thankful, first of all, because of the great inheritance we have and for everything God does for us on a daily basis. We need patience both at work and at home. We need to be patient with people as well as with the Lord to wait for His promises to be manifested in our lives. We need endurance or longsuffering to persevere and win in life. Finally, we need the joy of the Lord to give us the strength to go on each day.

Don't *ever* give up. Draw from the Lord the patience and endurance you need to go on. Be joyful and thankful!

133

REMEMBER YOUR PASTORS AND THOSE WHO TAUGHT YOU THE WORD OF GOD

Hebrews 13:7 (NLT)

Remember your leaders who first taught you the word of God. Think of all the good that has come from their lives, and trust the Lord as they do.

We all have people who influence our lives. One of those people is usually our pastor. We are to hold them in high esteem because of the position of influence and responsibility God has placed them in. Therefore, we need to remember our pastor in our prayers. We need to ask God to give him or her strength to go on, wisdom to lead the flock, and revelation in Him. Let's thank pastors for their work and sacrifices. Let's imitate their faith and follow their example of faithfulness to the Lord.

If you are currently not connected to a local church, ask God to place you in the one that pleases Him. It is important to be part of a church where they can help you and provide support in your life. The church is also a place where you will be able to supply your gifts and help others. Don't become too busy with work or home chores that you do not make time to attend church. You also need to make time with the Lord to grow and get to know Him at the personal level. If you don't make the time, it won't happen. Belonging to a church is another crucial element for your success in every area of your life.

134

REPLACE DOUBTS WITH HIS PROMISES

Psalm 94:19 (NLT)

*When doubts filled my mind, your comfort gave me
renewed hope and cheer.*

We all have, from time to time, sleepless nights when our minds wonder and our hearts become overwhelmed with doubts. The enemy's plan is to first attack our minds with thoughts of doubt about God's promises for our lives. If we entertain them and don't cast them out, those doubts will sink into our hearts. This is how he deceives us and eventually, if we allow him, we will move away from God's plan and will for our lives.

If you have doubts as to why you are in the job you are or in the company you are working at, ask God to help you remember your mission. Sometimes we are at a place to learn and attain new skills. Other times we are in a specific job to help others. When the time is right, God will move you to a new job. But instead of entertaining thoughts of doubt, seek God through His Word. Replace the doubt with a promise like this verse and receive the "new hope and cheer" from His comfort. Remember, His biggest promise is that He loves you.

135

STAY THIRSTY AND HUNGRY FOR GOD

Psalm 107:9 (NLT)

For he satisfies the thirsty and fills the hungry with good things.

During our lives, we experience seasons when we feel closer to God than others. During those times, we feel thirsty and hungry for Him so we go to church, read our Bible more often, and try to pray more than the usual. However, this is not enough to survive the attacks of the enemy on a daily basis. It is like living our daily lives on snacks alone where our bodies are not getting enough food to eat and are missing necessary nutrients. It is the same with our spiritual life. We can't expect to survive a spiritual attack if we are spiritually malnourished. We simply won't have what it takes to fight back, and we will lose the battle.

The workplace can be sometimes a place of peace or a battlefield. We need to be physically and spiritually nourished to do a good job and to deal with all the daily situations that arise.

Therefore, choose to always remain thirsty and hungry for God. Again, this is a daily choice. God is ready to pour out His love and all of Himself into you until you are full and satisfied. Only then you will be equipped to fight back and obtain the victory in every attack of the enemy, both at work and at home.

136

TAP INTO GOD'S GRACE

2 Timothy 2:1 (KJV)

Thou therefore, my son, be strong in the grace that is in Christ Jesus.

2 Corinthians 12:9 (KJV)

And he said to me, my grace is sufficient for thee: for my strength is made perfect in weakness.

During the course of our working lives, we will experience crisis — either at home or at work. How do we manage to get through it? By God's grace that is available through Jesus Christ. If we find we can't go on anymore, it means we are not tapping into God's grace. He will never leave us nor forsake us (Deuteronomy 31:8 NLT). He gives us the grace we need on a daily basis to live through every one of the situations we experience. When we are weak He gives us strength to go on because He is our source of strength.

Therefore, ask God for His grace on a daily basis. When crisis comes, ask Him for a double dosage. He will give it to you, and you will have the strength to go through it. His grace is sufficient unto *you*.

137

TAP INTO THE GIFT OF GRACE

Hebrews 4:16 (NLT)

So let us come boldly to the throne of our gracious God. There we will receive his mercy, and we will find grace to help us when we need it.

Hebrews 6:20 (NLT)

Jesus has already gone in there for us. He has become our eternal High Priest in the line of Melchizedek.

Jesus, as our High Priest, knows our weaknesses and represents us before God. He took this position willingly because He loves us.

Whenever you sin (in any area), go to God and ask for forgiveness. He will receive you with open arms and by His mercy He will heal your heart. He will also give you grace to help you go on. It is by grace you were saved to begin with, and it is also by grace that you can make it through life on a daily basis. Ephesians 2:8 (NIV) says, "For it is by grace you have been saved, through faith—and this not from yourselves, it is the gift of God."

His grace is always available to you, and there is a special kind of grace that God will give you to deal with every situation—including work. When you are drowning in work, are having health issues, and/or have family related activities going on, ask God for His grace to get you through. Some day you will look back and say, "How did I do it?" It was by His grace. Thank Him in advance for this gift.

THE GODLY WILL FLOURISH

Psalm 92:12-13 (NLT)

But the godly will flourish like palm trees, and grow strong like the cedars of Lebanon. For they are transplanted into the Lord's own house. They flourish in the courts of God.

This is a great promise of God to all of us. Sometimes we see the worldly people succeed and we wonder, is it worth it? Are the fight and sacrifices we make on a daily basis to live a godly life worth it? Yes and yes. The Bible reminds us of the wicked's short-lived success. Their final destination is eternal destruction. Our final destination is eternal life with God. Therefore, our efforts and focus must be in sharing the good news of the Gospel so more people can partake of eternal life. God makes us strong, like the big cedar trees that stand for years and years.

We, the godly, are transplanted directly to God's own house. What a privilege that is! We cannot take it for granted. His promise to us is that we will flourish in His presence and grow strong so we can do His work on earth.

Don't get weary in living a godly life for doing so is worth everything. Even if you work in a worldly environment, continue to be an example and the light to the world around you. You are strong in the Lord, and you will flourish.

139

THE LORD IS OUR SOURCE OF STRENGTH AND PEACE

Psalm 29:11 (NLT)

The Lord gives his people strength. The Lord blesses them with peace.

God is so powerful! He used His power to raise Jesus from the dead. The Holy Spirit gives us that same power, which is the source of our strength. This is one of the many benefits we have as children of God. We are weak but made strong in the Lord. He gives us the strength we need on a daily basis to fulfill the calling He has given us. He also blessed us with His peace that surpasses all understanding. The peace of God cannot be found in this world because it can only come from Him. Peace is another great benefit He gives us because He loves us.

When the stress of life with work and home responsibilities is getting to you, stand on His promise and go to the source of strength and peace—God.

140

THE LORD IS WAITING FOR PEOPLE TO REPENT

2 Peter 3:8-9 (NLT)

But you must not forget, dear friends, that a day is like a thousand years to the Lord, and a thousand years is like a day. The Lord isn't really being slow about his promise to return, as some people think. No, he is being patient for your sake. He does not want anyone to perish, so he is giving more time for everyone to repent.

You may have friends who know you are a Christian and mock you because you expectantly wait for Jesus to come back. Memorize the verse above to make your friends aware the reason He hasn't come back is because of people like them—to give them more time to repent and believe. God truly doesn't want to lose any of His sheep. But it is our choice after all. We have free will. It is because of God's mercy that Jesus hasn't come back yet.

If you are reading these words today and you are not saved, make a decision to accept Christ right now. Just tell Him you repent of your sins, you believe He died for you to have eternal life, and you want Him to be Lord of your life (John 3:16 NLT). You need to do three basic things: acknowledge that you are a sinner, believe in Jesus as your Savior, and confess to other people that He is your Savior.

If you are reading these words today and you are saved, continue to pray for your friends and loved ones and be a witness to them of the love of God, because time is short. God doesn't want anyone to perish—that includes you and your loved ones.

141

THE WORD IS OUR LIGHT

Psalm 119:105, 130 (NLT)

Your word is a lamp for my feet and a light for my path…
As your words are taught, they give light; even the simple can
understand them.

Some people jokingly say their babies should come with a manual. Well, they do. The Bible is our instruction manual on how to raise our children from the moment they are born and throughout their entire lives. It is also a guide for us on how to live our lives here on earth. It is for all people across cultures, generations, and backgrounds.

The Bible is the Word of God written for us and directed to us. It is divinely inspired by God through many people, and, together, it makes the perfect book. The Word can be read by anybody who is hungry to learn about God and to know Him personally. He gives us examples of successes and failures of His chosen people so we can learn. The Bible is a lamp unto our feet that lights up our path. The world we live in is dark, but we have the lamp, the light, which is God Himself.

Proverbs 4:18 (KJV) says, "But the path of the just is as the shining light, that shineth more and more unto the perfect day."

God wants every person to learn His Word. He has it available for all to read and learn His ways. He doesn't want anybody to be lost. It doesn't matter how little or much education you have. The Bible is for *you*. It is your manual for success in every area of your life—including work.

142

THERE IS PURPOSE IN OUR WORK

Ecclesiastes 2:26 (NLT)

God gives wisdom, knowledge, and joy to those who please him.

King Solomon was reflecting on work, all the effort it takes to create wealth, and the fruit of his work. He realized that the pleasure of working, and everything it brings, comes from the hand of God. Otherwise, working, work itself, and the fruit of it are all worthless without or apart from God.

When we obey God's Word and His direction to our lives, we are in His will. This pleases Him. The Bible tells us God gives wisdom, knowledge, and joy to those who please Him.

My desire is for you, as a working woman, to have a purpose in your work. Don't just work because you need the money. Don't treat your job just like work that produces a paycheck. Think of it as something purposeful; do it as unto the Lord and for others. You can find purpose in any job when you look at the big picture and know why God placed you there and work as unto Him.

Ask God to reveal to you why He placed you in the work-place you are. Ask Him to give you a purpose and to help you have an attitude of gratitude toward Him. Thank Him for your job and do it cheerfully. Ecclesiastes 3:13 (NLT) says "people should eat and drink and enjoy the fruits of their labor, for these are gifts from God."

WAIT EXPECTANTLY ON THE LORD

Psalm 5:3 (NLT)

Listen to my voice in the morning, Lord.
Each morning I bring my requests to you and wait expectantly.

David's plea to the Lord was a daily act of faith. Every morning he talked to God and made his requests known to Him. He then waited on God and expected Him to listen to his prayers and an-swer them. We often treat God as a magician. We tell Him what we want and expect Him to respond immediately, like magic! We don't wait patiently on Him. Other times we pray to God and don't even expect Him to hear or answer our prayer. Then we get discouraged and stop asking altogether. We lose our faith in God. Both extremes are wrong. We are to ask God to meet our needs and wait expectantly as David did.

When we wait on the Lord we put our faith, hope, and trust in Him. This act blesses God. He then gives us the grace we need to wait until His answer manifests. We must learn to wait pa-tiently because His timetable is not ours. He knows what's best for us and that includes the right time. When His timing comes, He will give us a solution better than any we would have thought of on our own.

If you need change in your workplace, a new boss, a different job, or want to change fields, wait expectantly from the Lord. Expect to receive whatever He thinks is best for you, not just what you asked Him for. Once you give your request to Him, sincerely believe in your heart that He will answer your prayer and thank Him in advance for the answer.

WE ARE SAVED BY GRACE THROUGH FAITH

Galatians 2:16 (NLT)

And yet we Jewish Christians know that we become right with God, not by doing what the law commands, but by faith in Jesus Christ. So we have believed in Christ Jesus, that we might be accepted by God because of our faith in Christ—and not because we have obeyed the law. For no one will ever be saved by obeying the law.

God promised Abraham a savior. God gave Moses the laws 430 years later to keep the people guarded until Jesus came. When Jesus realized God's promise on earth, the old system of the law was no longer needed. According to the old law, people were cursed if they didn't follow the law. But when Jesus died on the cross, He became sin and was cursed for us. "Cursed is everyone who is hung on a tree" (Galatians 3:13 NLT). So now that faith in Christ has come, we no longer need the law as our guardian. We are all children of God through faith in Jesus Christ. Therefore, we are united in Christ, and there is no more Jew or Gentile, slave or free, male or female—we are one in Christ Jesus. Once we belong to Christ, we are true children of Abraham. We are his heirs, and now all the promises God gave to him belong to us (vv. 9-29).

The message is, all humans alike, are saved by the grace of God through our faith in Jesus Christ. This was God's plan from the beginning; it is the same now, and will never change. The only thing we have to do is accept Jesus in our hearts and have faith in Him. He already did the rest to save us.

145

WE ARE TO BE STRONG

Psalm 18:32 (NLT)

God arms me with strength; he has made my way safe.

Most of us think of strength as being physical only. But we need to have emotional and spiritual strength as well to be successful in life. It doesn't matter how physically strong a person is. If they are not strong in the other areas, they are not going to make it through the storms of life.

We draw our strength in all areas from God. All we have to do is seek Him above all things and ask Him for strength. The more time we spend alone with the Lord, the stronger our relationship with Him is and the stronger we become.

The most important area to be strong is our spirit because it drives the other two areas of physical and emotional strength. When we are spiritually strong, we know our purpose in life, we have a strong faith, and we don't give up the daily fight as easily.

In the workplace, now more than ever, we must be strong working women. We must be strong to stand our ground and fight for what we believe. We must be strong to be able to meet all the demands of our jobs. We must be strong to make the right decisions on a daily basis, and then stand by the decisions we make.

Knowing and appropriating the Word of God and His promises gives us strength. The Bible gives us several scriptures that encourage us to be strong such as: "I can do all things through Christ which strengtheneth me" (Philippians 4:13 KJV); "If God is for us, who can ever be against us?" (Romans 8:31 NLT); "In all these things we are more than conquerors through him that loved us" (Romans 8:37 KJV).

146

WE EACH HAVE SPECIAL GIFTS

Ephesians 4:7 (NLT)

However, he has given each one of us a special gift according to the generosity of Christ.

In verse 6, Paul tells the church of Ephesus that we (both Jews and Gentiles) have one God, one faith, and one baptism, and God reigns over us all. But He chose to give special gifts to each one of us. God appointed Jesus to distribute the gifts as He ascended to heaven. He is generous, so there is more than one gift given to each person. He gave gifts to the church (apostles, prophets, evangelists, pastors, and teachers) for the purpose of edifying, equipping, and building up the body of Christ. But He also gave other gifts to each person so everyone can do their part and form (fitly put together) the entire body of Christ. We each have a gift, a responsibility, and a part to play in God's greater plan.

Do you know what your special and specific gifts are? If not, ask God to reveal them to you. You may have the gift of working with numbers, with people, or setting up events. You may be gifted in the area of sales, public speaking, or mentoring others. You are where you are for a purpose and your company needs all of your gifts to succeed. Are you using your gifts and talents at work? If not, start today.

WE WERE BORN TO KNOW HIM

Isaiah 43:10 (NLT)

"But you are my witnesses, O Israel!" says the Lord. "And you are my servant. You have been chosen to know me, believe in me, and understand that I alone am God. There is no other God; there never has been and never will be."

Because we are the seed of Abraham through Jesus and by our faith, this message is for us. We have been *chosen* to know God. What a privilege! The only one God—the true God—has chosen us to be His friends, to get to know Him, to fellowship with Him, and to enjoy all of His blessings. However, it is only by spending time with Him and reading His Word we get to know Him. When we know Him, it's easier to obey Him because we trust Him. When we know Him, we find out how much He loves us and cares about every detail in our lives. We realize He has a great plan for our lives, and His plan is far better than anything we could have ever dreamed up by ourselves.

We, as His chosen people, are His children and servants. We are His children because He adopted us and paid a price to purchase us through Jesus' blood. We are also His servants because we have work to do on His behalf here on earth. We each have an assignment that only we can complete. It is a unique calling that aligns with our personality, gifts, talents, and skills. Therefore, we must be willing to follow His plan, believe, and obey every step He directs us to do. Our goal at the end of our lives should be to hear God say to us "well done, thou good and faithful servant: thou hast been faithful over a few things, I will make thee ruler over many things: enter thou into the joy of thy lord" (Matthew 25:21 KJV). This reward will be better than any work or job we would have done in our lives.

Step into the privilege of being a chosen one and start knowing God personally and intimately. Build a relationship with your Creator and start enjoying the most fulfilled life you could ever imagine.

148

WEALTH AND HEALTH ARE GIFTS FROM GOD

Ecclesiastes 5:19 (NLT)

And it is a good thing to receive wealth from God and the good health to enjoy it. To enjoy your work and accept your lot in life—that is indeed a gift from God.

What is wealth to you? Wealth can have different meanings to different people. For some, it may simply mean to have a job, one car, a comfortable home, and to provide for their family. For other people, it means to have millions of dollars, many cars, homes, big toys, travel to exotic places, and have influence in their community or even the world.

I believe there are two kinds of wealth: the one that comes from the world that only brings sorrow and eventually destruction, and the one that comes from God that brings peace and joy. He brings wealth and adds no sorrow to it. When you dedicate your life to serve God and He gives you wealth, you must recognize it is His gift and use it for Him.

The same way when you are in good health, thank God for it and acknowledge it is a gift from Him. Don't take your health for granted. In today's world, being healthy is almost the exception, not the rule.

In all you do, enjoy the gifts of God—including your work.

149

WHEN WE WORSHIP GOD, WE WALK IN HIS LIGHT

Psalm 89:15 (NLT)

Happy are those who hear the joyful call to worship, for they will walk in the light of your presence, Lord.

We are all called to worship God. He created us to love Him, to fellowship with Him, and to worship Him. It is like a chain of events. When we worship Him, our hearts connect with His in a supernatural way. He then imparts His heart to us so we can walk in the light of His presence.

When we walk in His light, darkness and confusion dissipate, things become clear. We have His divine protection and the enemy can't overcome us. Verse 16 says that we will also rejoice all day long in His wonderful reputation. We rejoice in His name.

Therefore, make time to worship God. Don't let the busyness of your job, household chores, and other responsibilities rob you of this wonderful privilege. You will see new doors of opportunities and blessings when you walk in His light as a result of you spending time worshipping God.

150

WITH GOD ALL THINGS ARE POSSIBLE— INCLUDING SALVATION

Matthew 19:26 (KJV)

But Jesus beheld them, and said unto them, With men this is impossible; but with God all things are possible.

In the verses prior to this one Jesus confronted a rich young man who always kept all of the commandments and followed the law. But when Jesus asked him to sell everything he had and give the proceeds to the poor, he couldn't do it "for he had great possessions." Then, when Jesus told His disciples that it was very hard for a rich person to enter the Kingdom of heaven, His disciples were astounded and asked him, "Who then can be saved?" (v. 25).

We in our own ability cannot be saved. We cannot purchase salvation because Jesus already did that when He died on the cross for our sins. Jesus is not saying rich people won't go to heaven. It is a matter of the heart. People, rich or poor, who put their trust in riches, will not enter the Kingdom of heaven. Those who put their trust in God, and love Him above all, will.

No matter how many good deeds we do in this world, if we don't accept Jesus as our Lord and Savior, we will simply not go to heaven. Jesus is the *only* way to the Father. That is His *only* plan of salvation for humanity. There is no other. For us it is impossible to go to heaven on our own but with God all things are possible—including our salvation.

Seek Jesus. He is the truth, the light and the way. John 3:16-17 (NLT) say, "For God so loved the world that he gave his only Son, so that everyone who believes in him will not perish but have eternal life. God did not send his Son into the world to condemn it, but to save it." Romans 10:9-10 (NLT) says, "For if you confess with your mouth that Jesus is Lord and believe in your heart that God raised him from the dead, you will be saved. For it is by believing in your heart that you are made right with God, and it is by confessing with your mouth that you are saved."

FAITH

151

ALL THINGS ARE POSSIBLE IF YOU BELIEVE

Mark 9:23 (NKJV)

Jesus said to him, "If you can believe, all things are possible to him who believes."

A man brought his child possessed with an evil spirit to the disciples and they were not able to cast it out. At that point, the child's father, disappointed, told Jesus, "Do something if you can." Then Jesus replied, "If you can believe, all things are possible to him who believes." After that, the child's father said something that moved Jesus. He said, "Lord, I believe; help my unbelief!" The New Living Translation says it this way, "I do believe, but help me not to doubt!" (v. 24).

So often our spirit is willing and wants to believe, we really want to have faith, but our mind is going the other way, trying to rationalize everything and letting in doubt. The human mind is not capable of understanding the things of God. We need to put those thoughts down, believe with all our hearts, and ask God to help us believe. He is so merciful He even helps us believe when He knows we are trying our best and sincerely want to. Proverbs 3:5-6 (NLT) say, "Trust in the Lord with all your heart; do not depend on your own understanding. Seek his will in all you do, and he will direct your paths."

Don't stop believing for what is in your heart. Seek God with all your heart, mind, and soul, and He will help you. Remember, all things are possible to those who believe.

152

ALL WE NEED IS A LITTLE FAITH

Matthew 17:20 (NLT)

"I assure you, even if you had faith as small as a mustard seed you could say to this mountain, 'Move from here to there,' and it would move. Nothing would be impossible."

From the day we become Christian until the day we die, we are to walk by faith. That is the life of a Christian. Jesus tells us that if we had as little as a mustard-seed-size faith, we could do anything. That is because we are not the ones doing the miracles, God is. All He wants us to have is faith in Him that He can and will perform what we ask Him to do for us.

We have to *believe*! But how do we increase our faith? By hearing the Word of God repeatedly until it sinks into our hearts. In addition to believing, we have to *trust* Him that He will perform His promises in our personal lives, and we should *expect* them to come to pass. His promises, among many, include peace, joy, rest, love, protection, and, of course, the ultimate promise of salvation. They are all free gifts to us.

Once we have a little faith, we must put it to work and exercise it with the authority that God has given us. We start with small things and, as we pass the small faith tests, we will become more confident and our faith will continue to grow.

If you are having issues at work, if you are praying for a promotion, for a special client, project, a new boss or employee, or whatever it is, have faith that God will give you what you're asking for. Exercise your faith today.

153

BELIEVE, ASK, AND RECEIVE

Matthew 21:22 (NLT)

If you believe, you will receive whatever you ask for in prayer.

Jesus cursed the fig tree on the road because it had no fruit and immediately it withered up. The disciples were amazed, then Jesus said, "If you have faith and don't doubt, you can do things like this and much more" (v. 21). When we have faith and not doubt in our hearts that God can do what we're asking Him, He responds.

Some people abuse this scripture, however, and think God works like a genie. They ask Him for a house, a car, or material things, thinking they will just show up the next day on their driveway. First of all, God knows what we need. He knows our heart motives, and He also has a will for our lives. When we ask God for something that is clearly not in His will for our lives, He will not give it to us. A good example would be when a single woman asks God to give her somebody else's spouse. He will clearly not answer that prayer. Another example is if we ask God to get promoted to a specific job, yet don't posses any of the skills or experience necessary to do that job. In that case, we need to acquire knowledge and some additional skills to be considered for that position, then we can ask God for help.

We cannot expect God to give us things if we are not willing to do our part. The first step is to be in His will. We also have to work hard, get an education, obey Him, and have patience. Then believe we will receive what we ask for in faith and with no doubts.

154

DON'T LET UNBELIEF RISE UP IN YOU

Hebrews 12:15 (NLT)

Look after each other so that none of you will miss out on the special favor of God. Watch out that no bitter root of unbelief rises up among you, for whenever it springs up, many are corrupted by its poison.

God asks us to look after each other and keep each other accountable to stay in faith. We are also to guard our hearts from unbelief. It not only poisons us but it spreads to other people around us. The seed of unbelief must be rebuked and destroyed immediately; otherwise, it will grow in our hearts the same way as faith but with the opposite effect. Faith brings life; unbelief brings death.

How do you fight unbelief? Watch your words, watch your thoughts, and watch what you listen to. When you have done all you can, ask God for the gift of faith.

What and who are your input sources? TV, books, movies, the Internet, your work environment, and some friendships may influence you in a negative way by sowing seeds of unbelief in your heart. The same sources, however, can also sow good seed in your heart that eventually grows in faith. Therefore, seek friendships that will encourage you and keep you accountable in your faith walk. And, by all means, don't let unbelief rise up in you. Be like the boy's father who said to Jesus he believed but needed help with his doubts (Mark 9:24 NKJV). He admitted the problem we all have with unbelief, and God gave him the faith he needed when he needed it.

155

DON'T LOOK BACK. FIX YOUR EYES ON WHAT IS AHEAD.

Proverbs 4:25-26 (NLT)

*Look straight ahead, and fix your eyes on what lies before you.
Mark out a straight path for your feet; then stick to the path
and stay safe.*

When we desire to make a change in our lives, we have the tendency to want to look back. However, the Bible tells us we are to forget the past, look straight ahead, and fix our eyes on what lies before us. We are to set a straight path for our feet to walk on, and then stick to the path without getting distracted. Verse 27 says, "Don't get sidetracked; keep your feet from following evil." Since Jesus is the way, the truth, and the light, let's allow Him to set that path for us. He will walk with us on the narrow road that will lead us to the Father.

The business world, your family, and your community need you to be a decisive woman. Therefore, once you make a decision, don't look back; look ahead instead. Use the wisdom of God to make every plan, and use your faith to stick to the plan God gave you. As you walk your path, only look to Jesus for help. He is your guide when you lose direction and focus. He is your light when you have lost your own and your lamp runs out of oil. He is your friend when you feel alone and abandoned by your earthly friends. He is your joy when you lose it trying to stay on the narrow road. He is your shield when you fall and get hurt. He keeps you safe. And when you feel there is nothing to look forward to in this earthly life, don't get discouraged. What lies before you, as a believer, when your journey here is done, is an eternity with Jesus Christ in heaven.

156

FOCUS ON JESUS, NOT ON THE STORM

Matthew 14:29-30 (NLT)

"All right come," Jesus said. So Peter went over the side of the boat and walked on the water toward Jesus. But when he looked around at the high waves, he was terrified and began to sink.

Our daily Christian walk is like walking on water toward Jesus. Notice that when Peter was focused on Jesus and walking toward Him, he could do it. The moment he looked at the circumstances around him, he began to fear and sink. The high waves in this verse represent all the problems and issues we have to face in our lives. When we focus on Jesus only, He will get us through it all. He will help us do things (as Peter walked on water) we could have never done on our own. Jesus' compassion for us is so great that even when we are losing our faith, but we cry out to Him for help, He will immediately reach out to grab our hand. "Save me Lord!," Peter shouted, and "instantly Jesus reached out his hand and grabbed him" (v. 31).

If you are going through trials in your life right now at work or at home, don't lose your faith in Jesus. Acknowledge the storm, but don't focus on it. Instead, keep walking toward Him. He will guide you, comfort you, love you, and protect you as you walk on the water. Jesus is there for you always.

157

FORGIVE BEFORE YOU ASK

Mark 11:24-25 (NLT)

"Listen to me! You can pray for anything, and if you believe, you will have it. But when you are praying, first forgive anyone you are holding a grudge against, so that your Father in heaven will forgive your sins, too."

We hear verse 24 all the time. Ask, have faith, and you will get your prayer answered. But we hardly pay attention to an equally or more important thing we must do before praying in faith. "First forgive...," are the words Jesus used, "...anyone you may be holding a grudge against." Forgiving others is key to having our prayers answered. Not only that, but if we don't forgive others, God will not forgive our own sins. Without God's forgiveness, we are not going to enter His Kingdom. Being unforgiving is destructive in every way—physically, mentally, and spiritually. It is more destructive to our lives than to the person who offended us.

You can ask for anything in faith, but first you must forgive before you can receive your answer. Examine yourself on a daily basis and see if there is anybody who offended you whom you haven't forgiven yet. Of course, I believe the easier way to do this is to not get offended in the first place. At the moment the offense occurs, you have the choice to take the offense or to let it go. It is a decision you can make in an instant, but if you choose wrong, it can take you the rest of your life to forgive. It will be your baggage and burden for years until you give it to the Lord and have Him take care of it. God is looking for pure hearts and pure hearts don't have unforgiveness. The workplace is the perfect place to put this into practice on a daily basis, so start today.

158

GO TO GOD FIRST AND PRAY FERVENTLY

James 5:16

*The earnest prayer of a righteous person has a great power and
wonderful results* (NLT).
*The effectual fervent prayer of a righteous man
availeth much* (KJV).

When we become born again we are made righteous by the grace
of God. He listens to our prayers and responds.

Whenever you have a need of any kind, pray first. Ask God
for wisdom, grace, strength, favor, peace—whatever you need—
and He will help you. Always examine your heart to make sure
your motives are right. Then pray with fervency from your heart,
not casually, but with passion. The Bible tells us it is that kind of
prayer that has power and brings wonderful results.

In your job, when your workload is overwhelming, pray for
God to help you by multiplying your time and giving you ideas to
become more efficient. When you are out of balance and work has
taken over your life, ask God to help you prioritize your priorities
and bring you back to balance. Don't leave prayer as your last option because nothing else worked. Go to God first and apply this
principle to every area of your life.

159

GOD DOES HEAR AND ANSWERS OUR PRAYERS

Psalm 116:1 (NLT)

I love the Lord because he hears and answers my prayers.

Part of trusting God is knowing in your heart and believing that He does hear your prayers and that He does answer them. What are you praying for lately? What prayers have you been asking God that He has not answered yet? Are you expecting an answer from Him? I encourage you to continue to pray until you see the answer manifested.

Some prayers take longer to be answered than others, due to various reasons. Sometimes we are not ready to receive the answer and we need more preparation. Other times, we don't fully trust Him to perform what we're asking. Other times we may not be in His will, and He knows that what we're asking will harm us.

Every situation is different, every prayer request is different. If you are asking for a new job or for a work situation to be resolved, ask God to give you patience to wait for His perfect timing. If you are feeling He is not answering any of your prayers right now, thank Him for everything He has done for you in the past. This will lift your spirit and encourage you to continue to pray until He answers your prayer.

160

GOD GOES BEFORE YOU

Deuteronomy 31:8 (NLT)

*Do not be afraid or discouraged, for the Lord is the one
who goes before you.
He will be with you; he will neither fail you nor forsake you.*

Moses encouraged Joshua as he became the new leader of the Israelites, right before entering the Promised Land and crossing the
Jordan River. There are three important issues revealed in Moses'
words. First, if you are in any leadership position, you have the
opportunity to always encourage those under you. Moses continually told Joshua to not be afraid or discouraged, to finish the journey, to continue the fight, and to trust God in all things.

Secondly, Moses was confident in God's ability to help Joshua. Moses assured Joshua God was the one who would go before him, He would be with him, and would never leave him nor
forsake him. You, as a leader, need to be strong in your faith in
God. You must have a solid relationship with the Lord in order to
impart that confidence to those who look up to you. The people
you lead need that confidence in order to cross their Jordan and
do what they're called to do. You are the one who can encourage,
inspire, and motivate them to succeed with the assurance that God
will go before them and will help them.

The third important issue is that once you receive direction
and instructions from the Lord on what steps to take next, do it!
Don't be afraid. Don't get discouraged by circumstances or small
setbacks. Trust you heard from God. Go with your heart and know
beyond any doubt that God Himself is going before you, opening
doors for you, and protecting you. He is with you through His
Holy Spirit. He will never leave you nor forsake you.

161

GOD HELPS US THROUGH GRACE BY FAITH

Isaiah 41:10 (NLT)

Don't be afraid, for I am with you. Do not be dismayed, for I am your God. I will strengthen you. I will help you. I will uphold you with my victorious right hand.

Those are God's words for His chosen people of Israel. We must grab hold of those promises as well because we are Abraham's seed by faith. Galatians 3:14 (KJV) says, "The blessing of Abraham might come on the Gentiles through Jesus Christ; that we might receive the promise of the Spirit through faith."

If you have accepted and received Jesus in your heart as your Lord and Savior, then you qualify by faith to receive all of God's promises to His chosen people. You are a chosen one too.

Read this verse again and capture the depth of this promise. God the Father, the Creator of all, promises to help you, to lift you up when you're down, to strengthen you when you are weak, and to uphold you with His victorious right hand. What else can you want? He is the answer to all of your problems, hurts, desires, and needs.

It is difficult to believe these promises when you are going through hard times in your life. But God can help you and get you through. He will give you supernatural grace to withstand the attacks of the enemy and win the fight. It is a special and unique grace to deal with every situation—one at a time. "My grace is sufficient for thee: for my strength is made perfect in weakness" (2 Corinthians 12:9 KJV).

162

GOD LISTENS TO OUR REQUESTS WHEN THEY ALIGN WITH HIS WILL

1 John 5:14-15 (NLT)

And we can be confident that he will listen to us whenever we ask him for anything in line with his will. And if we know he is listening when we make our requests, we can be sure that he will give us what we ask for.

The Apostle John wrote this verse for all of us who believe in Jesus. The first step then is to believe Jesus is the Son of God and He died for our sins so we can go to heaven and have eternal life. This assures us that God listens to our prayers. We must notice, however, that He will give us whatever we ask for when it aligns with His will. Sometimes we ask repeatedly, with no results, for something that may be out of the will of God for our lives. So, how do we avoid frustration by asking for something that is not in His will? We ask God to reveal His will for our lives and for every circumstance. We also ask Him to exchange our worldly desires for godly desires. Then we can be confident He will grant us everything we ask for.

Have you been asking God for a new job, a promotion, or to switch careers and it's not happening? Ask Him what His will is for your career at this point in your life, then pray and believe He will listen and answer your prayers.

163

OUR FATHER KNOWS WHAT WE NEED

Matthew 6:7-8 (NLT)

When you pray, don't babble on and on as people of other religions do. They think their prayers are answered only by repeating their words again and again. Don't be like them, because your Father knows exactly what you need even before you ask him!

The Lord wants our prayers to be sincere, honest, and to the point. Jesus tells us that our Father already knows what we need, so there is no need to repeat words or prayers. God wants us to approach Him as a child approaches his dad. Kids are direct; they ask exactly for what they need. He wants us to ask because that is the way we acknowledge Him as our God, and it shows we trust Him.

Verses 9-14 show us how we are to pray. First of all, we are to honor Him. Then we ask for His will to be done here on earth (in our lives) as in heaven. We pray knowing we have need of things and, in faith, believing He will meet our needs on a daily basis. We ask for forgiveness, with a forgiving heart. We ask Him to keep us from temptation and to protect us from evil.

If you are in need of specific things in your life, ask God exactly for what you need, believing in your heart you will receive it. If you need a job, ask Him for one. He knows what you need and when you ask in faith, He will give it to you.

164

PRAY IN AGREEMENT WITH OTHER BELIEVERS

Matthew 18:19-20 (NLT)

"I also tell you this: If two of you agree down here on earth concerning anything you ask, my Father in heaven will do it for you. For where two or three gather together because they are mine, I am there among them."

In this verse Jesus gives us another clue on how to get our prayers answered. Having your individual faith is extremely important and critical to getting your personal prayers answered. But sometimes we need to join our faith with other believers' faith so we can be stronger and find support in one another. This is called the prayer of agreement. We must notice, however, that Jesus didn't say to pray with just anybody, He said "because they are mine." The people we choose to pray in agreement with have to be fellow believers in Christ. Because we are His, He is among us and the Father will answer our prayers.

If you need a new job, would like to change careers, or whatever the case may be, ask one or two fellow believers to join you in prayer. That's one thing believers can do for each other.

165

THERE IS A REWARD FOR STAYING STRONG IN YOUR FAITH

1 Peter 1:6 (NLT)

So be truly glad! There is wonderful joy ahead, even though it is necessary for you to endure many trials for a while.

While we are here on earth, we are going to live through trials and sufferings. We must endure every trial to succeed. The Bible says "these trials are only to test your faith, to show that it is strong and pure" (v. 7). Our faith is tried as gold is tried through fire to make sure it is real gold. To God, our faith is more valuable than gold. God is moved when we have faith—faith in Him, faith in His Word, and faith in what Jesus did for us.

Our reward for enduring and passing every test of faith is to receive "much praise and glory and honor on the day when Jesus Christ is revealed to the whole world" (v. 7). Our reward for trusting in Him will be the salvation of our souls.

Endure the trials you may be going through at work. If your faith remains strong after being tried, you will receive the rewards. The same applies if you're experiencing trials at home. Believe that God will take care of everything.

166

WE MUST HAVE CHILDLIKE FAITH

Psalm 116:6 (NLT)

The Lord protects those of childlike faith; I was facing death, and then he saved me.

Hebrews 11:1 (NLT)

What is faith? It is the confident assurance that what we hope for is going to happen. It is the evidence of things we cannot yet see.

Hebrews 11:6 (NLT) says that without faith it is impossible to please God. Why? Because it is only through faith in His Word and promises to us that we can be His true children. But our faith has to be like a child's—without questions or doubts. We, as parents, get irritated and even hurt when our children don't believe what we say and don't trust us. Sometimes we may have given them a reason not to trust us, but God has never given us any reasons not to trust Him. He never changes and always keeps His promises. It is up to us to choose to believe in Him and act on His Word so we can receive His promises.

We need to meditate on His Word and continually hear it until it sinks into our hearts and we can say, "I believe! I got it now!"

The Bible promises us that the Lord protects us when we have childlike faith, and we will walk in the Lord's presence as we live here on earth (Psalm 116:9 NLT). Christians are to live by faith, and that faith is to be like a child's.

167

WE PLAN. GOD MAKES
THE CONDITIONS PERFECT.

Ecclesiastes 11:4 (NLT)

If you wait for perfect conditions, you will never get anything done.

How many times we want to make a move, a change in our lives, and we don't because the perfect conditions are not there? We wait just a little more, one more day, one more thing to put in order, and many times we miss opportunities because we waited too long. In real life, we will never have the perfect conditions to make a step, to obey God by faith, or to make a change in our lives. We have to learn to take risks in faith and in wisdom.

Many people confuse being in faith with lack of planning. They have a "God will take care of me" attitude and don't want to do their part. That is foolish. For example: if you want to get a new job, don't quit the one you have in faith and then start looking, unless you can afford it financially. In my opinion, that is not faith. It is being irresponsible. I want to clarify that there may be circumstances where you may have to quit your job cold due to extreme circumstances like sexual harassment. But in most cases, you need to plan your exit.

Examine yourself. Take inventory of your skills, keep your network of contacts alive at all times. Research, plan, plan, plan. Planning is not lack of faith. It is wisdom. However, there comes a time when you are done planning and revising your plan. You turn your plan over to God and take the step. You plan with His guidance and do your best. Then let Him take care of the rest, and He will make all the conditions become perfect to allow you to make the move.

168

WHEN PERSECUTION COMES, LET THE HOLY SPIRIT SPEAK

Mark 13:11 (NLT)

But when you are arrested and stand trial, don't worry about what to say in your defense. Just say what God tells you to. Then it is not you who will be speaking, but the Holy Spirit.

Part of our destiny as Christians is to be persecuted and falsely accused because of our faith. This will happen to us at some point in our lives. Jesus warned His disciples these things will happen and encouraged them to not worry about defending themselves. Many times we forget we are not alone doing our jobs. We have the Holy Spirit within us. He is our defense attorney—the best in the world. He has our best interest as His first priority. He can take care of all the legal matters and defends us. He can tell us exactly what to do and say at the right time.

There are a few things we must do in order for the Holy Spirit to act on our behalf. The first thing is to not worry. Even though our spirit is in faith, and our flesh in fear at the same time, we must believe He is our defense and shield. Then we need to allow Him to take control of the situation. Finally, we have to act. This means we say and do exactly what He tells us to say and do without adding our opinion or thoughts to it. Then we give the glory to God for every situation He delivers us from.

If you are in a situation at work where you have been wrongly accused of something, let the Holy Spirit guide you on what to say. Turn your case over to Him. He will vindicate you and will bring the truth to light. Let Him do His job. Then give Him thanks for defending and delivering you.

169

WITH GOD NOTHING IS IMPOSSIBLE

Matthew 19:26 (NLT)

*"Humanly speaking, it is impossible.
But with God everything is possible."*

Jesus said those words to His disciples after they asked Him who could ever be saved. They thought it was too hard or impossible for any person to be saved on their own. But that's why the gift of salvation is just that—a gift given to us by God's grace. We receive salvation by faith.

This message, however, goes beyond salvation. With God, everything is possible. All we have to do is believe. He always provides a way out for every situation. He knows there is only so much we can handle, and He gives us the grace to go through every situation victoriously.

Are you facing a situation right now that seems impossible? Maybe it is, humanly speaking, but not with God. If you need a new job, or there is a difficult situation going on in your workplace, whatever that may be, for God it is not impossible. Ask Him for ideas, guidance, and the patience to endure until circumstances change—until you get your victory.

FAITHFULNESS

ARE YOU MANAGING YOUR GIFTS?

Matthew 25:15 (NLT)

He gave five bags of gold to one, two bags of gold to another, and one bag of gold to the last —dividing it in proportion to their abilities — and then left on his trip.

This is the story of a master who entrusted his gold to his servants. In this story Jesus states two things clearly: 1) He gives something to every person to manage on His behalf while He is gone, and 2) He gives these responsibilities according to every person's individual abilities. Nevertheless, to Him it is equally important that every person manages what He gives to their best of their ability.

The first step you need to do in order to manage God's gifts in your life is recognize the gifts come from Him. He gives both natural gifts, as well as spiritual gifts, to every person He creates.

The second step is to be grateful for what you have and don't compare your gifts to anybody else's. Don't be proud and ask God why He only gave you this or that or so few while He gave all these other gifts to somebody else. You don't have the right to ask. He has, however, the right to give whatever He wants to whomever He wants as the Creator.

The third step is to develop each and every gift He gave you. This is "investing" and "growing" His gold.

Finally, we are to live our lives as if He, our Master, is coming back today to ask us how we managed what He entrusted us with. Our goal should be to hear His words: "Well done, my good and faithful servant. You have been faithful in handling this small amount, so now I will give you many more responsibilities. Let's celebrate together!" (Matthew 25:23 NLT).

BE FAITHFUL IN SEEKING GOD'S WISDOM

Proverbs 2:8 (NLT)

He guards the paths of justice and protects those who are faithful to him.

Part of being faithful to the Lord is to seek Him first, above all things. In addition, we are to ask for His wisdom. The Bible says that when we pursue wisdom He will guard the paths of justice and will protect those who are faithful to Him. What a promise that is!

Listen to God's wisdom on a daily basis. That is part of being a faithful servant and follower of Jesus Christ. You need wisdom to be successful at work and at home.

BE FAITHFUL TO BELIEVE

Hebrews 3:12 (NLT)

Be careful then, dear friends. Make sure that your own hearts are not evil and unbelieving, turning you away from the living God.

We must guard our hearts from evil and unbelief—always. Every time we don't believe, every time we reject one of God's promises, our hearts harden and we move further away from Him.

Sometimes things may seem impossible; we see no way out, and we have no hope left. Those times are turning points in our lives. When the trials bring us down to the lowest points in our lives, we have to believe and stand on a particular promise by faith only. We also need to ask God to give us faith as a supernatural gift at that moment.

When Jesus was in his own country, He could do no works there because of their unbelief (Mark 6:1-6 KJV). All that God needs is our faith, and He will act. He wants us to be faithful to believe. He is also ready to give us the gift of faith when we ask.

Examine your heart and ask God if there are any areas of unbelief in your heart. Maybe you don't believe that He can give you the best job for you, or the husband you have been waiting for, or the children you desire… The list could be endless. You must have faith in every area of your life.

BE FAITHFUL TO THE END

Hebrews 3:14 (NLT)

For if we are faithful to the end, trusting God just as firmly as when we first believed, we will share in all that belongs to Christ.

Disobedient people get nothing from God. He withholds blessings from them because they choose to disobey His commands. They are rebellious and have unbelief in their hearts. The people of Israel could not enter the Promised Land for forty years because they disobeyed God and didn't believe. Even though God kept feeding them and protecting them while they were in the desert, they were still in unbelief. Therefore, when they rebelled, God said, "They will never enter my place of rest" (Hebrews 3:11 NLT). "For only we who believe can enter his place of rest" (Hebrews 4:3 NLT). This place of rest is a place of peace and joy in the Lord.

We must be faithful to the end, continue to trust God every day and as firmly as the day we got saved. When we continue to believe, we can receive and enter into the rest God has prepared for us. His promise is that we will share in all that belongs to Christ—including rest.

The questions for you today are: Do you trust God in everything? Do you believe in Him just as strongly as the first day you got saved?

174

FINISH YOUR RACE

2 Timothy 4:7 (NLT)

*I have fought a good fight, I have finished the race,
and I have remained faithful.*

These were some of Paul's final words to Timothy. Our number one goal in life should be to finish the race God placed before us and planned for our lives. We each have a unique race that only we can finish. During the race we must remain faithful to God's Word and direction in our lives. We do not run an easy race. That's why Paul said, "I have fought a good fight."

Jesus said that in the world we shall have tribulation but to be of good cheer for He has overcome the world (John 16:33 NLT). When we seek God first, we have His wisdom, peace, joy, grace, and all the benefits we receive from being His children, then we *can* finish the race.

Finish your race and stay faithful to the Lord. Then you will be able to say Paul's words when your time comes to meet your Lord and Savior personally.

175

FULFILL YOUR VOWS TO THE LORD

Psalm 76:11 (NLT)

Make vows to the Lord your God, and fulfill them.

God is a God of His Word. He keeps His Word and every one of His promises. He is faithful and doesn't change His mind. He does what He says He will do. We, as His children, are to imitate His example. We are to be women of *our* word. When we make a vow to God, He expects us to follow through. Nevertheless, because He knows our nature, He gave us the Holy Spirit to help us follow through with our vows.

It is easy to not keep our promises to God because He won't tell anybody. But when we make a promise to another person, they will be terribly disappointed if we don't fulfill it. Because we are to do everything as unto the Lord, we must follow through with our promises.

When you make a vow to the Lord and fulfill it, His promises in your life will come true. When you make a commitment to your co-workers, fulfill it just as if you made it to God. It doesn't matter if you committed to help somebody on a special project, participate in a committee to raise funds for a cause, or you promised your boss you would have a task done by the end of the day. Fulfill your commitments, and God will bless you.

176

GOD CARED FOR US SINCE THE MOMENT HE CREATED US

Psalm 71:6 (NLT)

Yes, you have been with me from birth; from my mother's womb you have cared for me. No wonder I am always praising you!

Some people are not introduced to the Lord until later in life. Other people are introduced to God's love at birth. And yet others are born into Christian homes, but choose to reject the things of God or simply ignore them. No matter who we are, He has always cared for us all. From the moment He created us in our mother's womb, He, God our Father, first loved us.

God patiently and lovingly waits for us to accept Jesus as our Lord and Savior. This means we accept His love for us and take the first step toward our daily walk with God for the rest of our Christian lives.

Knowing that God loves you and cares for you is a personal revelation in your heart. Your parents and friends can only tell you about God and their experiences, but in order for you to have that revelation, you have to experience Him yourself. The more you seek God, the more you will get to know Him and have a revelation of His love for you.

When you walk and live your life in the revelation of knowing He loves you, people around you are going to desire what you have. Those are opportunities to show them the love of God. Your workplace will always provide you with such opportunities.

177

GOD DOES NOT FORGET HOW HARD YOU WORK FOR HIM

Hebrews 6:10 (NLT)

For God is not unfair. He will not forget how hard you have worked for him and how you have shown your love to him by caring for other Christians, as you still do.

Sometimes you may feel you are wasting your time and energy by being a good worker in your company because you feel it's not making a difference. Other times you may feel that what you're doing for another person, at work or outside of work, whether they are a Christian or not, is not worth continuing because you don't feel appreciated.

Don't get weary in working hard for the Lord. Dedicate your natural, as well as spiritual, work to Him. God is a fair God, and He will not take for granted or forget the time and effort you invest when working hard for Him. He notices it and appreciates it.

The Bible says in verse 12 that if you work hard, "Then you will not become spiritually dull and indifferent. Instead, you will follow the example of those who are going to inherit God's promises because of their faith and patience." Therefore, continue working hard for the Lord with the expectation that this promise will come to pass in your life.

GOD IS A FAITHFUL GOD

Psalm 31:5 (NLT)

*I entrust my spirit into your hand. Rescue me, Lord,
for you are a faithful God.*

When you are distressed, entrust your spirit into God's hands and believe that He will help you. He is a faithful God and is always there for you. He will never leave you nor forsake you. But the process of believing takes trust and faithfulness on our part also. We are to be faithful to make time to spend with Him, in His presence—just because we love Him. God is faithful at keeping all His promises. His Word is full of promises for us. When we are faithful to read His Word, we will find more and more of His promises. In time of need, we can then stand on the verses where a specific promise is written and remind God of His faithfulness.

Therefore, give all your work-related issues to God. Put them in His hands, and He will help you.

179

GOD IS ALWAYS WAITING FOR US

Isaiah 30:18 (NLT)

But the Lord still waits for you to come to him so he can show his love and compassion. For the Lord is a faithful God. Blessed are those who wait for him to help them.

The prophet Isaiah encouraged the people of Israel to not return to Egypt to ask for help but to ask God instead and wait for His help. The story of the people of Israel and their mistakes are recorded in the Bible so we can learn from them and not repeat them. In time of famine, the Israelites were going back to Egypt looking for help instead of turning to God. Even though God had already taken them out of Egypt and performed many miracles for them, they refused to obey or seek Him.

Today, we act the same as the people of Israel. We get in trouble. God rescues us. We forget about it and get in trouble again. Instead of running to God and asking Him for help, we decide we have a better plan. A good example would be when we overcommit our time. We say yes to projects and additional responsibilities, and then we have no idea how we're going to deliver what we promised. Part of obeying God is to be good stewards of the resources He entrusts to us, and time is one of those resources. We need to ask Him for wisdom and to teach us how to manage our time. Even when we are in too deep and backing out seems to be the only way out, God has a better plan. He will give us ideas on how to get it done and teach us not to overcommit in the future.

God is always waiting for you to repent and run to Him. He yearns to demonstrate His love for you, and His compassion overflows when you return to Him. He is patient and faithful. So, don't run to the world for the solutions to your problems. Run to God and wait for Him to help you. He will come through.

GOD IS FAITHFUL TO ANSWER OUR PRAYERS

Psalm 65:5 (NLT)

You faithfully answer our prayers with awesome deeds, O God our savior. You are the hope of everyone on earth, even those who sail on distant seas.

God is a faithful God; therefore, He answers the prayers of those who diligently seek Him. He answers our prayers with awesome deeds because He loves us. Furthermore, He is the only hope for everyone on earth. That's why our ultimate goal is to bring people to Him. We are God's servants, and when we are at His disposal, He will use us.

If your prayers regarding a new job, a change in your career, or a work related situation are not being answered, don't despair. Sometimes, it's not the right time for your prayers to be answered. Ask God to give you patience and grace to wait until you get an answer. He is your hope, and He will answer your prayers in His divine and perfect timing.

GOD NEVER CHANGES

Hebrews 13:8-9 (NLT)

Jesus Christ is the same yesterday, today, and forever. So do not be attracted by strange, new ideas. Your spiritual strength comes from God's special favor, not from ceremonial rules about food, which don't help those who follow them.

God doesn't change. He is the same always. His Word doesn't change either because it is Him. Jesus is the Word of God made flesh. The truth is always the truth and the truth will set us free.

The world is full of false doctrines. There are new ones coming out all the time with the purpose of contradicting the Word of God. This is one of the enemy's tactics to confuse people—even Christians. Don't believe everything you hear. Always go back to the Bible to confirm what you are hearing or are being taught— even at your church. Ask God to give you a personal revelation and wisdom to discern between the truth and the enemy's lies. The Devil's work is to deceive people so they can't see the truth and deny Christ.

Trust God, for He never changes. Believe that His promises from His Word will come to pass in your life just as they did for the ones who believed in Him before us.

In the workplace you will find people from various backgrounds and beliefs. Guard your heart against influences or doctrines that come from sources other than the Word of God. Our spiritual strength comes from God alone, not from any ritual or false religion.

182

GOD RESCUES GODLY PEOPLE FROM THEIR TRIALS

2 Peter 2:9 (NLT)

So you see, the Lord knows how to rescue godly people from their trials, even while punishing the wicked right up until the day of judgment.

If you find yourself the only godly person in an ungodly environment, don't get discouraged. If you feel you are the only person striving to live a holy life and are tired of living in a sinful, immoral atmosphere, don't despair. God will rescue you out of that place.

The workplace can be an immoral, ungodly, and worldly environment to work in. I met someone once who used to be a topless dancer before she found Jesus. Imagine that kind of place as your everyday working environment! Other women may work in a white collar office environment that may seem on the surface like a good place to work, but it is corrupted inside.

It doesn't make a difference if it's stealing money, falsifying documents, adultery, or murder that is going on. If you are a godly woman, God will take you out of there as He did with Lot. Verses 7 and 8 say, "But at the same time, God rescued Lot out of Sodom because he was a good man who was sick of all the immorality and wickedness around him. Yes, he was a righteous man who was distressed by the wickedness he saw and heard day after day."

Trust God, and He will rescue you from any situation or environment and from all your trials.

183

Honor God by Honoring Marriage

Hebrews 13:4 (NLT)

Give honor to marriage, and remain faithful to one another in marriage. God will surely judge people who are immoral and those who commit adultery.

The workplace is full of opportunities for adultery and to destroy marriages. If you are a married working woman, keep your marriage sacred and don't open doors of opportunities for sin you will later regret. Give priority to your husband above all the after-hours commitments you may have with clients, co-workers, your male boss, or employees. There are certain things you can do to avoid the appearance of evil and opportunities for inappropriate behavior that eventually could lead to sin. For example: Avoid meetings or drinks after work alone with another man (single or married). The best way is to go out in a group. If you absolutely have to entertain a male client, take your assistant or colleague along or go to a very well lit restaurant where there is a business atmosphere.

If you are a single woman, also avoid the wrong appearance and avoid going out with married men. Adultery is a two-way street. It won't happen if one party will stop it or avoid it all together. Guard and save your body for your future husband—the one God is reserving for you. Honor God by honoring marriage. It is a serious issue to God and disobedience in this area brings severe consequences.

If you made a mistake and committed sin in this area but repented from your heart, God forgave you already. Now you need to forgive yourself as well and get back on track with God. He is a God of second chances and He is merciful.

IF YOU USE YOUR GIFTS, MORE WILL BE GIVEN TO YOU

Matthew 25:29 (NLT)

To those who use well what they are given, even more will be given, and they will have an abundance. But from those who are unfaithful, even what little they have will be taken away.

God gave each one of us gifts we must discover, treasure, and develop. Our goal should be to use each one of the gifts and talents God gave us at some point during our lifetime.

How do you discover, use, and manage every gift? First, you discover what your gifts are by asking God to reveal them to you. You, of course, need to listen to His answer. Then, ask Him what His priority is for your gifts to be used for His Kingdom. Go with the desires of your heart. They are one of His ways to reveal His gifts in you. Plan, prioritize, and develop your gifts. The Lord will give you opportunities to use every one of them.

In the workplace you will have the opportunity to use several of your gifts. If you have the gift of leadership, use it to lead people. If you have the gift of organization, use it to organize your job and help others get organized. If you speak another language, use it to reach people in that community. Because you will go through different stages in your life, you may not be able to use some gifts right now. Don't forget about them. At some point in your life, later on, God will need you to use them. The more you use what God has given you, the more responsibilities and gifts He will give you. Don't be like the unfaithful servant so that "even what little they have will be taken away." Instead, use all of the gifts He gave you and expect to receive even more.

185

SPEND TIME ALONE WITH GOD

Mark 1:35 (NLT)

The next morning Jesus awoke long before daybreak and went out alone into the wilderness to pray.

Praying before the day began was a common practice of Jesus. He often went alone to pray, just to be with His Father. By being with God, He got refreshed, renewed, and strengthened to continue His mission. Jesus gave us an example of how we can accomplish our mission here on earth.

Each one of us has a mission appointed by God that only we can fulfill. But we need to spend time with Him in order to follow His direction and to have the spiritual and physical strength we need to do His will. Sometimes, we are so tired we just need to be in His presence and wait for Him to speak to us. We need to rest in Him and quietly worship Him. Other times, we need to cry out for help and dump all of our problems and frustrations on Him. There will also be times of celebration when everything is going well. We must not forget to meet God in those moments too; celebrate with Him, and thank Him. That pleases Him.

Even if you don't have a place of wilderness in your home, choose a place where you can meet Him regularly. Soon that place will become like a sanctuary, where you go and rest in God. You need to be aware of God's presence in everything you do and include Him in your daily life. You also need time alone where you give Him your undivided attention, where you can talk to Him without interruptions and listen to His heart. This is the only way you will be able to accomplish what He's called you to do. When you are refreshed spiritually you are better able to focus on your work and experience more success in your job.

186

STAY FAITHFUL TO THE TRUTH

I John 2:24 (NLT)

So you must remain faithful to what you have been taught from the beginning. If you do, you will continue to live in fellowship with the Son and with the Father.

Peter tells us that if we stay faithful to what we have been taught from the beginning, the truth, the Word of God, then we will continue in fellowship with Jesus and the Father. When we deviate from the truth, we move away from God. When we are not living in the truth, we are living in deception, a lie. God has given us the Holy Spirit to teach us all truth. When we live in truth, we are living in Christ. Verse 28 says, "And now, dear children, continue to live in fellowship with Christ so that when he returns, you will be full of courage and not shrink back from him in shame."

In the workplace, we must remain faithful to what we have been taught from the beginning—the basic code of ethics in doing business—which is to be a person of honesty, truthfulness, and integrity. Are you remaining faithful to the truth?

187

STUDY THE WORD AND HIS COMMANDMENTS

Psalm 119:15-16 (NLT)

I will study your commandments and reflect on your ways. I will delight in your principles and not forget your word.

Working in the business world, we often find ourselves studying new regulations, industry policies, and trends so we can continue to grow professionally. This is extremely important for the success of our companies and of ourselves personally. Companies spend millions of dollars annually sending their employees to specialized training to further their education and to increase their knowledge in their field. This is all important. However, Christians need to also spend time studying the Word of God and His commandments. This is how we grow spiritually, which is more important than all of the above. If we don't continually learn more of the things of God and increase in the knowledge of Him, we will not grow.

Therefore, let's delight in His principles, study His Word and commandments, and obey them. He gave us the Word to teach us, instruct us, and guide us through life. In addition, he gave us the Holy Spirit to reveal to us the truth and to give us a clear understanding of His Word.

188

THERE IS ONLY ONE GOD

Deuteronomy 4:39 (NLT)

So remember this and keep it firmly in mind: The Lord is God both in heaven and on earth, and there is no other god!

Moses often addressed the nation of Israel and reminded them of all the awesome things God had done for them. He went through an account of everything God did, from taking them out of Egypt—feeding them, guiding them, protecting them—to the time when they were about to enter the Promised Land. The one thing Moses cautioned them most about was to not create any idols or to worship any images of anything. He reminded them God is the only god, and He is a jealous God. He warned them that if they forgot God and started worshiping other gods, they would surely perish in every way (Deuteronomy 8:19 KJV).

In today's world, there are gods all around us. A god is anything we focus all our time, energy, and resources on. It can be anything or anybody we place above God.

We all have weaknesses and areas we need to guard so they don't become our god. For some people, it may be alcohol, smoking, TV, a specific hobby, or even their children. For others, however, their job or career becomes their god. Why? Because that's what they focus their resources, find their self-worth, and center their entire life around.

If your career is an area of temptation for you, simply offer it, and everything you do, to the Lord. Obey what He tells you to do and give Him the glory for your successes. Put God above all, "Then you will enjoy a long life in the land the Lord your God is giving you for all time" (v. 40).

HOLINESS

189

ARE YOUR EARNINGS ENHANCING YOUR LIFE?

Proverbs 10:16 (NLT)

The earnings of the godly enhance their lives, but evil people squander their money on sin.

Earning money for the hard work we do is part of the satisfaction we get from working. It is one of the rewards and the fruit of our labor. God wants to reward us for that work. The Bible tells us the earnings of the godly enhance their lives. The key word is godly. Being godly is a lifestyle, and part of that is using God's wisdom to spend our earnings. The way we spend our money determines if our lives will be enhanced or not. Unfortunately, nowadays there are a lot of Christians who mismanage their money and spend it on sin just as unbelievers do.

Where do we draw the line on how we spend our money? I believe when we use our earnings as God leads us, we give glory to Him. God leads each one of us to do different things with our money. Our priorities should be to give to His Kingdom as He directs us and to meet the needs of our families by paying our bills. We need to learn to manage our money and live within our means to avoid the trap many Christians and non-Christians alike fall into—bankruptcy. Therefore, let God direct your use of money and your earnings will enhance your life.

190

GOD HELPS US BECOME HOLY

James 1:21 (NLT)

So get rid of all the filth and evil in your lives, and humbly accept the message God has planted in your hearts, for it is strong enough to save your souls.

When we accept Jesus in our hearts, we are going to spend the rest of our lives getting rid of filth and evil things. But that's okay. God never asks us to become holy overnight. He knows it is a lifetime process, and He knows we can't do it without His daily help. When we humbly accept the message of salvation, we accept we are sinners and that only with God we can do all things—including becoming holy and living a holy life.

The first step in becoming holy is asking God to reveal to you the areas you need to change and clean up. Even though we all have many areas, don't worry, He won't overwhelm you by giving you a long list. Instead, He, in His great love, will only give you a few areas at a time to work on. He will give you the faith, patience, and grace to help you change each one. In the workplace, take notice of the little things you could change such as treating everyone with respect, not becoming angry easily, and helping others when you see the need.

God is sensitive and merciful, He will change you little by little, taking care of every wound and healing you in the process. He will mend your heart from every hurt. He will forgive every sin that made you dirty and will make you clean as white snow (Isaiah 1:18 KJV). He will save your soul.

191

God Protects the Godly

Psalm 97:10-12 (NLT)

You who love the Lord, hate evil! He protects the lives of his godly people and rescues them from the power of the wicked. Light shines on the godly, and joy on those who do right. May all who are godly be happy in the Lord and praise his holy name!

Being a godly person is difficult, and it seems it is getting harder and harder as darkness gets darker in these last days. But, don't get discouraged. The Bible says that in the last days darkness will be darker but also the light will shine brighter. It is time to press for godliness and holiness as never before and not be ashamed of it. Wicked people are proud of being wicked. They announce it, are loud, and invasive into our lives with their evil agenda. Why don't we invade them with the Gospel? Why are we keeping God to ourselves? It is time for us, the godly people, the church of Jesus Christ, to rise up stronger than ever and fight against evil. It is our job, our destiny! Don't be afraid of being a Christian. Don't be ashamed of saying you believe in God and that Jesus is your Savior.

In the workplace, stand up for what you believe. There is a professional and respectful way to do it. Don't compromise your beliefs. Look at what the Bible says. God protects His godly people and rescues you from the wicked. His light shines on you and gives you His joy.

192

GOD SMOOTHES OUT THE ROAD OF THE RIGHTEOUS

Isaiah 26:7 (NLT)

But for those who are righteous, the path is not steep and rough. You are a God of justice, and you smooth out the road ahead of them.

When we seek God first and wholeheartedly, He makes us pure and righteous. When we strive to live a holy life, God sees our efforts and rewards us with His blessings. Smoothing out the road ahead of us is one of those blessings. The road we have to walk while we are in this world is rough, dangerous, steep, and dark. But when we walk with Jesus at our side, He lights our road so we can see where we're going. He takes care of the problems and goes ahead of us to confront the enemy and fight on our behalf. Then, the road becomes narrow, smooth, and safe for us to continue our walk.

If you are doing your best and striving to live a holy life, don't despair when you see the wicked succeed. God is a God of justice and their turn will come when they will vanish. "The steps of the godly are directed by the Lord. He delights in every detail of their lives… Don't be impatient for the Lord to act! Travel steadily along his path, He will honor you, giving you the land. You will see the wicked destroyed" (Psalm 37:23, 34 NLT).

If you find yourself right now on a rough road—either at work or at home—stop what you're doing and seek God with all your heart. Examine yourself to see if you have missed His direction at some point, repent if necessary, and ask Him to make your road smooth. He will listen to your prayers and answer your plea. He will not desert you. He loves *you*.

193

GOD WATCHES OVER THE PATH OF THE GODLY

Psalm 1:6 (NLT)

For the Lord watches over the path of the godly, but the path of the wicked leads to destruction.

The Bible exhorts Christians to live godly and holy lives. But what does it really mean to be godly? The previous verses in Psalm 1 describe being godly as those who do not follow the advice of the wicked or stand around with sinners. They instead delight in doing everything the Lord wants. They think about God's laws day and night. "They are like trees planted along the riverbank, bearing fruit each season without fail. Their leaves never wither, and in all they do, they prosper" (vv. 1-3).

Being godly these days means the same. When we entrust God with our lives, study and meditate on His Word, and obey what He asks us to do—we are godly. He promises us then to watch over our path. God has a path, a plan, for each one of us. But we must have the revelation of His will for our lives so we can walk on that path.

Everything you do each day, such as your work, is part of your path. Therefore, be thankful for the job you have and work as unto the Lord, knowing it is part of what He wants you to do. Trust the Lord with your job because He wants to bless you through it. Your part is to thank Him, work hard, and give Him the glory for all your accomplishments. The basic requirement as a godly person is to love God, and one way you love Him is by being thankful.

JESUS HELPS US LIVE A GODLY LIFE

2 Peter 1:3 (NLT)

As we know Jesus better, his divine power gives us everything we need for living a godly life. He has called us to receive his own glory and goodness!

The only way we can get to know Jesus better is by spending quality time with Him in prayer and reading His Word. He gives us all His promises in the Bible. As we get to know Him, we will live our lives according to His promises that teach us the way to a godly life. "Knowing God leads to self-control. Self-control leads to patient endurance, and patient endurance to godliness. Godliness leads to love for other Christians, and finally you will grow to have genuine love for everyone" (vv. 6-8).

Peter gives us the key to love each other, the succession of events, and the virtues we are to develop. Jesus has everything we need to be successful in our pursuit of living a godly life. This applies to every area of our lives—home, church, and work. Verse 10 says, "Work hard to prove that you really are among those God has called and chosen."

We, on our own, cannot live a godly life. But we can with Jesus' help and His divine power.

KEEP A HUMBLE HEART

Proverbs 29:23 (NLT)

Pride ends in humiliation, while humility brings honor.

What do you do or say when you are praised for your accomplishments? How do you react? Many working women don't know how to receive praise or a compliment the right way. They have the wrong understanding of humility. Being humble is not denying an accomplishment by belittling it or just saying "it was nothing," when it took a lot of effort, hard work, and dedication. Being humble is a matter of the heart. How does your heart react every time you are praised? Does it get enlarged in pride? Do you think to yourself "Wow, I'm great, *I* did it all by myself" or do you give the glory to God for every one of your successes? Do you thank Him for giving you all the gifts and talents you have? Do you thank Him and say, "*We* did it Lord."?

But how do you become and stay humble? Having a thankful heart is one way. In the workplace, if you are part of a team, always give credit where it is due. If you are a manager, make sure you praise your employees and thank them for helping you look good. Remind your team their individual success depends on the success of the team and vice versa. It is a two-way street. If you participate in a sports team, you know that to win a game, every team member must play their part to their best. Every person has to be disciplined and dedicated to even be part of the team.

Proverbs 27:21 (NLT) says, "Fire tests the purity of silver and gold, but a person is tested by being praised." When we receive praise, it is a test to our heart to see if it's pure or not. Every time we give God the glory and thank Him, we pass the test and move on, knowing our heart is pure. Then honor comes by itself.

196

LEARN TO CONTROL YOUR TONGUE

James 3:2, 5 (NLT)

We all make many mistakes, but those who control their tongues can also control themselves in every other way... So also, the tongue is a small thing, but what enormous damage it can do.

We all have a tongue, and we all use it a lot. Unfortunately, we use it sometimes to build and other times to destroy. The Bible says, "And the tongue is a flame of fire. It is full of wickedness that can ruin your whole life. It can turn the entire course of your life into a blazing flame of destruction, for it is set on fire by hell itself... but no one can tame the tongue. It is an uncontrollable evil, full of deadly poison" (James 3:6-8 NLT). Verse 10 says, "And so blessing and cursing come pouring out of the same mouth. Surely, my brothers and sisters, this is not right!"

Wow, those are powerful statements about the tongue. Yet most of us have said things over the course of our lives we later regret. Therefore, it is important to learn to control our tongue so we are able to control ourselves in other areas of our lives. What a difficult task we have! But with God's help nothing is impossible.

Start practicing tongue control by seeking opportunities to use your mouth at work to encourage your co-workers, give advice to a friend in need, and congratulate them when they do a good job. Choose to say nice things about your company, products, and colleagues instead of gossiping. Choose to say kind words instead of angry, hurtful words when co-workers offend you. The Bible says in Luke 6:45 (KJV) that out of the abundance of the heart, the mouth speaks. Examine what's in your heart as the more godly things you put in, the more godly things your mouth will pour out.

197

LET YOUR LIFE SHINE BRIGHTLY BEFORE THE WORLD

Philippians 2:15 (NLT)

… You are to live clean, innocent lives as children of God in a dark world full of crooked and perverse people. Let your lives shine brightly before them.

Some of you may be thinking it is impossible to live a clean life when we live in this world. But it is not impossible. Remember that anything is possible if you believe (Mark 9:23 NLT). You must first know that you are not trying to do this on your own. You can only do it with God's help. You may also have other Christian friends who can help you and you can be accountable to. If you are a new believer, look for friends who are also believers. Join a church where you can get connected and make new friendships. Unfortunately, you may have to leave some relationships behind if they drag you to your old sinful behaviors.

You also need to follow Paul's instructions to the church to "Fix your thoughts on what is true and honorable and right. Think about things that are pure and lovely and admirable. Think about things that are excellent and worthy of praise" (Philippians 4:8 NLT). What you think and meditate on is vital to your way of life. What you read and put in your mind goes to your heart. Then whatever is in your heart comes out of your mouth and ultimately dictates what you do with your life.

In addition to taking control of your thoughts, you must love others as God loves you. That is what really matters and what helps you keep your life pure and clean. When your heart is right with God, He helps you shine brightly before the world. The place where you work is part of *your* world that needs *your* light to shine brightly.

LET'S MAKE A HIGHWAY

Isaiah 40:3-5 (NLT)

"Make a highway for the Lord through the wilderness. Make a straight, smooth road through the desert for our God. Fill the valleys and level the hills. Straighten out the curves and smooth off the rough spots. Then the glory of the Lord will be revealed, and all the people will see it together."

God spoke those words to His people of Israel through the prophet Isaiah. We are to live our lives today with the expectation that Jesus is coming back, and we must be preparing ourselves daily. We have spots, wrinkles, and rough places that need to be fixed and straightened out. We need to make our temples smooth so God can dwell in us. As we each make our roads straight, the entire body of Christ will work together toward the same goal. Then we, as one body, can receive and handle His glory.

How do you, as an individual, accomplish such a big task? The first step is self-examination on a daily basis by asking yourself questions such as: Am I treating everyone at work with respect and dignity? Am I treating my family, friends, and co-workers in a loving way? Secondly, ask the Lord to help you identify areas in your life you need to change and repent of any sin (anything that keeps you or takes you away from God). Thirdly, always have a thankful heart because if it wasn't for God's plan to send Jesus to save you, you would not stand a chance.

Finally, by spending time with the Lord praying, reading, and meditating on His Word, you will be changed; the roads of your life straightened and smoothed out. Verse 8 says, "The grass withers, and the flowers fade, but the word of our God stands forever."

You may think it is impossible to get straightened out, but for God all things are possible. He helps you with your own highway on a daily basis.

LORD, TEACH US YOUR WAYS

Psalm 86:11 (NLT)

Teach me your ways, O Lord, that I may live according to your truth! Grant me purity of heart, that I may honor you.

Psalm 86:11 is a prayer I want to keep close to my heart and live out. When we know the ways of the Lord, we can live in His truth. By studying and meditating on His Word, we get to know Him and receive a revelation in our hearts of the truth. We can then live our lives according to what He wants for us.

The King James Version of the Bible says the second part of this verse this way, "Unite my heart to fear thy name." When we ask God to put in our heart the fear of His name, our heart becomes pure. When our heart is pure, God can mold it and transform it into the heart He wants us to have — His heart. Remember, He made us in His image.

When we live our lives according to this truth, we become a light to the world and are able to influence people for His Kingdom. This applies for our work, home, and community involvement.

PRACTICE SELF-CONTROL DAILY

1 Peter 1:13 (NLT)

So think clearly and exercise self-control. Look forward to the special blessings that will come to you at the return of Jesus Christ.

Exercising self-control is critical to achieve success in every area of our lives. We, as the church, are called to be holy and we need self-control to do it. Even though we cannot become holy on our own, we have God's grace to help us, and His Spirit has already made us holy (1 Peter 1:2 NLT). Nevertheless, we have to do our part, which is to think clearly before we act, and to exercise (practice) self-control.

At home, for example, you can exercise self-control by watching what you eat and not over eating, by exercising regularly, by turning off the TV when there are shows you shouldn't be watching, and by spending time with the Lord, among other things. At work, you can exercise self-control by not overworking, by controlling your temper in difficult situations, and by not participating in office gossip.

Therefore, practice self-control on a daily basis and look forward to the reward and special blessings you will receive when Jesus comes back.

201

SEEK GOD FROM YOUR HEART

Psalm 14:2 (NLT)

The Lord looks down from heaven on the entire human race; he looks to see if there is even one with real understanding, one who seeks for God.

God constantly looks for people who are earnestly seeking Him and whose hearts are pure. When we seek God, we must examine our motives. Are we seeking Him because we understand our need of Him or to take advantage of His blessings? When we seek Him, it must be with the understanding that we are His children whom He loves. We are His servants whom He trains and expects work to be done for His Kingdom. We are His stewards whom He will ask later how we managed His resources. In every area, we are accountable to God.

The Bible tells us that if we seek, we shall find. God wants us to find Him. He is always ready to give us His love, forgiveness, and blessings. But even though He wants us to choose Him, He doesn't force us because He gave us free will to choose. We bless

Him when we, out of our free will, choose to seek Him. We bless Him when we are interested in knowing Him. We bless Him when we want to spend our time with Him rather than doing anything else the world has to offer. Those moments of fellowship with the Lord fill our hearts with His love so we can then overflow and spill that love into other people's lives. It is in those moments that we learn from Him the most.

The people you work with need the love of God, and you may be the only one God can use in your workplace. Therefore, purpose in your heart to be one God picks out from the crowd because your heart is seeking His when He is looking down from heaven.

202

STAY PURE BY OBEYING GOD'S WORD

Psalm 119:9 (NLT)

How can a young person stay pure? By obeying your word and following its rules.

If you are a young working woman just starting out your career and working life, it is important you stay pure in your heart. This not only includes purity of your body, but it also means you need to protect your mind and heart. Look for relationships that will help you stay positive, productive, and respectful of those in authority. Stay away from negative people, whiners, complainers, and gossipers, for they will take you down their path of unhappiness.

Stay tuned to what God tells you personally to do and obey and follow His commands always, not only when it's convenient. Don't compromise your beliefs just to fit in. He will take care of you. For example, if your friends at work participate in gossiping, just choose to not participate.

Therefore, be an example to other young working women. Don't be ashamed to be pure and always remember to stay humble. Striving to be pure doesn't mean you are better or superior to others. Jesus was pure all His life on earth yet He was the most humble person that ever lived. He stayed pure with God's help and by obeying His Father's Word and following all His commandments. With God's help, you can be pure too.

203

STRIVE TO LIVE A PURE AND BLAMELESS LIFE

2 Peter 3:14 (NLT)

And so, dear friends, while you are waiting for these things to happen, make every effort to live a pure and blameless life. And be at peace with God.

The Bible says that when Jesus comes back many things will happen. Heaven and earth will cease to exist as we know them and "everything around us is going to melt away (v. 11)." While we are waiting for these things to happen, we are to live holy, pure, and blameless lives. Again and again, we are reminded of how important this is to God. In fact, God commands us to be holy, and He never commands us to do anything we cannot do. Therefore, it must be possible for us to be holy.

Striving to live a holy life is a daily fight, a daily decision, and a daily prayer. It is our choice just as we choose to be saved. We have to want to be holy. We have to ask God for His grace to overcome temptation, believe that He knows our hearts, and put action into our words.

Start today by making small changes in your life. For example, don't tell lies at work (this includes exaggerating results), don't backstab a co-worker, don't say negative things about your boss or your company—every little change you make counts, and God sees your effort. This is vital to your success in your Christian life. Be an example of holiness to those in your workplace, your family, and friends.

 204

THE INNER BEAUTY IS MORE PRECIOUS TO GOD THAN THE OUTWARD

1 Peter 3:4 (NLT)

You should be known for the beauty that comes from within, the unfading beauty of a gentle and quiet spirit, which is so precious to God.

As working women, we sometimes focus on our outward appearance, how smart we are, or how much education we have achieved. We believe these are the assets we need in order to be successful at work. All of those things are very important; however, we also must focus on our inner beauty. That is what is most important and precious to God. The Bible defines inner beauty as a "gentle and quiet spirit."

Do you posses a gentle and quiet spirit? Gentle means to be calm, tender, and moderate, among other things. Quiet means also to be calm, tranquil, and peaceful.

The key is to trust God and ask Him to change us on a daily basis. He will help us become godly women and have a quiet and gentle spirit. Therefore, don't get discouraged. Remember, our lives are a daily walk with God.

205

THOSE WHO LIVE A GODLY LIFE WILL DWELL ON HIGH

Isaiah 33:15 (NLT)

The ones who can live here are those who are honest and fair, who reject making a profit by fraud, who stay far away from bribes, who refuse to listen to those who plot murder, who shut their eyes to all enticement to do wrong.

God is speaking to His people through the prophet Isaiah about the future Jerusalem, which He will make "his home of justice and righteousness" (v. 5). People were asking which one of them could live in the presence of God when their time came. Then the Lord answered (on verse 15 above) who were the ones who would live and "dwell on high" (v. 16). Notice that it is the ones who "shut their eyes to *all* enticement to do wrong." To God it is just as wrong to make a profit by fraud or to take bribes as it is to plot murder. In His eyes, it is all sin, and He treats it the same—as sin. They all lead to one same consequence, which is death and separation from God. As humans, even when we are saved, we will sin. The important thing is we repent and ask God's forgiveness through Christ.

As working women, we must always watch our conduct. We must be an example of honesty and fairness to others. We must examine our hearts constantly to make sure our motives for doing business are pure. We are to treat our customers and employees fairly. They are the reason we are in business in the first place.

God wants us to live godly lives and follow His example. "The godly are directed by their honesty; the wicked fall beneath their load of sin" (Proverbs 11:5 NLT).

206

WE ARE TO BE HOLY AS GOD IS HOLY

1 Peter 1:14-16 (NLT)

Obey God because you are his children. Don't slip back into your old ways of doing evil; you didn't know any better then. But now you must be holy in everything you do, just as God—who chose you to be his children—is holy. For he himself has said, "You must be holy because I am holy."

God chose us to be His children and, as His children, we are to obey Him, imitate Him, and be holy. As a matter of fact, He commands us to be holy as He is. How do we even begin the process of becoming holy? We are born again by choosing Him. Once we make that step, we have a revelation of what is right, holy living, and what is wrong. Therefore, we have to fight to not go back to our old ways of sinful living. For example, if you used to lie about your time card and wrote down hours you didn't work, stop that behavior. If you used to gossip at work about your company and co-workers, don't participate anymore. If you used to mistreat co-workers and your employees, start walking in love and treat them with respect and dignity. By doing these simple changes, you will see immediate results in your work environment.

God has special mercy on those who don't know the truth and are living in sin. However, once we receive the revelation of truth we have a responsibility to be like Him. Jesus gave us the example of how to live a holy life here on earth. He made himself human to show us that, with God's help, we can be holy. He gave us an example of how to succeed in every area of our lives.

Examine yourself to see if there are areas in your life where you may be slipping back to old behavior or sin. And if you are, ask for His forgiveness and strength and guidance. Strive to be holy on a daily basis.

207

WHEN WE DO WHAT'S RIGHT, WE ARE RIGHTEOUS AS CHRIST IS

1 John 3:7 (NLT)

Dear children, don't let anyone deceive you about this:
When people do what is right, it is because they are righteous,
even as Christ is righteous.

Doing what is right consistently is difficult. In the workplace, we are confronted daily with situations where we need to decide to do what is right—no matter the cost. Many of us compromise the truth and not do what is right mainly for fear of losing our jobs. Very few women who work don't really need to work. Therefore, when our job is on the line, what do we do? According to the Bible, we are always to do what is right—no exceptions.

When we do what's right, we are righteous as Christ is. We will have to trust God with all our heart that He will protect us and provide for all our needs. Our job is a need and, therefore, He will provide it for us. We have to believe and trust that He will never leave us nor forsake us—especially when we are doing what is right.

208

YOU ARE A SLAVE TO WHATEVER CONTROLS YOU

2 Peter 2:19 (NLT)

They promise freedom, but they themselves are slaves to sin and corruption. For you are a slave to whatever controls you.

In this passage, Peter is talking about false prophets. He warns us about them and their tricks to deceive people. Peter says, "They promise freedom." Yet they don't know what it takes to give freedom. Jesus is the only one who can give us freedom. The truth will set us free and Jesus is the only truth. "They themselves are slaves to sin and corruption." That is a warning sign for us to be watchful. False prophets live in sin and have corrupted hearts.

"For you are a slave to whatever controls you." This applies to all of us. Is there a bad habit you have and are trying to be delivered from? It doesn't have to be the big things such as addiction to pornography, drugs, or alcohol. How about smoking? How about gossiping, watching too much TV, overeating, anger, or other things? These are examples of behaviors that can control people's lives. If they control you, you are a slave and need to be set free.

Therefore, ask God today to deliver you and make a commitment to Him to stop whatever it is that is controlling you. He will set you free and give you grace to overcome if you go to Him with a repenting heart.

LEADERSHIP

209

ARE YOU A WORLDLY LEADER OR A GODLY LEADER?

Matthew 20:26-27 (NLT)

But among you it should be quite different. Whoever wants to be a leader among you must be your servant, and whoever wants to be first must become your slave.

Jesus explained to His disciples how kings and leaders of the world take advantage of their people. Christians, on the other hand, who want to be leaders and have positions of authority in God's Kingdom, must become a servant to their people. It is the opposite of how our human flesh thinks it should be. A leader is not a true godly leader until that person learns to humbly serve others.

Jesus, who is God's Son, didn't come to be served, but to serve others and to give His life as a ransom for many (v. 28). Jesus is our ultimate example of a servant leader. Knowing He is the Son of God, He became a servant to serve all of us.

In the workplace, as you are promoted into higher levels of management and leadership, remember to imitate Jesus and become a servant to your employees. This means you have their best interest at heart, you pray for them, care for them, pay fair wages, and are honest, trustworthy, truthful, and loving. By being a godly leader, you provide an opportunity to your employees and your company to have an environment where loyalty and faithfulness can flourish.

210

ARE YOU ONE OF GOD'S WORKERS?

Matthew 9:37-38 (NLT)

He said to his disciples, "The harvest is so great, but the workers are so few. So pray to the Lord who is in charge of the harvest; ask him to send out more workers for his fields."

Jesus said those words after being with multitudes of people who went to Him with their problems. He was only one and He saw the great need of having more of Him on earth. As we become born again, when we ask Jesus to come into our lives, we become God's laborers and workers of His field. The harvest is God's, but He needs us to work it for Him.

Most of us consider ourselves good workers. In fact, we welcome and look for opportunities for promotion. As workers of the Kingdom of God, our attitude toward new opportunities should be the same, and we should ask ourselves some questions. Are we doing a good job for God? Are we bringing in the harvest? Are we looking to be promoted in the Kingdom of God? With God our jobs are not just a title. In His Kingdom, the higher the position, the more responsibility we have with people's lives. Jesus said, "And whosoever of you will be the chiefest, shall be servant of all" (Mark 10:44 KJV). The higher we go in God's positions, the more we have to serve others.

Therefore, let's ask God for more workers to help us with the great task we have ahead. But also, let's ask Him to help us be the best workers we can be for His Kingdom.

211

BE A FAIR LEADER

Deuteronomy 1:16 (NLT)

I instructed the judges, "You must be perfectly fair at all times, not only to fellow Israelites, but also to the foreigners living among you."

Moses gave the instructions above to his judges when he appointed them to help him rule God's people. If you have a position of leadership at work, you must also be fair to all your employees. Sometimes Christians may favor other Christians at work because we are brothers and sisters in Christ. However, the Bible tells us we are to treat everybody the same—Christians and non-Christians. We will always have to interact and live among people from various cultures and religious backgrounds. Instead of feeling righteous and superior to them, we must have the compassion of God and be a witness. One way to show them the love of God and being a witness is by being fair.

In addition, from the legal standpoint, we have to comply with the laws protecting all employees. But we need to go beyond that. There are subtle ways in which we can show favor for some people over others and that is also wrong. Verse 17 says, "When you make decisions, never favor those who are rich; be fair to lowly and great alike."

Examine your heart to ensure you are being fair with everybody in all you do and at all times—especially if you are in leadership.

212

BE A GODLY LEADER

Deuteronomy 16:19 (NLT)

You must never twist justice or show partiality. Never accept a bribe, for bribes blind the eyes of the wise and corrupt the decisions of the godly.

These instructions were given to the judges and officials of the tribes of Israel. These standards are still valid today for any position of authority and for anybody who has the power to make decisions.

Finding leaders with integrity these days is, unfortunately, the exception and not the rule in our society. We hear in the news about company leaders and people in government positions who twist justice, accept bribes, and show partiality toward one issue or another.

There are two key points we must notice. One is that, as Christian women, we have the responsibility to vote and appoint leaders that will not do these things. They are to be people of character, honest, truthful, and godly. We are to take that responsibility seriously and research and learn about the people who are running for public office.

The second key point is that if we are one of those appointed leaders to serve the community, then we are to live by those godly standards instructed by God Himself. The same principles apply if we are in a leadership position at work. We are still serving the people under us and have the responsibility to make godly decisions. God gives us specific instructions: don't twist justice, don't show partiality, and don't take bribes of any kind (this includes a promised promotion, a special client, a bigger raise, or anything given to us in exchange for something else). We are to be examples of godly leaders.

213

GOD PUT HUMANS IN CHARGE

Psalm 8:5-6 (NLT)

For you made us only a little lower than God, and you crowned us with glory and honor. You put us in charge of everything you made, giving us authority over all things.

God created us all in His own image so He could fellowship with us for eternity. But we must not forget He is the Creator and we are His creation. As His creation, we have been given the authority to rule over everything else He created on this earth. Because He made us in His image, He gave us one thing He did not give to any other of His creations — the will to choose. We have the choice to love and obey Him, or to reject Him and go our own way.

By disobeying God, we are choosing to give control over everything He gave us to Satan. It all started with disobedience and continues to be the main reason why our lives can get messed up. When we obey God and do His will for our lives, we regain that control. In addition, He directs our steps and teaches us how to rule and use the authority He gave us. Without His guidance, we tend to use that authority for personal gain instead of using it to give glory to God.

As a Christian working woman, purpose to follow God's lead in everything you do. Represent Him with honor so He can get all the glory for all of your accomplishments. Use your influence in the workplace for His Kingdom. Use the authority He gave you to fight the enemy. Remember, you *can* be a successful working woman because you have Him in your life. How you act and conduct yourself in the business arena will say more than any words you speak.

214

GOD'S BASIC REQUIREMENTS FOR LEADERS

Exodus 18:21 (NLT)

But find some capable, honest men who fear God and hate bribes. Appoint them as judges over groups of one thousand, one hundred, fifty, and ten.

This is the first instruction on how to be a good leader that God gave to Moses. In order to be a leader, God required four basic characteristics:

1) *Be Capable*: We must possess some level of skill to lead a group in the various areas of business.

2) *Be Honest*: We must be honest people, always doing what's right, and being truthful.

3) *Fear God:* We must fear, honor, and revere God; this is a lifestyle.

4) *Hate bribes:* We must not accept bribes under any circumstances.

Our main interest and focus should always be to serve those under us by leading them to the best of our ability and with the wisdom of God by the Holy Spirit. Christian working women are called to be leaders in one way or another. The most basic leadership task is leading people to Christ by our example.

Ask God to help you cultivate these character traits in your life so He can use you as a leader in His Kingdom.

215

JESUS PREPARED FOR HIS CALLING

Matthew 4:1-2 (NLT)

Then Jesus was lead out into the wilderness by the Holy Spirit to be tempted there by the Devil. For forty days and forty nights he ate nothing and became very hungry.

God has a special and unique calling for each one of us, and we all need preparation to fulfill it. Part of that preparation is to be in the wilderness and experience temptations from the Devil. Jesus was lead by the Holy Spirit to go to the wilderness to be tempted. The Devil didn't come until Jesus was at His weakest point in the flesh, after He had been fasting for forty days and forty nights. At the same time, however, that's when He was the strongest in the Spirit because He had prepared through prayer and fasting to endure temptation.

There are some key things we must do to prepare and be ready to fulfill the calling of God in our lives. Spiritually, we must be willing to be lead of the Spirit into uncomfortable places. We must live a life of prayer and fasting—prayer, to be in constant communion with the Lord; fasting, to constantly submit our flesh and become stronger in the spirit. Then we must pass every test from the Devil so we can move on to the next step in God's plan for us. We also need to learn to be bold in the spirit and use our authority given to us by Jesus. He said, "Get out of here, Satan" (v. 10) and "then the Devil went away"… (v. 11). We can and should do the same.

Since part of our calling is our careers, we also must prepare to get to the place where God wants us to be. We need to continually educate ourselves, sometimes do jobs we don't particularly feel comfortable with, and be bold and assertive to survive in the business world. Jesus' ministry began after this preparation was completed. He prepared for His calling and so should we.

216

THREE KEY TRAITS LEADERS MUST HAVE

Deuteronomy 1:13 (NLT)

Choose some men from each tribe who have wisdom, understanding, and a good reputation, and I will appoint them as your leaders.

Wisdom, understanding, and a good reputation are the character traits God told Moses to look for in the leaders Moses was to appoint to help him lead His people. These are key traits you must have to be a successful leader. The question is how do you acquire them? *Wisdom* is a gift from God you can simply ask for if you're lacking it and He will gladly give it to you. In these days, you need godly wisdom not worldly wisdom to do your job. *Understanding* comes the same way, by asking God to open the eyes of your understanding, so you are enlightened by the truth of His Word. Only by reading His Word, meditating, and studying it, will you acquire the *knowledge* that only comes from Him.

By doing God's Word and obeying His commandments, you establish a *good reputation*. When you don't compromise what you believe and always do what is right and pleasing to God, He rewards you with good reputation. As a Christian, you are responsible for having a good reputation because you represent Him here on earth.

Therefore, ask God to show you if you need to develop as a leader in any of these areas.

217

WE ARE TO PRAY FOR THE LIGHT

Psalm 82:5 (NLT)

But these oppressors know nothing; they are so ignorant! And because they are in darkness, the whole world is shaken to the core.

The world has had wicked people and oppressors since the beginning of time. The Bible says they know nothing. They are ignorant of the things of God because they don't know Him and reject Him. Because they reject God, they reject and oppress His people too, all of us. Furthermore, because they don't have God, they walk in darkness. God is the truth and the light of the world. Anybody who walks without Him walks in darkness. It is because there are wicked people in the earth walking in the lack of knowledge of God that "the foundations of the earth are out of course" (King James Version of the verse above).

One of our responsibilities as Christians is to pray for those in authority—even for the wicked and oppressors—so they receive the light of the world, Jesus. However, it is every person's choice to accept Christ. Every person has free will to accept Him or not.

Our job is to pray for the light and to be a light to the world as representatives of Christ. Let's not forget the workplace is part of the world we can be a light to.

OBEDIENCE

218

ALWAYS PRAY FOR THOSE IN AUTHORITY

I Timothy 2:1-2 (NLT)

I urge you, first of all, to pray for all people. As you make your requests, plead for God's mercy upon them, and give thanks. Pray this way for kings and all others who are in authority, so that we can live in peace and quietness, in godliness and dignity.

Part of our daily prayer life must include praying for those who are in authority. All the positions of authority are ordained of God (Romans 13:1 NLT) and, therefore, we are to obey and respect them.

During our working life we will encounter bosses who are not very easy going or loving. It is not easy to pray for them when they don't treat us right, yet the Bible says it is our responsibility to do so. We are to ask God for mercy upon them and give Him thanks for them. This doesn't make much sense in the natural, but it works because God put it in place.

In your daily prayers, don't forget to include your boss and all the people in authority over you (your husband, if you are married; your city officials; state representatives; and our president of the United States). "This is good and pleases God our savior, for he wants everyone to be saved and understand the truth" (I Timothy 2:3-4 NLT).

BE A TRUE DISCIPLE

Matthew 7:21 (NKJV)

"Not everyone who says to me, 'Lord, Lord,' shall enter the kingdom of heaven, but he who does the will of My Father in heaven."

It doesn't matter how much we pray and read the Bible, as the Pharisees and false prophets did in the time of Jesus. If we continually disobey God, we may reach a point when we deny our salvation and we may not enter the kingdom of heaven. Sometimes, we think that if we are going to church often, reading the Word, or even attending a prayer group, we are walking with God. On the surface people may think, "Wow, that person is very religious." They are right. "Religious" is the correct word. But God is not looking for religious people. He is looking for true disciples of Jesus. "The decisive issue is whether they obey my Father in heaven" (Matthew 7:21 NLT), Jesus said to His disciples later.

God is the only one who sees everyone's hearts. You can only see the surface, which is not important in the end. In the workplace, it doesn't matter how much you talk about church and God. What matters is how you act and conduct yourself. What matters is that you obey what God has asked you to do, not compromise His Word, and always do His will. When you obey the Father, you are then a true disciple of Jesus.

220

Bring Joy and Insight to Your Job

Psalm 19:8 (NLT)

The commandments of the Lord are right, bringing joy to the heart.
The commands of the Lord are clear, giving insight to life.

The commandments of the Lord are not complicated. They are simple, to the point, and very clear. Humans make them hard to understand because we mix them up, twist them, and misinterpret scripture to accommodate our lifestyle. Society has changed the basic commandments and now accepts sinful behaviors as normal. But God is very clear about sin, and we cannot change the way God sees it. What He says is sin, is sin, no matter how we paint the picture. To Him, adultery and fornication are as sinful as murder or theft.

We are to love the sinner and hate the sin. We are to help our brothers and sisters to get out of a sinful lifestyle so they can experience the blessings of God. At the same time, we must not judge others because we are all sinners and we all need salvation. God loves us all the same.

Obeying God's commandments brings joy to your life because you stay in fellowship with Him. The book of Proverbs contains a wealth of wisdom tips and insights to help you live a godly life. Therefore, take time to study Proverbs and obey what God tells you personally to do in your life. As a working woman, you have a great opportunity and responsibility to bring light to the workplace. You can bring joy and insight to your job and spread the love of God in your office.

221

CHOOSE TO BE FAITHFUL

Psalm 119:29-30 (NLT)

Keep me from lying to myself; give me the privilege of knowing your law. I have chosen to be faithful; I have determined to live by your laws.

This was David's prayer to God. David considered it a privilege to know the law of God. By God's grace we were chosen to be His children. That is also a privilege we must not take for granted. We, the Gentiles, have been grafted into the olive tree, into His chosen people. He made us part of His family by His grace and through our faith. The first step is to accept Jesus in our hearts as our Lord and Savior. Then as we grow in our Christian walk, we can take advantage of the privilege of having His laws and commandments available to us.

David also stated he has chosen to be faithful and is determined to live by God's laws. One thing is to know the laws; another thing is to choose to obey them. It is every person's choice to be faithful to the laws and to determine to live by them. Even though we are now under the new covenant of grace, we still have to follow God's commandments and adopt a godly and holy way of life. It is our choice.

In the workplace these days it is hard to find people who are faithful to their company, to their work, and to their managers or employees. It's a look-out-for-yourself mentality. However, the Bible tells us to be faithful. If we choose to be faithful, God will take care of us.

David prayed, "Make me walk along the path of your commands, for that is where my happiness is found" (v. 35). Choose to be faithful and you will be happy.

222

CHOOSE TO BE FAITHFUL AND OBEDIENT

Psalm 103:17-18 (NLT)

But the love of the Lord remains forever with those who fear him.
His salvation extends to the children's children of those who are
faithful to his covenant, of those who obey his commandments!

Salvation is extended to our children's children. But they have to choose it personally. What a promise that is! When we choose to be faithful to God's covenant and obey His commandments, we can expect to receive this benefit fully. We also learn to fear God (honor, respect, revere Him) when we are faithful and obedient.

Through faithfulness, we persevere; we stick with God no matter what we experience in the world. We trust Him completely and blindly. This act blesses Him greatly, and it touches His most inner part—His heart. Then, as a Father, He pours out His love and blessings upon us.

Through obedience, we stay away from evil things that could destroy our lives. We stay in God's will and on course to complete the plan He has for us.

Therefore, choose to be faithful to spend time with the Lord no matter how busy you are at work. Set up a time and schedule it as the most important VIP (Very Important Person) meeting. Choose to obey Him, and His love will overwhelm you.

223

DO YOU HAVE A WILLING AND OBEDIENT HEART?

Matthew 4:20, 22 (NLT)

And they left their nets at once and went with him… They immediately followed him, leaving the boat and their father behind.

After Jesus started His ministry He began calling His disciples. In verse 20, Jesus called Simon (Peter) and his brother Andrew. They left what they were doing (their profession and job) to follow Jesus *at once.*

Then Jesus found two other brothers, James and John, and they *immediately* left their boat (again their jobs) and their father (their family). The key words here are "at once" and "immediately." The question to us is, are we ready to leave everything behind for Jesus if He asks us to do so? Part of our preparation to fulfill the calling of God in our lives is the willingness to leave our current lives behind and follow Him. It is to leave behind old habits, friends, family, homes, jobs, careers, etc. for His sake.

The Lord doesn't usually ask every person to leave everything behind for His cause. But He does ask us to leave those things that will keep us from being close to Him and prevent us from fulfilling our calling. Leaving things behind to follow God is our choice daily and in every area of our lives.

The other key is obedience. Are we obeying God at once, or are we doing things when it's convenient or not at all? Willingness and obedience are critical to our success in fulfilling the calling of God in our lives.

224

DON'T DRAW ATTENTION TO YOURSELF BY WHAT YOU WEAR

I Timothy 2:9 (NLT)

And I want women to be modest in their appearance. They should wear decent and appropriate clothing and not draw attention to themselves by the way they fix their hair or by wearing gold or pearls or expensive clothes.

This verse may seem a little extreme for our days, but Paul was referring to women who wear exuberant, inappropriate clothes, and are provocative to men. We, as Christian women, must be modest and not draw attention to ourselves. We must be careful to not be the one in the office all the men look at in a lustful way because of the clothes we wear. If those men have sinful thoughts because of our inappropriate clothes, we are responsible before God.

There are beautiful, modest, professional looking outfits you can wear without causing unneeded waves at work. I'm referring to not wearing the mini-skirts, super low cut blouses, super tight or see-through tops, etc. Now that the business casual attire has become a norm, you need to choose your wardrobe more carefully. Remember, you are a representative of Christ.

The bottom line is, we are to make ourselves attractive by the good things we do, not by how we look (v. 10). On the other hand, we are to take care of our bodies (God's temples) and always look good and appropriate for the occasion. God is into the details, and He wants us to look good and feel good about ourselves.

225

Don't Fool Yourself...Do the Word

James 1:22

And remember, it is a message to obey, not just to listen to. If you don't obey, you are only fooling yourself (NLT).
But be ye doers of the word, and not hearers only, deceiving your own selves (KJV).

God gave us His Word as the foundation on which to base our lives. If we don't obey His Word, we can't expect to receive any of the promises and blessings. We are just fooling ourselves, not God. He knows our hearts and, therefore, knows when we are serious and mean what we say.

In other words, walk the talk. This is an expectation of all of us in the working environment. If leaders of a company don't do what they promised to their employees and shareholders, they will quickly lose people's confidence and it can mean the end of the company. The same way, God expects us to do the Word and follow His commandments. However, unlike the world, He never loses hope and will always wait for us to repent and obey. He never loses His confidence in us and—because He gave us a free will—He patiently waits for us to choose Him.

Choose today to be a doer of the Word. Verse 25 says, "But if you keep looking steadily into God's perfect law—the law that sets you free—and if you do what it says and don't forget what you heard, then God will bless you for doing it."

226

ENJOY DOING GOD'S WILL

Psalm 40:8 (NLT)

I take joy in doing your will, my God,
for your law is written on my heart.

God's will for humanity is to live in fellowship with Him while we are here and for all to go to heaven when we die. He also has a unique will for each person. He gives us guidance and direction on how to live our lives through the Bible. He gives us direction for our personal lives by us spending time with Him alone.

When we seek God and ask Him to reveal His will for us, He does. Then we have the choice of doing His will or ours.

How do we align our will with His? When we have His laws written on our hearts, we desire to please Him and doing His will becomes easy. In order for us to have His laws written on our hearts, we have to know what they are. Therefore, we need to read the Bible and study His laws. These laws, however, are not the burnt offerings, sacrifices, or old rituals the people of Israel used to do. His laws are all founded on the main one—the law of love. We are to love God above all things and with all our heart. Then we are to love one another and treat others as we want to be treated (Matthew 22:37-40 NLT). He also gave us the Ten Commandments to follow always. There are other laws we also need to know, such as the law of sowing and reaping—what you sow is what you reap.

Whether we like it or not, these spiritual laws are as real as the natural laws in the universe (such as the law of gravity). God put all these laws in place from the beginning.

Know God's laws and write them on your heart so you can enjoy doing His will always.

227

EVEN JESUS LEARNED OBEDIENCE THROUGH SUFFERING

Hebrews 5:8 (NLT)

So even though Jesus was God's Son, he learned obedience from the things he suffered.

We all go through painful periods of time during the course of our lives. Yet it is during those situations we seek God the hardest, we get closer to Him, and we are the most willing to obey Him. I believe that is one of the reasons He allows certain things to happen in our lives. We need to see those experiences as opportunities to grow—especially in the areas of obedience and faith.

We also experience situations where, if we would have obeyed God in the first place, we would have avoided a lot of suffering. Other times, we forget to ask God to direct our path. Then, when we go on our own, we wonder what went wrong and why. When we ask Him for direction, He receives us, refocuses us, and gives us the grace to continue and fix the situation.

If you are experiencing a difficult situation right now (at work or at home) and are suffering, ask God to show you if there may be areas where you need to obey His direction. Ask Him for guidance and grace. Once you are done with this experience, don't repeat it by flunking the test of obedience. Obey and move on.

228

FINISH YOUR RACE BY KEEPING YOUR EYES ON JESUS

Hebrews 12:1-2 (NLT)

Therefore, since we are surrounded by such a huge crowd of witnesses to the life of faith, let us strip off every weight that slows us down, especially the sin that so easily hinders our progress. And let us run with endurance the race that God has set before us. We do this by keeping our eyes on Jesus, on whom our faith depends from start to finish.

Jesus endured His own race here on earth. He "who for the joy that was set before him endured the cross, despising the shame" (v. 2 KJV). Jesus' reward for finishing His race is all of us living eternally in heaven with Him. Now, He is our helper during our race. He is the author and finisher of our faith, from the moment we start our race until we finish.

Don't give up running your race at work and at home despite the suffering, the circumstances, or whatever situation you are going through. Cling to Jesus and He will help you continue the race. When you keep your eyes fixed on Jesus only, everything else will seem small. You will have the strength to fight, to get up, and finish your race. "For God had far better things in mind for us that would also benefit them, for they can't receive the prize at the end of the race until we finish the race" (Hebrews 11:40 NLT). "Them" in this passage refers to our fathers in the faith—what they started, we have to finish. They finished their race. Now we must finish ours so they can receive their prize together with us.

In order to finish our race, we also have to strip ourselves from sin and things of this world that are slowing our progress. We cannot afford the weight of sin on our lives. We must finish our race!

FOLLOW GOD'S WRITTEN INSTRUCTIONS

Joshua 23:6 (NLT)

So be strong! Be very careful to follow all the instructions written in the Book of the Law of Moses. Do not deviate from them in any way.

Joshua's final words to the people of Israel compelled them to stay in the Word of God. There are several words we need to pay attention to. The first exhortation from Joshua is to be *strong*! If we are not strong in our faith and our commitment to serve the Lord, we won't succeed. Next, he says to *be very careful* to follow all the instructions written in the Book of the Law of Moses. If we are not careful, but take those instructions lightly, we will not follow them and once we disobey, God will lift His protection from over us. It is important also to follow *all* the instructions, not only the ones we agree with or the ones that are convenient at the moment.

The next key words are to not *deviate* from those instructions in *any way*. That's why God gave the instructions to Moses and asked him to write them down. It is easier for us to follow written instructions than verbal because we can read them repeatedly until we understand. We can read them out loud so our ears can hear them, and we can also pass them from generation to generation without changing them. Those commandments have not changed for us even to this day. They are the basis of Christianity.

Ask God to help you keep those instructions in front of you at all times, with the first two being the most important ones. They are to love God above all and with all your heart, mind, and soul and to love your neighbor as yourself. You need to apply these basic, but most important commandments, in the workplace as well as in the home.

230

GIVE FREELY AND GOD WILL BLESS YOU

Deuteronomy 15:10 (NLT)

Give freely without begrudging it, and the Lord your God will bless you in everything you do.

As Christian women in the workplace, we must set an example of a giving people. In this verse, God is instructing the Israelites to give to their own people in need and to people from other nations as well. If someone needed something, they were to give gladly and not with a bad attitude. Verse 8 tells us to "Instead, be generous and lend them whatever they need."

The Bible says there will always be people in need around us. When God blesses us with resources, we are to share them with others. In the workplace, we have the opportunity to share our resources of time, knowledge, and experience with other people. We must not become so busy with our own work that we miss those opportunities. If we help others, God will bless us in everything we do. That is a great promise and incentive for all of us to help each other.

231

HOW TO BE PREPARED IF YOU EVER LOSE YOUR JOB

Matthew 7:24 (NLT)

Anyone who listens to my teaching and obeys me is wise, like a person who builds a house on solid rock.

Because of the times we live in, job security is unpredictable. The companies we now work for may not be here tomorrow. Therefore, we need to be prepared to move on if we lose our jobs. There are things we can do to prepare for the unexpected. Some of those things are to keep our résumés updated, continue our education, always learn new things, and refine our skills.

Keep your contacts and network active at all times. Know your skills, your talents, and gifts so you can improve and develop them. They are assets that will help you get a new job.

Preparing is important and necessary; however, no matter how ready we may be, if we are not planted on the solid Rock, Jesus, when things happen it will be very difficult to recover. It is like building our house's foundation on solid rock. When the storms come, the house will not be moved or destroyed. We need to put our trust in Him alone. Only then will we overcome any situation the world may bring to us—including losing our jobs.

232

In the End, We Will All Be Judged

Ecclesiastes 12:13-14 (NLT)

Here is my final conclusion: Fear God and obey his commands, for this is the duty of every person. God will judge us for everything we do, including every secret thing, whether good or bad.

The verse above contains the final words and conclusions of King Solomon, the wisest man (aside from Jesus) that ever lived. He dedicated his life to study wise and foolish people, what made them wise, and what made them foolish. He studied the lifestyle of both wise and foolish people alike and found out the bottom line is for every person to obey God's commands and to fear (honor, revere) Him.

Wisdom starts when we fear and obey God. He created us with that ability. Then He can pour out all His blessings upon us. God also created us with a will and the option to choose Him or not. We have the power to choose life or death and God makes us accountable to Him for our choices. Despite the fact the entire Bible tells us, advises us, and guides us toward choosing life and God's ways, we still get to choose. The Bible also shows us very clearly what the consequences are for those who obey and for those who choose to disobey. Still, some people will not choose God. They will choose the pleasures of the world and, eventually, death. And even though God forgives our sins and they are wiped clean through Jesus, the Bible says the day will come when we will all be judged for our choices, for everything we ever did, big and small, whether good or bad, and we will then receive our reward accordingly.

Choose life. Choose to love and fear God. Choose to obey all of His commands and be an example to others so they choose to follow God too.

233

KEEP YOURSELF PURE SO GOD CAN USE YOU

2 Timothy 2:21 (NLT)

If you keep yourself pure, you will be a utensil God can use for his purpose. Your life will be clean, and you will be ready for the Master to use you for every good work.

As Christians, we are called to be holy, to be pure, and live a godly life. It is an everyday fight for as long as we live here on earth. The temptations are all around us. We all have weak areas in our lives the enemy knows about. He will continually test us in the same area for as long as we fail until we conquer the temptation. Once we conquer one area, he will move to another one to continue the testing.

In the workplace you may encounter many temptations such as gossiping, becoming jealous, drinking, betraying a friend, stealing company resources (including excessive time spent chatting and socializing instead of working), etc. The opportunities to not stay pure are countless. The only way you can stay pure is by spending time with the Lord, meditating on His Word all the time, and choosing your friendships carefully.

We are to love everybody with the love of God. Yet the Bible says in 2 Corinthians 6:14 (NLT) "Don't team up with those who are unbelievers. How can goodness be a partner with wickedness? How can light live with darkness?" Therefore, we are not to fellowship (have an intimate friendship) with unbelievers. We are to love them but strive to stay pure so God can use us for every good work.

234

LET'S CHOOSE LIFE!

Deuteronomy 30:15 (NLT)

Now listen! Today I am giving you a choice between prosperity and disaster, between life and death.

In the verse above, Moses continues to exhort and encourage the Israelites to make the choice for God. In the previous verses he explains in detail all the blessings that will overtake them if they choose to obey and love God. He also explains in detail all the curses God will put on them if they disobey and choose to worship and love other gods. The key concept is: loving and obeying God is *our* choice.

God created us with the freedom to choose life or death. He will not make the choice for us. It is up to each one of us. What He does, however, is give us detailed scenarios of the consequences of our choice.

Our Christian walk is a daily choice for life or death. Even when we accept Jesus as our Lord and Savior, it doesn't prevent us from making our daily choices for life or death. Every day at work, for example, we have the opportunity to get offended or to forgive, to treat people wrong or to walk in love, to steal from our company or to be honest. Verse 19 says, "Today I have given you the choice between life and death, between blessings and curses… Oh, that you would choose life, that you and your descendants might live!"

Sometimes the choice is not very clear. The world will present opportunities and situations where you truly don't know which way to go. It can look wonderful on the surface, but it could mean suffering for you down the road. At that point, ask God for wisdom to make the right choice. When He gives you peace about a specific direction in which to go, that's your clue to choose that option. "Choose to love the Lord your God and to obey him and commit yourself to him, for he is your life" (v. 20).

235

LET'S LOVE GOD FOR WHO HE IS

Deuteronomy 30:10 (NLT)

The Lord your God will delight in you if you obey his voice and keep the commands and laws written in this Book of the Law, and if you turn to the Lord your God with all your heart and soul.

Moses continually talked to the Israelites and encouraged them to obey God's voice and His commands. In the previous verses, Moses reminded them of everything God did for them, the blessings they could experience from following God, and the curses that would fall on them when they disobey God.

God's expectations for Christians today have not changed. All He asks is that we obey Him and love Him back with all our heart and soul. He already loves each one of us and wants His love to be reciprocated, just because we choose to. He wants us to love Him for who He is, not for what He can provide or give us.

When we put other things first such as our jobs, careers, or even our family, we are not loving Him back. When we make Him our first love, then He delights and takes pleasure in us. His blessings then come upon us and some of them include our jobs, careers, family, and everything else.

The Bible gives us all the guidelines, instructions, advice, commands, and direction we need to live our Christian life in a godly way. It teaches us how to love God with all our heart and soul. Loving Him half way doesn't work. He wants our commitment and undivided love, which we show by our actions. Therefore, let's love God with all our hearts and without reservations.

236

LISTEN AND OBEY

Psalm 81:13-14 (NLT)

But oh, that my people would listen to me! Oh, that Israel would follow me, walking in my paths! How quickly I would then subdue their enemies!

God has not changed. He, to this day, still only asks of us to be obedient—to listen and obey Him, to follow Him all the days of our lives. In this psalm, God is talking to the Israelites. Because they did not listen to God and, instead, they worshipped other gods, they walked away from His will. Then they wondered why their enemies were taking them over and defeating them in every battle. The Israelites were upset at God for not defending them, yet refused to repent of their sin of disobedience in the first place.

Sometimes, God gives us direction on what to do on a specific situation at work, and we choose to disobey. We want to take matters into our own hands instead of following His lead. When things start to go wrong, we wonder why and complain to God.

If you find yourself in the situation described above right now, ask God to show you where you disobeyed. Ask Him for His guidance, then listen and obey. You will see how circumstances will start to change in your life.

237

LISTEN TO GOD'S BELOVED SON

Mark 8:34 (NLT)

Then he called his disciples and the crowds to come over and listen. "If any of you wants to be my follower," he told them, "you must put aside your selfish ambition, shoulder your cross, and follow me."

When Jesus was here on earth, He continually gave instructions to His disciples on how to conduct their lives as Christians. He also taught them how to do the things He was doing here such as healing people, casting out devils, and teaching the Gospel. Every person who makes a decision to follow Christ becomes His disciple. As one, we must follow His instructions including putting aside our selfish ambition, shoulder our cross, and follow Him. We have to carry our cross while we are here. The cross means to endure anything and everything up to losing our earthly life for the sake of the Gospel. Most of us will not have to experience that extreme, but our cross is also to put aside our fleshly desires on a daily basis. Our cross is choosing to be godly versus worldly.

God, the Father, is pleased when we listen to what Jesus says. During the transfiguration of Jesus (when He appeared with Moses and Elijah), a cloud came over them and a voice came from the cloud saying, "This is my beloved Son. Listen to him" (Mark 9:7 NLT). God asked the disciples to listen to the teachings and the words of Jesus. We are His disciples as well, so this is for us. We must listen to what Jesus tells us through His Word. It is all recorded in the Bible for us.

Everything you need to succeed in your professional life, as well as your family life, is in the Bible. Read it, study it, and meditate on the words of Jesus. If you are going through hardship right now, believe that God will help you. If everything is going well, then don't forget to be thankful to the Lord, the One who helped you succeed.

LOVE AND OBEY GOD WITH ALL YOUR HEART

Deuteronomy 10:12-13 (NLT)

And now, Israel, what does the Lord your God require of you? He requires you to fear him, to live according to his will, to love and worship him with all your heart and soul, and to obey the Lord's commands and laws that I am giving you today for your own good.

Even though these were Moses' instructions to the Israelites, the instructions apply today to our lives as Christians. The journey is difficult, and our Christian walk is a daily fight. But God sent Jesus to die for our sins and to become the ultimate sacrifice of blood to purchase all of us. The first step to loving God is to accept Jesus as our Lord and Savior. When Jesus was here on earth, He lived His life as an example for us to follow. Then when He left, He gave us His Holy Spirit to guide us and help us on our daily walk.

God is not complicated. He is simple and has given us a choice to follow Him from our free will. He gives us the choice between life or blessing and death or cursing. He wants us to choose life, to choose Him who provides the blessings (Deuteronomy 11:26 KJV). But it is our choice alone. He will not force us.

Don't let the busyness of life rob you of choosing God and His blessings. If your job or career is taking too much of you (your time, your focus, your effort, and your energy) don't allow it to become your god. There is only one God—The Father who loves you and chooses you. Now it's your turn to choose Him back.

239

LOVE COVERS A MULTITUDE OF SINS

1 Peter 4:8 (NLT)

Most important of all, continue to show deep love for each other, for love covers a multitude of sins.

God's first command to us is to love Him above all things and with all our hearts. The second command is to love each other as He loves us. This sometimes seems impossible, yet there is a way. We can ask God to give us His love—the God kind of love—to love people. We ask Him to give us His compassion for people so we can start seeing them through His eyes not ours. I have tried this with a couple of people in my life I was having trouble loving, and God changed my heart. When I saw them with the heart and eyes of God, my perspective changed, the things that used to bother me disappeared. Since that moment, I was able to love them with the love of God.

When we love people with God's love, we are able to see beyond their faults. We are able to hate the sin and love the sinner. I encourage you to try this with those you are having trouble loving—whether they are your co-workers, friends, or relatives.

240

LOVE GOD, NOT MONEY

Hebrews 13:5 (NLT)

Stay away from the love of money; be satisfied with what you have. For God has said, "I will never fail you, I will never forsake you."

Many people's hunger for money is such that they become greedy (regardless of sex, age, or cultural background). They want to pursue certain jobs, careers, or fields just because they know they are lucrative. Be aware of that trap of the enemy. Those individuals are the most unhappy ones because, when they make it to the top, they realize they have sacrificed a lot along the way. They wake up all of the sudden alone and lonely. They have left behind friends, family, marriage, and all the ones who really care for them and whom they used to care about.

Avoid becoming one of those individuals and go back to the basics. Follow the desires of your heart. Ask God to reveal what those are if you are not sure. Then pursue those desires. If God put them there, He will help you and equip you to be successful in those areas. He will also bless you in every other area of your life. It is His promise to never fail us, leave us, or forsake us. And most of all, love *God* not money.

241

Never Forget What God Has Done for You

Deuteronomy 8:19 (NLT)

But I assure you of this: If you ever forget the Lord your God and follow other gods, worshipping and bowing down to them, you will certainly be destroyed.

We like to read and talk about the blessings that come when we obey God and His commandments. Yet there is another side we don't like to hear about, the consequences that will happen to us if we don't obey God and choose to worship other gods.

Just as the blessings are a promise if we obey, the curses are also a promise. Verse 20 states that "just as the Lord has destroyed other nations in your path, you will also be destroyed for not obeying the Lord your God." Later on, Moses told the Israelites on chapter 9, verse 19, "How I feared for you, for the Lord was ready to destroy you. But again he listened to me." Moses fasted and prayed for forty days and forty nights and begged God not to destroy them.

The Bible clearly says that if we choose to follow other gods (like money, fame, power, prosperity itself, etc.), we will certainly be destroyed. Why? Simply because when we choose to walk away from God, we walk away from His divine protection and plan for our lives. We are on our own in this world where Satan reigns. Satan will destroy us and God will allow it.

The Israelites had Moses to intercede for them. Sometimes, when you are living a sinful life, you wonder why things keep going well… it is because you have somebody interceding for you. Most importantly, once you accepted Jesus as your Savior, He always intercedes for you. Therefore, praise God, and thank Him for those who intercede for you. Keep your eyes focused on God and never forget what He's done for you.

242

OBEDIENCE AND LOVE GO TOGETHER

I John 3:10 (NLT)

…Anyone who does not obey God's commands and does not love other Christians does not belong to God.

Obeying God and loving our Christian brothers and sisters is crucial for us to succeed in our Christian walk. But most importantly, that's how we know if we belong to God or not — if we are children of God or not.

Obeying God's commands may seem hard because obeying Him is a constant fight between our flesh and our spirit. But let's not forget that we control our actions, and we make the choices. Loving other Christians is sometimes harder than loving a stranger because Christians have the ability to hurt us more. However, we can be victorious in both areas of obedience and love with the help of the Holy Spirit.

When Jesus left the earth, He left us with the Holy Spirit—His Spirit—so He can now live in each one of us. The Holy Spirit guides us, leads us, and convicts us. He teaches us the truth and reveals the love of God to us so we can love others with His love that conquers all. Verse 18 says, "Dear children, let us stop just saying we love each other, let us really show it by our actions."

In the workplace you have daily opportunities to show the love of God by your actions. These days, "showing" God's love versus "telling" people about God's love may be the only opportunity you have to put this principle into action.

Finally, 1 John 5:3 4 (NLT) say, "Loving God means keeping his commandments, and really, that isn't difficult. For every child of God defeats this evil world by trusting Christ to give the victory."

243

OBEY AND PLEASE GOD AND YOUR REQUESTS WILL BE ANSWERED

1 John 3:21-22 (NLT)

Dear friends, if our conscience is clear, we can come to God with bold confidence. And we will receive whatever we request because we obey him and do the things that please him.

When we obey God by doing what He says in His Word and do the things that please Him, we are in fellowship with Him. When we examine ourselves on a daily basis and are in fellowship with God by abiding in Him continually, our conscience is clear. Then we can go to God with great and bold confidence knowing He will answer whatever we request.

The only way you can obey God and do what pleases Him is by spending time with Him, one-on-one. Therefore, schedule a time in your calendar to just worship Him, praise Him, and be with Him, in His presence. Treat that appointment as your most important one of the day for it is what will sustain you, refresh you, and renew you to accomplish everything else. If you drive your car to work, turn off the radio and use that time to talk with God. Other times, play music that inspires you to worship and praise Him. If you ride a bus or train to work, use that time to read and meditate on the Word or read a book to help you grow spiritually. This is your part of the deal. God is always ready to do His part and to bless you.

OBEY GOD BECAUSE YOU LOVE HIM

I John 2:5 (NLT)

But those who obey God's word really do love him. That is the way to know whether or not we live in him.

If you want to be a witness at work, live your life as Jesus did—in obedience. Jesus obeyed His Father simply because He loved Him. When we obey God's Word and His commandments, people will notice and will want to be around us. On the other hand, we may also be criticized and persecuted. However, when we know who we are in Christ, our self-esteem shouldn't suffer. Being a *Christian* working woman is nothing to be ashamed of.

If part of God's direction for your life is to work, then do it with all your heart and as unto the Lord. If you want to stay home and raise your children, obey God now for what He has you doing and believe He will give you the desires of your heart.

Imitate Jesus and obey God just because you love Him. There are many other reasons why we should obey God but love for Him should be our primary one.

OBEY GOD IN FAITH

John 15:14 (NLT)

You are my friends if you obey me.

Luke 11:28 (NLT)

"But even more blessed are all who hear the word of God and put it into practice."

Jesus went to the cross by faith, knowing it was the only way humanity would be saved. This is the ultimate sacrifice and example of obedience by faith that Jesus as a human did.

Many times God asks us to do things that don't make sense in our minds. Other times we simply don't want to do them. It is in those instances we must obey in faith, knowing God always wants the best for us and He orders our steps.

In the workplace, you will have many opportunities to obey or disobey God. For example: if you see a group of employees telling dirty jokes or gossiping, your flesh may want to participate just to fit in, but your spirit will be telling you, "No, stay where you are." Obey God by keeping your heart pure and not hearing corrupt communications. Remember, it is easier to disobey. But even when it is difficult to obey God's direction in your life, it is worth it and you will be blessed.

246

OUR REWARD FOR SEEKING HOLINESS IS THAT WE WILL SEE THE LORD

Hebrews 12:14 (NLT)

Try to live in peace with everyone, and seek to live a clean and holy life, for those who are not holy will not see the Lord.

God commands us to live a clean and holy life. It is a simple truth, that if we don't, we won't see the Lord. Even though it is a simple truth and a very clear command, it is very hard to follow when we live on this earth surrounded by sinful opportunities. However, with God nothing is impossible. He knows we can't follow His commands on our own so He sent us the Holy Spirit. He convicts us every time we are in sin. He gives us wisdom and discernment to help us decide between right and wrong.

As we grow in the Lord and experience the Christian walk, we are able to say no to the carnal, unclean, or unholy things we did before we accepted Jesus. The closer we get to God, the holier we become and the easier it is to say no to the flesh. Our reward will be that we *will* see the Lord.

247

READ GOD'S LAWS DAILY

Deuteronomy 17:19 (NLT)

He must always keep this copy of the law with him and read it daily as long as he lives. That way he will learn to fear the Lord his God by obeying all the terms of this law.

God gave specific guidelines for those He chose to be kings of the Israelites. First of all, he had to be someone chosen by God. He would be a man who must not build up wealth for himself, must not have many wives, and must make a copy of God's laws and keep them. By reading and obeying God's laws daily he would learn to fear God. Verse 20 states, "This regular reading will prevent him from becoming proud and acting as if he is above his fellow citizens." This principle is crucial for today's leaders at any level.

If you are in any kind of leadership position—whether it is in public office; in your own business; or volunteer at an association, your neighborhood, or church—this applies to you. The Bible says that those who are the chiefest of all are the servants of all (Mark 10:44 KJV). The higher you are in leadership positions, no matter where or what you do, you have a higher responsibility to serve those under you.

Don't allow pride to sneak into your life because of the position you hold at any place. God placed you in that position for a purpose. Instead, allow Him to use you to further His Kingdom on earth. How? By letting Him guide you and by obeying Him. Love the people He put under you, pray for them, treat them with respect and dignity, trust them, and help them be successful. You will then see God's blessings manifested in your life, and you will make a difference.

248

SEE, UNDERSTAND, AND DO WHAT'S RIGHT

Isaiah 42:20 (NLT)

"You see and understand what is right but refuse to act on it. You hear, but you don't really listen."

God kept telling the people of Israel what to do and what was right, but they continually refused to obey. Therefore, they had to suffer the consequences of their disobedience. God expressed His frustration in the previous verse. "Who in all the world is as blind as my own people, my servant? Who is as deaf as my messengers? Who is as blind as my chosen people, the servant of the Lord?" (v. 19).

Why is it so hard for us to obey, to listen, to believe that what He's telling us is what's right? Simply because we are human beings living in a fallen world. But with His help, we can listen and obey. We can do what is right and choose to do right every time.

Let's not be as God's people were back then; let's change the trend and be working women that always do what's right. Let's act on His Word and do the right thing. Let's hear and listen to what the Lord is saying to us. Then we will be an example to other business people and friends. It is okay to do the right thing. We don't have to compromise to fit in. Let's stand firm on what we believe is right according to our source of truth, which is the Bible.

249

SERVE, OBEY, LISTEN, AND CLING TO GOD

Deuteronomy 13:4 (NLT)

Serve only the Lord your God and fear him alone. Obey his commands, listen to his voice, and cling to him.

The Bible warns us there will be false prophets in the world, people who will say things that will come to pass. There will also be people, including our own friends and relatives, who will try to persuade us to worship other gods. Even though, in this verse, Moses was talking about worshiping other nations' gods or gods their ancestors never knew, I believe today there are things that have the potential of becoming our gods if we let them.

Anybody or anything that influences us to move away from God, we need to separate from. When we have a personal relationship with the Lord, we learn to know His voice. Anything else or any other voices, we are to discard and not listen to. We are to cling to God. That is the only way we will know and recognize false gods. The only way to know His voice and cling to Him is by spending time with Him alone.

Don't allow the voice of worldly success or attractions distract you and take you away from the only one true God. Even your job can become your god if it is the one thing that you give the most attention and energy to. Allow God to bless you through your job by focusing on Him and putting Him first in your life.

250

STAY ON YOUR PATH

Deuteronomy 5:32-33 (NLT)

You must obey all the commands of the Lord your God, following his instructions in every detail. Stay on the path that the Lord your God has commanded you to follow. Then you will live long and prosperous lives in the land you are about to enter and occupy.

I believe the words of encouragement Moses told the people of Israel still apply to us today. If we break down this verse into smaller pieces, we can see the first thing to do is to stay on the path. This means don't divert to the right or to the left. Don't look back either, only move forward on the path "that the Lord your God," not anybody else, not your parents, not your spouse, not your boss, or your friends, has "commanded" you. God commands a path for each one of us that we must follow and obey.

It is also important to know that God is into details, as verse 32 clearly states. His path for each person is very detailed—to our every moment here on earth. The key is for us to know the details of His plan and then to obey and act in faith on every detail and step He asks us to do.

We all miss details on a daily basis because we are human. But, that's okay. God is merciful, and He helps us through the Holy Spirit and forgives us when we repent from our heart.

Even in this messed up world, there is a Promised Land for you that you can only enter with God's direction and protection and by your faith and obedience. Your ideal job is part of your Promised Land. Don't give up. Stay on your path.

251

STUDY, MEDITATE, AND OBEY HIS WORD

Joshua 1:8 (NLT)

Study this Book of the Law continually. Meditate on it day and night so you may be sure to obey all that is written in it. Only then you will succeed.

Before Moses died, he entrusted Joshua to finish the mission God had given him, which was to bring the people of Israel to the Promised Land. Moses was Joshua's mentor and friend. After Moses died, Joshua probably felt inadequate, alone, vulnerable, and somewhat disoriented. How could he fill Moses' shoes? How will the people of Israel treat him? Will they respect him and follow his leadership? Then God Himself *charged* Joshua with his mission. He confirmed to Joshua *he* was now accountable to God for the fulfillment of his calling. On one hand, God made him responsible for this tremendous task. Yet, on the other hand, He assured him that He was with him. God *commanded* Joshua to be strong and courageous, to not be afraid or discouraged, and promised him He would go with him wherever he went (v. 9). In addition, God gave Joshua the key to his success—study and meditate on the Book of the Law day and night and obey everything it says.

Just like Joshua, we all have a mission, a plan that God has for each one of us. Everything we do must be with the end in mind of bringing more people to His Kingdom. God has given us the Bible, His written Word, in addition to His Holy Spirit—something the people of Israel didn't have—to help us through our journey. He gave us the tools. Our part is to study, meditate, and obey His Word. This is the only way we will succeed and fulfill our calling.

If you recently took over somebody's position as a leader or received new responsibilities, know that God put you there for a reason. Be strong and courageous knowing God is with you always.

252

There Is a Reward for Those Who Accept Discipline

Hebrews 12:11 (NLT)

No discipline is enjoyable while it is happening — it is painful! But afterward there will be a quiet harvest of right living for those who are trained in this way.

Part of growing in the Lord is receiving continued discipline from Him. When He is done disciplining us in one area, He will move on to the next one. We can all relate to the pain we feel while it's happening. But I'm sure we can also relate to the good feeling we experience when we are done with the process. Part of being successful in this life is recognizing when God is disciplining us.

Ask God to help you identify areas where you need to grow and change. Then ask Him to help you change. He will give you the grace you need. In the workplace, there may be some areas you need to be disciplined in. For example, are you participating in gossip in your office? Are you being loyal to your employer by working hard and not leaking confidential information to the competition? Are you being honest with your employees, customers, or vendors? These are some examples. I'm sure you can come up with more areas to look into. When you are "trained in this way," meaning you are used to continual discipline, there is a "harvest of right living" waiting for you.

253

WALK IN FREEDOM

Psalm 119:45 (NLT)

I will walk in freedom, for I have devoted myself to your commandments.

When we walk in obedience, and we choose to follow God's commandments, we walk in freedom. Every person wants to be free. People die for freedom because it is an innate right God gave us when He created us. But the true freedom comes from knowing God Himself. When we devote ourselves and make decisions to follow God's ways, we are free. We are free in spirit even when our circumstances look otherwise. Look at Paul; even when he was thrown into prison, he was a free man and he acted as a free man. How? By seeing himself as a child of God with a mission and purpose here on earth.

Only by spending time with the Lord will we find true freedom as He reveals His plan for our lives and as we find our purpose and mission in life.

You may think you are stuck with the job you have. But you are free to leave if you are not happy. Just ask God to give you wisdom and direction for your next step and make sure you obey His guidance. There is no perfect workplace or environment, but there is a place where God wants you to be to accomplish His plan. That's where you need to be and where you will find freedom in the area of work.

254

WE ARE TO OBEY OUR SPIRITUAL LEADERS

Hebrews 13:17 (NLT)

Obey your spiritual leaders and do what they say. Their work is to watch over your souls, and they know they are accountable to God. Give them reason to do this joyfully and not with sorrow. That would certainly not be for your benefit.

Part of our responsibilities as Christians is to pray for our leaders and those in authority and to obey them. We have to trust God that He is speaking to them and giving them direction to guide and teach their flock. Their responsibility is to lead the sheep and obey God with the direction they are given. They are accountable to Him for what they teach and for their actions.

When everybody in the congregation is walking in agreement, then the pastor can focus on preaching the Word of God instead of dealing with strife and division issues among the people. We are all different, yet God asks us to live in unity. How do we accomplish that? By knowing what our gifts are and by valuing and appreciating the gifts in others. Therefore, we need to ask God to place us in the right part of the body of Christ where our gifts can be used and developed.

In the workplace, pray for your leaders and especially for your boss. Ask God to give him or her wisdom and grace to lead the team you are part of. Then obey their direction and do your part. When you are faithful to obey your spiritual leaders as well as your work leaders, God will bless you for your obedience and faithfulness.

WE BELONG TO GOD BY OBEYING HIS COMMANDMENTS

1 John 2:3 (NLT)

And how can we be sure that we belong to him?
By obeying his commandments.

Jesus bought us with a price. The price is His blood. All He asks of us is that we love Him back. How do we love Him? Verse 5 says, "But those who obey God's word really do love him. That is the way to know whether or not we live in him." Obeying God's commandment is a daily act.

If things are not going right in your life, examine and ask yourself if you are obeying His Word. It's very simple. When we are in obedience, we are in His will and His blessings come to us because we are close to Him. When we are in disobedience, we are out of His will and living in sin. We are choosing to separate ourselves from God and we experience the consequences of sin in our lives.

One commandment we must obey is to love each other. Are you walking in love at work and at home?

WE CAN ALL BE FISHERS OF MEN

Mark 1:17 (NLT)

Jesus called out to them, "Come, be my disciples, and I will show
you how to fish for people!"

The first two disciples Jesus called where Simon (Peter) and his brother Andrew. They were fishermen by profession so Jesus told them something they could relate to. Even though they were trained and experienced fishermen, they needed training and experience on how to catch men for God.

We have different professions and work in different fields. We train, go to school, seminars, attend specialized classes, and get experience in our field by working at it every day. We work hard and try to do a good job at what we do. Yet Jesus calls us to also be fishers of men. He is willing to train us and give us one-on-one time with Him so we can learn from Him and His expertise.

There are people He will call away from their current professions to go into full-time ministry. But the majority of us are called to help Jesus get as many people into the Kingdom of God as we can right where we're at. This is every Christian's common high calling. God has a special plan for each person and their individual life, but He has a universal plan that each Christian is called to do as well.

There are several ways we can do the job of fishing for men. One is to support those in ministry financially. We can help those who are called to go to distant places to preach the Gospel as well as the local pastors—those who are teaching the Word at their local churches where God placed them. Another way is to invite people to church where they can hear the Word of God. A third way is by each one of us talking to people about the good news of the Gospel and winning them to Christ. I believe we can do these three things while we are working where God placed us and also be successful at fishing for men.

257

WE MUST BE HUMBLE AND OBEDIENT

Philippians 2:8 (KJV)

And being found in fashion as a man, he humbled himself, and became obedient unto death, even the death of the cross.

Philippians 2:12-13 (NLT)

... And now that I am away you must be even more careful to put into action God's saving work in your lives, obeying God with deep reverence and fear. For God is working in you, giving you the desire to obey him and the power to do what pleases him.

Paul tells us in his letter to the people of Philippi that Jesus was humble to the point of laying down His deity and becoming human. Furthermore, He died a criminal's death on the cross. The King James Version of the Bible says He was obedient unto death, even the death of the cross. If we are to be like Jesus, we must be humble and obedient. We must obey God with deep reverence and fear. We have to take the calling of God in our lives seriously and obey what He tells us to do. When we obey, He will give us even more desire to obey Him and the power to do what He wants us to do.

Are you doing what God is asking you to do—both at work and at home? Are you following Jesus' example of humility by remaining humble regardless of the position you hold in your company?

258

WHEN GOD SPEAKS, WE MUST LISTEN

Hebrews 12:25 (NLT)

See to it that you obey God, the one who is speaking to you. For if the people of Israel did not escape when they refused to listen to Moses, the earthly messenger, how terrible our danger if we reject the One who speaks to us from heaven!

One of the most important things God asks us to do is to obey Him. When we are living our lives according to His will, we are obeying Him. But when we are in disobedience, we are living in sin. It was because of disobedience that humanity fell. That is the first sin Adam and Eve committed, and the same sin all of us continue to commit over and over again. It is because of God's mercy that He continues to forgive us when we repent. He gives us a new chance with every new day. It is because of His grace that we can start all over again.

If God is speaking to you right now and asking you to do something, you must obey Him. Once you obey Him on this step, He will give you the next one. Sometimes you may wonder why He is not speaking to you. Trace your steps back and examine your heart to see if there was a step He told you to do and you haven't done it yet. Your life is a daily walk, and you have to listen and obey God every step of the way and in every area. What is He telling you to do in regards to your work?

WORK ALWAYS AS UNTO THE LORD

Ephesians 6:7 (NLT)

Work with enthusiasm, as though you were working for the Lord rather than for people.

In this verse, Paul is referring to slaves and masters. Even though we are workers and not slaves (although sometimes we may feel like one), we have to follow this command—to work with enthusiasm as if we are working for the Lord.

In the workplace, there are leaders and followers, managers and employees. Our attitude is crucial in being successful at work. If you are an employee, offer your work to the Lord and work hard. When you change your perspective, it will be much easier to be diligent and dedicated to your work. If you are a business owner, share your enthusiasm for your company and treat your employees right and with respect. Then you will have happy, loyal, and faithful employees.

SUCCESS

260

ACQUIRE A LIFE-LONG LEARNING ATTITUDE

Mark 4:25 (NLT)

To those who are open to my teaching, more understanding will be given. But to those who are not listening, even what they have will be taken away from them.

Jesus encouraged His disciples to always be open to listen and continue to learn from Him because the higher their desire was to learn, the more they understood. On the contrary, people who don't care or listen to the things of God drift away and forget even the little they know.

To be successful in the corporate world and our personal lives, we need to become life-long learners. This is true in the natural as well as in the spiritual area. We cannot grow in our spiritual journey with God if we don't spend time learning from Him and are not open to His daily teaching to us. Jesus, through His Holy Spirit, is willing to teach us how to live our lives and be successful in every area.

Jesus said those who are open to His teachings will receive more understanding because the things of God are understood with the spirit, not with our human minds. When we open our hearts to learn about the things of God, our spiritual understanding is illuminated and we receive revelation—the moment when we "get it."

Purpose in your heart to be open to a life-long learning attitude both professional and spiritually. This will ensure a well-balanced successful life here on earth.

261

AVOID COMPLAINING AND ARGUING

Philippians 2:14-15 (NLT)

In everything you do, stay away from complaining and arguing, so that no one can speak a word of blame against you. You are to live clean, innocent lives as children of God in a dark world full of crooked and perverse people. Let your lives shine brightly before them.

In our lives, both at work and at home, there are always reasons for us to complain and reasons to argue with other people. The Word tells us to do the opposite—to live our lives clean and innocent, to be an example to other people, to walk in love, and shine our light before them. When we do this, no one can speak anything against us. We accomplish this by following the example of Jesus. He did it by spending time with the Father. That is the only way we will ever become more like Him. Little by little we will learn to not be bugged by worldly things, to really walk in love, and see things from a different perspective—His.

Schedule time with the Lord and spend time with Him so you are able to avoid complaining and arguing.

262

BE OPEN TO NEW IDEAS

Proverbs 18:15 (KJV)

The heart of the prudent getteth knowledge; and the ear of the wise seeketh knowledge.

Successful people are always looking for new ideas and how to improve current processes. No matter what you do or where you work, always look for new ideas. Welcome change and be open to doing things in a new way. You can transform an old job into a brand new one just by implementing new ideas and ways of doing things. The New Living Translation version of this verse says it this way: "Intelligent people are always open to new ideas. In fact, they look for them."

Make an effort to be more open. Ask God for new ideas to implement in your job and in your business. When you get the ideas, implement them (if it's within your realm of authority) or seek the appropriate approval. If you are a manager, always be open to your employees' ideas. They will be grateful you considered them even if you don't end up implementing them.

263

BE WILLING TO HELP OTHERS

Proverbs 3:27 (NLT)

Do not withhold good from those who deserve it when it's in your power to help them.

As we grow in our careers and become more successful and influential, we will enjoy many more opportunities to help develop and guide other individuals. As a leader, it's important to not withhold good from those who deserve it—especially when we have the power and ability to help them.

When you help others, it shows you are not afraid of sharing success. Some of those you helped will remember you and be loyal to you in the future. You should also never forget those who helped you get where *you* are today. You can help others in several different ways. Sometimes it may be a word of recommendation for a promotion, encouragement for a project well done, or praise for individuals in front of their colleagues. Not only is helping others a rewarding experience, but in the end you will gain their favor and be a witness to them of the love of God.

264

BE WILLING TO WORK HARD

Proverbs 12:24 (NLT)

Work hard and become a leader; be lazy and become a slave.

Sometimes we think executives and leaders within a company tend to acquire their positions simply because they are lucky or know the right people. We may even feel that certain leaders don't deserve their positions. But, instead of becoming jealous or envious, we should strive to learn from them. We need to observe and take hold of the qualities that helped them achieve success. The majority of these people are hard working and spent years in school acquiring the education they needed to succeed. Then they spent years working at various jobs acquiring the necessary skills and needed experience to handle the responsibilities they now have.

If you're not willing to work hard, don't expect to be promoted to the highest positions of your company. God wants to bless you, but He also expects you to work hard. Otherwise, you will always be the worker and will not grow to *leader*. Even if you hold a support or entry-level position in your company, you can be a leader by being a good employee. Leaders work hard. Are you a leader?

265

DON'T REPAY EVIL FOR EVIL

1 Peter 3:9 (NLT)

Don't repay evil for evil. Don't retaliate when people say unkind things about you. Instead, pay them back with a blessing. That is what God wants you to do, and he will bless you for it.

When someone offends you at work, you have the choice—at that moment—to get offended or not and to retaliate or not. The easy thing to do is to get offended and to pay them back for what they did to you. In fact, it feels good at the moment. But you will regret it later. What follows is bitterness and resentment. Paying them back does not take away the offense or the hurt. Instead, you must choose to forgive that person and bless them. That is what God wants us to do. At the moment, it will be hard to do because it goes against your flesh. But God will bless you for it, and His blessings are always best. They will overtake you.

Furthermore, God will vindicate you when you are innocent and don't take matters into your own hands. He will clear your name and your reputation. "He will make your innocence as clear as the dawn, and the justice of your cause will shine like the noon-day sun" (Psalm 37:6 NLT).

266

FAITH AND PATIENCE ARE KEY TO YOUR SUCCESS

James 1:2-4 (KJV)

My brethren, count it all joy when ye fall into divers temptations; knowing this, that the trying of your faith worketh patience. But let patience have her perfect work, that ye may be perfect and entire, wanting nothing.

Part of living in this world is to experience trials and temptations. James encourages us to use those trials as an opportunity for joy because it is by going through those experiences that we grow and learn to be patient. When we become "perfect" (or mature in patience), we arrive at a spiritual place where we are entire and want nothing.

God allows us to go through those trials so we can grow in Him—in faith and patience. Remember, the test is on what we believe. When we pass those tests, our faith is stronger and we move on to the next level of maturity in the Lord.

Faith and patience are two crucial ingredients to your success in life. If you are experiencing trials at work or at home, ask God, in faith, for wisdom to know what to do and for patience to help you get through it. The first key is to have faith and believe God will answer you and help you out of that situation. The second key is to have patience while you wait for His answer. If you do this, you will come out in the end more mature and patient—wanting nothing.

267

GO TO GOD FOR REFUGE

Psalm 16:1 (NLT)

Keep me safe, O God, for I have come to you for refuge.

In our lives we have times when we don't know where to turn. Every avenue we look into for a solution is shut down. We keep thinking and brainstorming in anguish, trying to figure it all out on our own. It is in those times we must go to God for refuge. He wants to be our refuge, our comforter, our savior. When we pray this prayer to Him, He will come through for us and will keep us safe.

It takes understanding to realize we can't do it alone. "It" means our lives. We can't live a true successful life without involving God. The world's definition of success is not godly success. There are many successful people in this world that are not happy, regardless of their fame, material possessions, or profession. On the other hand, there are people that don't have many material things that live successful lives. Why? Because God fills in the blank for all the other things they don't have.

The Bible also says there will be poor people in the world always. There are poor people who are happy and those who are miserable. What is the difference? The ones that are happy have the Lord and His joy in their lives. They understand their need for Him, and they seek Him.

It is not a matter of being rich or poor. It is a matter of having Jesus in our hearts or not. It is a matter of involving God in every decision we make. To live a successful and balanced life, we must have the Lord with us, in every step of our life here on earth. To be successful is to live the will of God for our lives every day. If we do that, when our turn comes to meet our Creator, He will say to us "Well done!... You are a trustworthy servant" (Luke 19:17 NLT), and we will be able to say we fought a good fight, finished our race, and remained faithful (2 Timothy 4:7 NLT).

268

Hard Work Brings Wealth that Grows

Proverbs 13:11 (NLT)

Wealth from get-rich-quick schemes quickly disappears; wealth from hard work grows.

Wanting to get rich quick is a normal tendency of every human being. But the satisfaction of working hard and watching your wealth grow throughout the years is a true blessing. Avoid the temptation of joining or starting get-rich-quick schemes. These opportunities may look good on the outside, but too many times they are filled with empty promises and shattered dreams.

When you are given something you didn't work hard to achieve, you don't have the same appreciation for it. The value of it to you is nearly none. It's like giving an Olympic gold medal to someone who has never trained in anything. That person is probably going to give it away, sell it, or forget he ever received it. However, a true champion who diligently trains and works hard to win that gold medal will always appreciate it.

Get-rich-quick schemes may come and go, but hard work brings happiness, contentment, and lasting wealth that grows.

HAVE A GOOD ATTITUDE

Philippians 2:5 (NLT)

Your attitude should be the same that Christ Jesus had.

Always having a good attitude in life is crucial to success, yet it is not always easy. We live in the world, and we will face tribulation and problems while we are here. We are not to ignore them, but we are not to let them rule and take over our lives either. We take control, confront the situations, and fight the good fight of faith. When we know that God is with us to guide us, comfort us, and give us peace, we should then gain the attitude of a conqueror. Jesus was humble and obedient to God. He also trusted God and believed Him.

Philippians 4:4 (NLT) says to "Always be full of joy in the Lord. I say it again—rejoice!"

Verse 6 tells us, "Don't worry about anything; instead, pray about everything. Tell God what you need, and thank him for all he has done." These scriptures help us keep a good attitude.

PLAN AND WORK HARD AND YOU WILL PROSPER

Proverbs 21:5 (NLT)

Good planning and hard work lead to prosperity,
but hasty shortcuts lead to poverty.

During the course of our working lives we will have opportunities to take shortcuts. In the short term it may seem like the right thing to do and it may feel good. But long term, we may be leading ourselves to poverty. We must be women who plan for the long term instead of just for the moment. Planning our careers, educating ourselves, and working hard will lead us to prosperity.

Preparation and planning is a daily lifestyle. Therefore, we must always prepare ourselves for the next step. When we do, more opportunities will present themselves to us. We also need to prepare spiritually so God can give us new assignments. When we do our part, God will do His.

271

PURPOSE TO REMAIN FRUITFUL ALWAYS

Psalm 92:14 (NLT)

Even in old age they will produce fruit; they will remain vital and green.

In this verse, Moses is referring to the godly. In verse 12 he says, "But the godly will flourish like palm trees and grow strong like cedars of Lebanon." I plan to be a godly woman who will continue to produce fruit, be vital, and healthy even in my old age. Do you see yourself that way too?

Are you of old age now and still working and being productive? Then I'm proud of you. Some women start saying they're old when they're in their thirties, forties, or even fifties. If you retire at fifty-five or sixty-five, you still may have thirty to forty years to live. What are your plans? If you work for God, you will never retire. You have work for an eternity—to rule and reign with Him forever. Your time here is only preparation. I'm planning to continue my learning, preparation, and training until the day I meet Him personally in heaven. Do you?

Change your perspective with regards to work. When you work for the King, the Most High, our Father God, He will never lay you off, His benefits are the best, and He pays with His riches in glory!

It's never too late to go back to school, start your own business, or start a new career. Follow your heart through the leading of the Holy Spirit. Be fruitful.

SEEKING ADVICE IS VITAL TO SUCCESS

Proverbs 15:22 (NLT)

Plans go wrong for lack of advice; many counselors bring success.

Often times we think we can do things alone and we don't need advice from anybody. God encourages us to work in teams and with many counselors to be successful.

Don't be too proud to seek advice when you are faced with a difficult situation at work or when you are given a new project to manage. Ask God for direction as to whom to seek advice from and who should be part of your team. Different people bring different opinions and experiences to the table that can help you succeed. If you are a business owner, consider a team of professionals (counselors) to help you in your business planning.

SELF-CONTROL IS KEY TO SUCCESS IN BUSINESS

James 1:19-20 (NLT)

Dear friends, be quick to listen, slow to speak, and slow to get angry. Your anger can never make things right in God's sight.

There are many opportunities in the workplace to become angry. For example: the vendor didn't deliver what he promised, your employee didn't follow your directions and messed up, your customer is never satisfied with your product or service, your boss treated you unfairly, etc. I could go on and on.

Even though we may have good reasons to be upset, the Bible tells us to do the opposite—to listen to other people first, to be slow to speak, and slow to get angry. This seems to go against our nature. In fact, many times it feels good to be angry. Yet the Bible also tells us why we should not get angry—it "can never make things right in God's sight."

Self-control is a must if you want to be successful in the business world. It is a sign of maturity in the spiritual realm and professionalism in the natural realm. Therefore, practice self-control and train yourself by listening to people, waiting to speak, and by not getting angry so easily. I'm sure you will have plenty of daily opportunities to practice in your workplace.

274

THERE IS WORK FOR ALL OF US

Psalm 104:23 (NLT)

Then people go off to their work; they labor until the evening shadows fall again.

Every person is called to work every day and their entire life. There is no retirement in the Kingdom of God. He has work for us for eternity. This doesn't mean, however, we work ourselves to the ground and burn out. There is a balanced way to work, attend to our family, and have recreation in our lives.

I also want to clarify that women who choose to stay at home raising their children doesn't mean they don't work. Maintaining a home is hard work and raising children in addition is a 7 x 24 job. They simply choose not to pursue a job or career outside of the home.

Even though most women who work need the extra income, the goal should be to reach a point where a career is a choice, not a need. Choose to work because you want to, and choose a career or job in a field you love and enjoy. You will then have a much better chance to succeed. If you choose to stay home, be happy and enjoy being at home. Whatever you decide to do, make sure it aligns with God's will for your life.

275

WE ARE TO WORK HARD

2 Thessalonians 3:6, 15 (NLT)

...Stay away from any Christian who lives in idleness and doesn't follow the tradition of hard work we gave you...
Don't think of them as enemies, but speak to them as you would to a Christian who needs to be warned.

As Christians, we believe God will provide everything we need. However, trusting God to provide and meet all our needs doesn't mean we can be lazy. To the contrary, God has called us to be hard workers. This doesn't mean women who don't work at a job outside of their home are lazy either. The responsibility of women who have children is primarily to raise them. In today's society more and more women have to, or choose to, work outside of the home. Either way is fine as long as we each are following God's will in our lives and what He's asked us to do.

Christians are to be an example of people who work hard and do it as unto the Lord. When we do that, others will want to imitate us because we will be successful in everything we do. At the same time, we are not to look down on those who idle. The Bible says to stay away, meaning to not imitate their behavior. Therefore, we are to love them and encourage them to work hard instead.

276

WHEN YOU FEAR THE LORD, YOU WILL ENJOY THE FRUIT OF YOUR WORK

Psalm 128:1-2 (NLT)

How happy are those who fear the Lord—all who follow his ways!
You will enjoy the fruit of your labor.
How happy you will be! How rich your life!

Fear of the Lord is a key to seeing the fruit of your work. Psalm 127:1 (NLT) says that unless "the Lord builds a house, the work of the builders is useless." When we fear the Lord and follow His ways, then everything we do has meaning—including our work.

There are several things that work together. The first one is to be in the will of God and, therefore, to be in the place of work and field He wants you to be in. Whether you're starting your career or have been working for a while, it is extremely important that you are where God has called you to be. The fulfillment, enjoyment, and satisfaction you get from your job are the rewards for being in His will. And even though there may be jobs you don't enjoy much, just know that those are transition periods and preparation for the next steps.

The second important thing is to recognize that working without a purpose is worthless. It doesn't matter what you do. You must do it as unto the Lord and with pure motives. Love your job, educate yourself, and enjoy the privilege of working in the field of your choosing.

Third, and most importantly, is to know that without fear of the Lord and obedience to His commandments, everything we do is in vain. God is the reason for everything we are and do and everything we will ever accomplish.

WITH GOD'S HELP WE WILL DO MIGHTY THINGS

Psalm 108:12-13 (NLT)

Oh, please help us against our enemies, for all human help is useless. With God's help we will do mighty things, for he will trample down our foes.

Our fight on earth is not against flesh and blood (meaning against other people) "but against the evil rulers and authorities of the unseen world, against those mighty powers of darkness who rule this world, and against wicked spirits in the heavenly realms" (Ephesians 6:12 NLT). Therefore, human help is useless. We need God's supernatural help to win every battle.

Don't try to fight this war or daily battles on your own against the enemy of your soul. You are not meant to live your life alone, but with God. Only with His help and intervention you can succeed. He is interested in helping you in every area of your life. Give God a chance to help you with your work life as well. That is the only way you will find true success.

WORK HARD—BOTH IN THE NATURAL AS WELL AS THE SPIRITUAL REALM

2 Timothy 2:6 (NLT)

Hardworking farmers are the first to enjoy the fruit of their labor.

There are many scriptures that emphasize how important it is for us to be hard workers. God didn't create us to be lazy. There is work to do on earth for God. This applies to the natural as well as the spiritual realm. God has given us natural gifts we must use for His glory. Our goal should be to find a job that aligns with our natural talents and abilities. Then it is easy to learn, improve ourselves, enjoy the job, and be successful at it. Sometimes we may have to do tasks that don't necessarily fit our gifts. But let's not despair. These are opportunities to acquire new skills, improve in the areas we don't like as much, and continue to look for something that matches what we love doing.

God has also deposited in us spiritual gifts that we must discover, improve, and fully utilize for His Kingdom. We develop our spiritual gifts by first identifying what they are. Then we need to ask God to give us opportunities to grow by serving in those areas. We can serve by joining a prayer group, a Bible study, or volunteering at our church or community.

When we are hard workers in both the physical and spiritual areas, God will bless us and we will be the first ones to enjoy the fruit of our labor.

279

WORK HARD AND PROSPER

Proverbs 13:4 (NLT)

Lazy people want much and get little, but those who work hard will prosper and be satisfied.

Deuteronomy 8:18 (NKJV)

And you shall remember the Lord your God, for it is He who gives you power to get wealth, that He may establish His covenant which He swore to your fathers, as it is this day.

Deuteronomy 8:18 says to not forget the Lord when everything is going well. God gives you the "power to get wealth." What you do with that power is up to you. Working hard and to the best of your ability is a way of using that power. It is a promise of God that when you work hard you will not only prosper but will also be satisfied. So many people work many jobs during the course of their lives and are never satisfied or happy, why? One reason could be that they don't know God and, therefore, don't know His plan or calling for their lives. But another reason could be that they haven't worked hard at any of their jobs. They're just doing the job to get a paycheck and, therefore, don't move on and prosper.

Purpose yourself to work hard and you *will* prosper and be satisfied.

280

WORK HARDER IF YOU HAVE A CHRISTIAN BOSS

I Timothy 6:2 (NLT)

If your master is a Christian, that is no excuse for being disrespectful. You should work all the harder because you are helping another believer by your efforts.

We have heard many stories of Christians who work for other Christians and don't perform to their best, don't follow through, and are simply lazy. This is a bad testimony for unbelievers. Why should they become a Christian when this is the example they see? Why should they employ or do business with a Christian? This is exactly what ruins Christianity's reputation! They might as well stay heathen and hire hard working heathens.

If your boss is a Christian, pray for him or her and join his or her team as a hard working contributor to help the company succeed. Then your example will influence others to want to be a part of this company. This will be a great testimony.

WORK HARDER THAN THE WORLD

Proverbs 24:33-34 (NLT)

A little extra sleep, a little more slumber, a little folding of the hands to rest — and poverty will pounce on you like a bandit; scarcity will attack you like an armed robber.

A common mistake Christians can make is to think that because we trust God we don't have to work hard to prosper and succeed in life. To the contrary, as Christians, we have to work harder than other people in our field, whatever that may be. We not only have the responsibility to represent Christ on earth, but there is much to be done and accomplish for His Kingdom. Jesus was a hard worker, and we are to follow His example. Even the ultimate work He did for us — the cross — He had to do Himself. He worked hard for us. God didn't do it for Him. He did it on His own as a human but with God's strength.

Let's be an example to the world and work hard always as unto the Lord. He is so worth it! It's the least we can do to thank Him for what He did for us.

YOU CAN SHARE MORE THAN THINGS WITH THOSE IN NEED

Hebrews 13:16 (NLT)

Don't forget to do good and to share what you have with those in need, for such sacrifices are very pleasing to God.

As you gain knowledge and experience during your working life, don't forget to take time to help other women who are just starting out. Sharing what you have is not only about material things, but also about sharing the knowledge and experience you have acquired. Mentoring younger women is a rewarding experience, and you can be of great influence to those you help. Don't see them as a threat but as a friend you can help succeed.

When you help others, God will see you get your reward. Don't forget, however, to ask God for opportunities to share the most precious gift you have been given—the gift of salvation. You will do much more for a person by sharing salvation than anything else. I know you are supposed to be politically correct in the workplace, but God will give you wisdom as to when and whom you can share His precious gift with. This will, for sure, be pleasing to God.

283

YOUR PLANS CAN SUCCEED

Proverbs 16:3 (NLT)

Commit your work to the Lord, and then your plans will succeed.

We all have plans we want to realize and be successful in executing. The King James Version of this verse says "commit thy works unto the Lord, and thy thoughts shall be established." Every one of our plans starts with a thought, an idea. When we commit our lives to God it includes our work and every area of our lives. When we commit our work unto the Lord, He will help us realize those plans and our thoughts will be established. Our plans will succeed.

Therefore, remember to commit your work to the Lord on a daily basis.

THANKFULNESS

284

BE THANKFUL FOR WHAT GOD HAS DONE

Psalm 9:1 (NLT)

I will thank you, Lord, with all my heart; I will tell of all the marvelous things you have done.

God loves the heart of a thankful person. When we are thankful to Him for all the things He has done for us, He wants to bless us even more. When we are going through bad things or circumstances in our lives, we tend to forget all the blessings God has given us in the past. It is in those times we need to remember what God has done for us and truly thank Him for every gift and blessing He has given us.

When we bring these things to our remembrance, it helps us get through the current situation. Our faith also increases, and we are able to trust Him again through yet one more thing in our lives. Thanking God is vital to our success in every area of our lives.

At home, thank Him for your house, husband (if you are married), children (if you have any), your friends, and family. At work, thank Him for your job, your boss, your employees (if you are in management), your peers, and friends. Thank God for letting you be His child. Tell people of the marvelous things God has done for you.

285

BEING THANKFUL TRULY HONORS GOD

Psalm 50:14, 23 (NLT)

"What I want instead is your true thanks to God; I want you to fulfill your vows to the Most High." "…But giving thanks is a sacrifice that truly honors me. If you keep to my path, I will reveal to you the salvation of God."

Psalm 51:17 (NLT)

The sacrifice you want is a broken spirit. A broken and repentant heart, O God, you will not despise.

The people of Israel used to give many offerings to God to obtain forgiveness for their sins. Many people turned this into a tradition with no true meaning or repentance from their hearts. God has not changed today. He has been and will always be, interested in one thing—our hearts. He just wants us to be thankful to Him for everything He has done for us, starting with salvation. What a gift! We must thank God daily and every moment for it. Giving thanks from the heart is what He's after—a broken and repentant spirit willing to be changed, forgiven, and loved by God.

With today's lifestyle we all try to do too much. Sometimes we commit ourselves to serve in work committees, kids' activities, and even church activities—some out of guilt and sense of obligation. These activities may be good, but before we commit to anything new, we must make sure it will not take away time with the Lord. It is better to spend that time with Him than to be occupied with one more thing to do. We honor God by having a thankful heart and spending time with Him.

286

BURST OUT IN THANKSGIVING

Psalm 28:7 (NLT)

The Lord is my strength, my shield from every danger. I trust in him with all my heart. He helps me, and my heart is filled with joy. I burst out in songs of thanksgiving.

What a promise this is to us! In this verse, David is telling the Lord how much he trusts Him—with all his heart. We must follow David's example of trust and thankfulness. For all the little and big things the Lord does for us on a daily basis, we ought to be bursting out in thankfulness.

You have much to thank God for. When you are feeling down (and we all have those days), just start thanking God by faith. After a few minutes, and a few things you say to thank Him, His Holy Spirit will fill you up with joy. That joy will start expanding in your heart until you are ready to burst.

Thank God for your job every day. If you are in transition, thank Him for the right job He has for you. We are to be women of thankful hearts.

287

CULTIVATE A THANKFUL HEART BY SHARING WHAT THE LORD HAS DONE

Mark 5:19 (NLT)

But Jesus said, "No, go home to your friends, and tell them what wonderful things the Lord has done for you and how merciful he has been."

Jesus performed a miracle in a man's life by casting out many evil spirits. The man immediately wanted to leave his town and go with Jesus, but Jesus told him to go home instead and tell his family and friends about everything the Lord had done for him.

We all have a personal story or testimony to tell others about God's mercy and what He has done for us. It is important to keep this in remembrance and share it with others. This is the best way to win someone to the Lord. By sharing, we also record His deeds for us in our hearts and cultivate a thankful heart.

Having Jesus in our lives is a gift we must share with others. The best place to start sharing is with our own family and friends because they know us well and can see the changes in our lives more clearly than strangers. In the workplace we must be careful because there will be people that will not want us to share anything about our relationship with the Lord. However, God will give us opportunities to share at the appropriate moments and with people who need to hear our story. We can share our life story in a way that is personal, yet non-intrusive to others.

Therefore, don't be afraid to share what the Lord has done for you in your life. Do it as a gesture of gratitude toward God. It is the least you can do in return for all He's done for you.

288

DON'T BE IMPRESSED WITH YOUR OWN ABILITIES

Proverbs 3:7-8 (NLT)

Don't be impressed with your own wisdom. Instead, fear the Lord and turn your back on evil. Then you will gain renewed health and vitality.

Sometimes we forget the reason we are so smart and successful is because our Creator made us that way, and we owe it all to Him.

Don't be impressed with your own wisdom. Instead, thank God for the talents and gifts He placed in you, and ask Him how you can use them for His glory.

The Bible promises you that you will gain renewed health and vitality if you fear (revere, honor) the Lord. You need both health and vitality in order to be successful in your life. Therefore, the next time you enjoy success in your work life (a promotion, a raise, or recognition at work for a job well done), don't forget to praise God from Whom all wisdom and blessings flow.

289

Don't Let Wealth Be the Center of Your Life

Psalm 62:10 (NLT)

Don't try to get rich by extortion or robbery. And if your wealth increases, don't make it the center of your life.

Although there are people who make their riches by oppressing others or simply by stealing, we don't think of ourselves in that way when becoming wealthy. However, even when we become wealthy through hard labor and honest work, we run the same risk of making wealth the center of our lives. In the end, no matter how we create our wealth, we will end up removed from God if we make money the center of life, our god.

We can, however, guard our hearts from this trap by giving to the Kingdom of God and by being humble. In other words, we need to obey His prompting to share our wealth, give to our church and to people in need, and thank Him for what we have.

Your work can make you wealthy and that is okay. Just remember to always give the glory to God. He gives you the power to get wealth to begin with (Deuteronomy 8:18 KJV).

290

DON'T FORGET WHERE
YOUR SUCCESS COMES FROM

Deuteronomy 8:10 (NLT)

When you have eaten your fill, praise the Lord your God
for the good land he has given you.

For most of us it is easy to be humble when we are starting out our careers, when nobody knows us, and we are at the bottom of the ladder. But as we grow in our careers, obtain promotions, education, and higher positions of responsibility and visibility, we become vulnerable. The Bible warns us it is in our times of success when the enemy enters our lives through pride—but only if we let him.

God doesn't mind if we are successful. In fact, He wants us to succeed in every area of our lives. But He does ask us to "not become proud at that time and forget the Lord your God, who rescued you from slavery in the land of Egypt" (v. 14).

The key to staying humble is to give God the glory for every success, gifts, talents, or material wealth we may have. Moses told the Israelites God took them out of Egypt and performed all those miracles so that "you would never think that it was your own strength and energy that made you wealthy" (v. 17). I believe the same applies today. We all have an Egypt to be rescued from and God does miracles for all of us. Our part is to always remember God loves us and that's why He rescues us. Praise the Lord your God for everything you are and have—including your job.

GIVE GOD ALL THE GLORY—ALWAYS

Psalm 115:1 (NLT)

Not to us, O Lord, but to you goes all the glory for your unfailing love and faithfulness.

During our working lives we will have triumphs and victories we celebrate. Some examples include being promoted, moving to a particular area within our company, being recognized publicly for our accomplishments, obtaining a degree, etc. It can be anything that brings glory to ourselves. In those moments, we have the opportunity to become proud or to give all the glory—*all* of it—to God.

How do you stay humble when everything is going well and you're on top of the world? By getting on your knees at home in front of the Lord to thank Him, by recognizing that He is the reason of your success, knowing that without Him you are nothing, by doing everything you do as unto Him, and by not forgetting Him.

Give God the glory for everything you are, everything you have, and everything you do on a daily basis. He deserves the glory because of His unfailing love for us and His faithfulness.

GOD IS SO GOOD TO US

Psalm 13:6 (NLT)

I will sing to the Lord because he has been so good to me.

Psalm 103:2 (NLT)

Praise the Lord, I tell myself, and never forget the good things he does for me.

The biggest thing God did is to send His Son Jesus to die for us so we could be saved. Jesus came to give us abundant life. This means He came to restore our relationship with the Father so we could fellowship and be with Him for an eternity. Wow, what a plan, and how undeserving we are! How can we forget this? If nothing else, let's thank God for salvation every day of our lives on earth.

In addition to salvation, while you are living this life, you must notice the other small, simple things God does for you simply because He loves you. I challenge you to write a list of all the things you have, every talent and gift you possess, every person He put in your life, and all the nature around you. You will find yourself writing for a long time. God did all that for *you.*

Sometimes you may get wrapped up in your career and neglect your relationships, including your family. Remember, the most important gift God has given you, after salvation through Jesus, is other people. Therefore, you need to allocate time to nurture them. God put every person in your life for a purpose. You have the ability to influence their lives, and they have the ability to influence yours. Thank God for your current job (or for a new one if you are in transition) and don't take for granted all the other things and the people He blessed you with. When you are surrounded by all the people you love—that is heaven on earth.

GOD TAKES PLEASURE IN OUR THOUGHTS ABOUT HIM

Psalm 104:34 (NLT)

May he be pleased by all these thoughts about him,
for I rejoice in the Lord.

While meditating on the Lord's goodness, I started naming all the things He is to me, and to all of us, if we let Him. After many words that came to my mind I soon ran out of English words to call Him. Then I read this passage and wondered if He is pleased when we think of Him in those terms and the answer is, absolutely! What earthly father doesn't enjoy and is not pleased in knowing that his children think good thoughts about him? Imagine then, how much more it pleases God when we meditate on Him, on His person, and His attributes.

I encourage you to think of words, adjectives, and descriptions of God and what He is to you, and write them down. You can get started by saying He is your loving Father, your Savior, your teacher, your friend, your helper, your encourager, your cheerleader, your hope, your source of life… When you think these thoughts about Him, He will be pleased and you will be blessed.

LEARN TO BE CONTENT

Philippians 4:11 (KJV)

Not that I speak in respect of want: for I have learned in whatsoever
state I am, therewith to be content.

When parents have a thankful child, they want to bless him or her. God, just like a parent, wants to bless us even more because it pleases Him when we are thankful.

Thank God every day for all the gifts and talents He gave you. Thank Him for all He's done for you, starting with what Jesus did to save you. Thank Him for where you are right now in your life. Even though circumstances may not look good at the moment, thank Him in advance for helping you and delivering you from adversity. Learn to be content in whatsoever circumstance (situation or season in your life) you are while continuing to press toward the next mark He gives you.

Sometimes you may not be happy with your current job. Learn everything you can while you're there, thank God for the job you do have, and press on and prepare for a new job. Sometimes God keeps you in a place just to be a witness to somebody or just because you're the only light that can shine for Him in that environment. When you are content, you have peace and joy and you are indeed a light to shine for Him.

295

MEDITATE ON THE LORD

Psalm 63:6 (NLT)

I lie awake thinking of you, meditating on you through the night.

Those are David's words to God. He is a great example of how we are to praise God, lift Him up, and honor Him. David thought very highly of God and meditated on Him with these words: "Your unfailing love is better to me than life itself… I will honor you as long as I live… You satisfy me more than the richest of foods. I will praise you with songs of joy." (Psalm 63:3-5 NLT).

Even when we purpose to take time to meditate on God and on His Word, it doesn't happen as often as we would like it to. Yet this is how we get to know Him personally. We can meditate any-time during the day if we just set aside a quiet moment to ponder and think of Him. We can think about how much He's done for us and how much He loves us.

We all have different schedules, and what works for one person may not work for another. You may be able to take short walks during your lunch break, go to a nearby park or just an open meeting room where you can close the door and have private time with God. Otherwise, set aside time before you go to work in the morning, during your commute to work, or before you go to bed. We can all find or make the time to be with the Lord and meditate on Him, if we make it a priority.

296

We Were Created by God's Power and to Glorify Him

Romans 11:36 (NLT)

For everything comes from him; everything exists by his power and is intended for his glory. To him be glory evermore. Amen.

God created every one of us by His power. He has given us every-thing we have and made us who we are in Christ—one of God's beloved children. We must not forget that. When this revelation is present in our lives, we feel confident and know we can do all things through Christ, the One who strengthens us.

Thank God every day for your life, your family, your job, and for all the gifts He has given to you. The purpose of everything He created is intended to bring glory to Him. You were created to glorify God with your life and in all you do. This includes your workplace.

TRUST

297

Choose God to Be Your Shelter and Protection

Psalm 91:1, 9-10 (NLT)

Those who live in the shelter of the Most High will find rest in the shadow of the Almighty… If you make the Lord your refuge, if you make the Most High your shelter, no evil will conquer you; no plague will come near your dwelling.

Psalm 91 is a scripture we need to read often because it reminds us of God's promises to us and how much He wants to protect us. This Psalm tells us there are several things we must do in order to have God's protection.

First of all, we have to live (constantly be) in the shelter (under the cover and protection) of God in order to find rest—the rest we want and need to be conquerors, to live in peace. Verse 9 states, however, that we will be protected from evil's destruction only if we *choose* to make the Lord our refuge and our shelter. This means it is our choice to make God our place of protection. How do we live in the shelter of the Almighty? In verses 14-15, God answers that question when He says, "I will rescue those who love me. I will protect those who trust in my name. When they call on me, I will answer; I will be with them in trouble. I will rescue them and honor them."

In summary, there are three main things we must do in order to live in the Lord's shelter: We must *love* Him, we must *trust* in His name, and we must *call* upon His name. All of these, we must *choose* to do from our hearts.

Choose today to trust God. Choose Him as your shelter and protection and you will find rest in every area of your life.

298

DON'T TRUST MONEY.
TRUST THE LIVING GOD.

I Timothy 6:17 (NLT)

Tell those who are rich in the world not to be proud and not to trust in their money, which will soon be gone. But their trust should be in the living God, who richly gives us all we need for our enjoyment.

As we grow in our careers, get promoted to higher places of responsibility, and our income increases, God tells us two main things not to do: 1) to not be proud, and 2) to not trust in money. He will not work with anybody who has pride in his or her heart.

How do you avoid pride in your heart? By always honestly thanking God for what He has done for you and for what He has given you. Remember, He is the one who gave you the power to get the wealth to begin with (Deuteronomy 8:18 KJV).

How do you avoid trusting in money? Again, by thanking God and by using your money to do good and by giving generously to those in need, always being ready to share with others whatever God has given you (I Tim. 6:18 NLT). God wants to bless you in every way, but He wants you to share it with others.

299

DON'T BE AFRAID. JUST TRUST JESUS.

Mark 5:36 (NLT)

*But Jesus ignored their comments and said to Jairus,
"Don't be afraid. Just trust me."*

Jairus had just heard his daughter died. Messengers came to tell him the news and told him it was too late to bring Jesus to his house. They said, "Your daughter is dead. There's no use in troubling the Teacher now" (v. 35). But then Jesus did something we must learn to do. He ignored their comments. He simply told Jairus to trust Him.

Many times all we do is hear the negative comments people, even though well-intentioned, bring to us. Because of these comments, we give up asking God and quit praying. Even though we must not ignore reality and facts, we must also never take our eyes off Jesus. He is the only one who can help us and all He asks us is to trust Him. In addition to having faith, we have to trust Him personally and believe He will help us and perform His Word in our lives.

If you are looking for a job or are going through difficult times in your life right now, don't listen to the negative comments of people around you. Surround yourself with people that can believe with you and encourage you. Be open, of course, to making some changes to improve your situation (such as getting additional training if you need to). But the most important thing to do is to keep focused on Jesus and trust Him with all your heart.

300

DON'T PUT YOUR TRUST IN HUMANS

Isaiah 2:22 (NLT)

Stop putting your trust in mere humans. They are as frail as breath. How can they be of help to anyone?

It is sad to see how people trust men more than God in many, if not all, areas of their lives. In today's job market, we cannot trust other people or companies to provide us a job for life. It simply doesn't work that way anymore. Companies are bought and sold as an everyday occurrence with little thought of the employees' well-being. It is a look out for yourself environment. Our only source for a job is God. He is the only one we can trust to provide and meet every need in our lives—including our jobs.

It is unhealthy for a leader to promise job security for their employees and say they will never be fired. This is a manipulative and controlling tactic that creates a dependency on the employer from the employee's part. In that environment, employees don't have an incentive to improve their performance, and they get lazy. The company ends up with unmotivated employees causing productivity to decline. Those same employees become deadweight employees who can't be fired because the leader doesn't want to break his promise. At the same time, it creates a false sense of loyalty on the employee's part. They think they can't leave the company because they are not being loyal to their leader. It is a lose-lose situation in every way.

We are to be loyal and trust God only to provide for our job security, not trust a man, or a company. We are to obey God and go where He wants us to go. We are to do our best and be the best employee we can wherever God places us.

301

Don't Worry about Tomorrow

Matthew 6:34 (Weymouth)

Do not be anxious, therefore, about tomorrow, for tomorrow will bring its own anxieties. Enough for each day is its own trouble.

Do you worry about tomorrow? Do you worry about losing your job? Did you know that worry is the opposite of faith? Fear and worry rob us of God's peace and rest. In His Word, God tells us to not worry. In fact, He commands us not to worry. Why? Because worry shows lack of faith and trust in Him. When we worry, we are telling God that what He says in His Word doesn't work, so we are coming up with a better solution ourselves.

Did you know that God has feelings? God, as a Father, gave up His only Son and sacrificed Him so we may have life. By worrying, we are saying that what Jesus did was not worth it to us and that hurts God. Yet He doesn't keep track of hurts, and He forgives us on a daily basis.

God gives us grace for one day at a time. Each day has its troubles—sometimes big and other times small—either way, we must confront and resolve each one.

Therefore, don't worry about the future. Give it to the Lord. Work hard today and know that He is in charge and in control of your life.

302

GIVE YOUR BURDENS TO THE LORD

Psalm 55:22 (NLT)

Give your burdens to the Lord, and he will take care of you. He will not permit the godly to slip and fall.

How often do you feel burdened to the point of giving up? Most of us feel the burdens of life to be overwhelming at some point during our lives. The Bible tells us to give our burdens to the Lord for He will help us carry them. He cares for us and is always willing to carry us through every situation.

Anything can become a burden when there is no grace. But through His grace we are able to handle the trials of life and overcome difficult situations. Giving our burdens to God means we trust Him fully. It means we know He loves us and He will never abandon us.

Your work should not be or become a burden to you. If it is a burden right now, ask God what His will for you is, what your next step should be, and to help you carry your burdens. He will not let you fall. Remember, with Jesus, the yoke is easy and the burden is light (Matthew 11:30 KJV).

GOD GIVES US THE DESIRES OF OUR HEARTS

Psalm 37:4-5 (NLT)

Take delight in the Lord, and he will give you your heart's desires. Commit everything you do to the Lord. Trust him, and he will help you.

God places desires in our hearts. When we delight in Him (take time to be with Him, spend time in His presence, and fellowship with Him), He will give us those desires. When we commit ourselves to do everything unto the Lord, He will help us achieve our goals. In other words, when we spend time with Him, we give Him an opportunity to change us, to exchange old desires with new ones. Therefore, when we desire what He put in our hearts, He will help us achieve those desires because He put them there in the first place.

Are you spending enough time with the Lord to give Him the opportunity to place those desires in your heart? What kind of job do you desire to have? Are you in the industry you desire to be?

GOD IS OUR FORTRESS IN TIMES OF TROUBLE

Psalm 37:39 (NLT)

The Lord saves the godly; he is their fortress in times of trouble.

More often than not, we get in trouble all by ourselves. Other times, we find ourselves in a mess by association. Our family, our company, or friends get in trouble, and we are included because we are part of them.

There are various levels of trouble. Sometimes we create a problem at work because of something we said or did. Usually, those situations can be resolved quickly by clarifying things or with a simple apology. Other times, however, the difficult situation we experience is a consequence of sin. For example, if we are caught stealing from the company, we will not only lose our job but will probably go to jail as well.

The consequences of our sin are both in the spiritual realm as well as in the natural. Sin is simply separation from God. Our spirit is meant to be in fellowship with God, so when we separate ourselves because of sin, we are lost. The way to restoration is repentance. Once we repent, God forgives us, and we move on spiritually with Him. David said, "But I confess my sins; I am deeply sorry for what I have done" (Psalm 38:18 NLT). Then God heard him and David said later, "I waited patiently for the Lord to help me, and he turned to me and heard my cry. He lifted me out of the pit of despair, out of the mud and the mire. He set my feet on solid ground and steadied me as I walked along" (Psalm 40:1-2 NLT).

Even though God restores our spirit, we still have to face the consequences such as losing our job and even going to jail in the example above. God allows those things to happen so we don't take advantage of His grace and we learn from our mistakes. God is indeed our fortress in times of trouble because we can always go to Him.

305

GOD IS OUR REFUGE

Psalm 62:8 (KJV)

Trust in him at all times; ye people, pour out your heart before him: God is a refuge for us.

As Christians, we are to trust God always. When we are burned out, overwhelmed, and confused, we can trust Him and pour out our hearts before Him. He will listen, guide us, refocus our lives, bring clarity to our minds, and lovingly keep us in His arms. He is our refuge at all times.

Therefore, when challenging times come and you find yourself in trouble, don't run away from God—run *to* Him with all your might. Talk to God as a friend, share your heart, and He will give you comfort.

God is your refuge at work too. When no one will listen, He will. When others talk behind your back, He won't. When you are burned out from being overworked, He will lift you up and will make your burden light. Don't forget, God is your refuge, and He's always ready to receive you in His arms.

306

GOD IS YOUR SHIELD, YOUR ROCK, YOUR GLORY, AND YOUR REFUGE

Psalm 3:3 (KJV)

But thou, O Lord, art a shield for me; my glory, and the lifter up of mine head.

Psalm 62:7 (KJV)

In God is my salvation and my glory: the rock of my strength, and my refuge, is in God.

Sometimes you may feel as if everybody around you in the workplace is against you. Other times you may feel alone because there are no other Christians around to fellowship with. Yet other times, even when you are among Christians, you may feel persecuted and judged. Whenever you feel that way, run to God, for He is your shield, your glory, and the only one who will lift up your head. He loves you, believes in you, and will always encourage you to go on. He gives you a purpose to go on. He is your rock, your source of strength, and your refuge. Call on Him.

307

GOD ORDERS OUR STEPS

Proverbs 16:9 (NLT)

We can make our plans, but the Lord determines our steps.

Psalm 37:23 (KJV)

The steps of a good man are ordered by the Lord; and he delighteth in his way.

When we seek God in everything we do, He not only helps us with our plans and gives us godly ideas, but He also determines and orders every one of our steps. God delights in us and is interested in every detail of our lives. He wants to be involved and be an active participant of our daily decisions. He is right there walking with us and ready to give us His insight and advice at any moment and for every moment.

If, at any time, you don't know where you're going or you've lost track of your steps, stop and ask God. He will redirect you, refocus you, and order your steps again.

308

GOD WILL LEAD US TO THE ROCK WHEN WE ARE OVERWHELMED

Psalm 61:2 (KJV)

From the end of the earth will I cry unto thee, when my heart is overwhelmed: lead me to the rock that is higher than I.

Sometimes at work there is so much to do that, when combined with all of our other responsibilities at home, we become overwhelmed. When our heart is overwhelmed, we tend to lose focus of our priorities. When we are stretched physically and mentally by the demands and pressures of life, everything becomes blurry and our ability to set and keep priorities is hindered considerably.

It is in those moments we must cry out to God from our hearts. We must ask Him to lead us back to Him, to refocus our efforts, and to help us prioritize our actions. We need to put Him first again. His perspective is higher than ours. He is our rock and our fortress, and as such, we can turn to Him for protection and shelter. He will lift us above our circumstances so we can clearly see everything from above—from His perspective. When that happens, I assure you, your mind will become clear again and your heart will cease to be overwhelmed.

309

GOD'S JUSTICE AND LAWS ARE ETERNAL

Psalm 119:142, 160 (NLT)

Your justice is eternal, and your law is perfectly true…All your words are true; all your just laws will stand forever.

God and His Word are one. They are both true and eternal. Therefore, all His traits and everything about Him are eternal. Because He created us in His image, we are also eternal—with a beginning but with no end. His plan is for us to live with Him and reign for eternity.

Whenever you think and meditate on the Lord and what He is, think of Him as forever, always, unchangeable, with no beginning or end. That is how His mercy, love, patience, grace, joy, peace, and all of His attributes are. That's what He is toward us.

If you feel you are being treated unfairly in any area of your life, be assured it is only for a short while. God is a just God, and His justice is eternal, so at some point He will help you get out of that situation, the truth will be revealed, and you will be free. If you are not being treated fairly at work, let God vindicate you and let Him do His work to bring justice to the situation. Trust in Him and His Word and believe they are always true.

310

HAVE COMPLETE CONFIDENCE AND FAITH IN JESUS

Mark 4:40 (NLT)

And he asked them, "Why are you so afraid? Do you still not have faith in me?"

Jesus and His disciples were in their boat crossing a lake when a fierce storm arose. The disciples were afraid they were going to drown and went to wake up Jesus who they found peacefully sleeping in the back of the boat. Then Jesus asked His disciples the question above. It is insulting to Jesus when we have Him in our hearts, yet don't have faith in Him to deliver us from the storms.

When we accept Jesus into our hearts as our Lord and Savior, we are telling Him we believe in His ability to save us from every-thing—including going to hell. How can we believe He saved us from eternal damnation in hell, but we don't have enough faith to believe He can get us through the storms in our lives?

When Jesus was inside the boat with His disciples and a storm developed all around them, He was sleeping in peace. How could He do that? Simply because He had complete confidence in His Father, and He knew that no matter what was going on in the world around Him, the Father would take care of Him. This is a revelation we must appropriate in our hearts.

If you accepted Jesus, then He is in you now and all that He is and represents is inside of you, in your spirit. Having Him in your life means you have His power, His anointing, peace, love, joy, and everything else God wants you to have to be successful in Him.

Meditate on this today and know that Jesus is in you. Have complete faith, trust, and confidence in Him. Know that no matter what you are going through in your life, Jesus is in control, and He will deliver you.

311

In God, We Have Everything We Need

Psalm 23:1 (NLT)

The Lord is my shepherd; I have everything I need.

We all have needs, and God knows each one of them. Matthew 6:32-33 (NLT) say, "Why be like the pagans who are so deeply concerned about these things? Your heavenly Father already knows all your needs, and he will give you all you need from day to day if you live for him and make the Kingdom of God your primary concern."

The first need God wants us to realize we have is the need of Him in our lives. Life without God is empty and purposeless. When we recognize we need Him and accept Him in our lives, we then have a purpose to live. By making His Kingdom our priority, He meets all our needs. These needs are not only material such as food, clothing, and a home. We have many other needs He also fulfills such as rest, strength, wisdom, and love. Psalm 23:2-3 (NLT) say, "He lets me rest in green meadows; he leads me beside peaceful streams. He renews my strength. He guides me along right paths, bringing honor to his name."

Jesus is our shepherd. We are His sheep. As a shepherd, He knows us very well and knows what we need on a daily basis, not only to survive, but to be successful. We, as His sheep, must trust Him unconditionally. We need to obey Him, follow His direction, and trust Him that He knows what's best for us.

As a working woman, you have many needs that go beyond a job. You need rest, balance, love, good friendships, stability, and many other things that are unique to you. Give your needs to the Lord. Tell Him what David told Him in Psalm 23:6 (NLT), "Surely your goodness and unfailing love will pursue me all the days of my life, and I will live in the house of the Lord forever."

312

IT IS IMPOSSIBLE TO PLEASE GOD WITHOUT FAITH

Hebrews 11:1, 6 (NLT)

What is faith? It is the confident assurance that what we hope for is going to happen. It is the evidence of things we cannot yet see… So, you see, it is impossible to please God without faith. Anyone who wants to come to him must believe that there is a God and that he rewards those who sincerely seek him.

Hebrews 11:1 (KJV)

Now faith is the substance of things hoped for, the evidence of things not seen.

Faith in God—not faith in faith—is the substance and bottom line in walking out our Christianity. It is by faith that we accept Jesus into our lives as our Lord and Savior. By faith we believe God raised Him from the dead. Therefore, it is impossible to please God without it because faith is what connects us to His love—the foundation of Christianity. We cannot seek Him sincerely from our hearts without faith, without believing in Him. Since God knows us, He knows when we come to Him with sincere hearts. Then He rewards us with His blessings.

God can do anything in your life when you believe in Him. Jesus said in Mark 9:23 (NKJV), "If you can believe, all things *are* possible to him who believes." What do you believe? When you are in the will of God by obeying what He's asking you to do, following the desires of your heart, and believing He will come through for you, things *will* happen.

JESUS IS READY TO HELP US IN OUR SUFFERING

Hebrews 2:18 (NLT)

Since he himself has gone through suffering and temptation, he is able to help us when we are being tempted.

Why is it that sometimes when we go through trials and temptations, we don't go to God first? Our tendency is to figure things out on our own first. Jesus went through every kind of suffering and temptation anybody could ever go through in their entire lives. He became a human being so He could experience real life, real suffering, and real temptations. He died for us and went to hell for three days to declare His victory over evil. He conquered death and overcame suffering and every kind of temptation. He did it so He could be there for us when we experienced those things.

Jesus is always waiting for you to call on Him and ask for help. If you are going through trials at work, at home, or with your physical body, run to Jesus. He has the answers. He will help you and meet you where you are because He understands and loves you.

JUST TRUST GOD

Psalm 111:5 (NLT)

He gives food to those who trust him; he always remembers his covenant.

Food is something we need to survive, and God knows it. We need natural food to nourish our bodies, and we need spiritual food to nourish our spirit. God always remembers His covenant, and if we trust Him, He will meet all our needs.

If you are currently going through change in your life and are feeling overwhelmed, start trusting God. If you are in a transition period right now, if you have lost your job, or are deciding to start your own business, this is for you. God's promise to you is that He will meet all your needs (Philippians 4:19 KJV). All you have to do is trust Him. Tell him how you feel, and ask Him to help you trust Him more.

God knows you need your job. Ask Him for direction, then when He gives it to you, trust Him and act on His plan.

LET THE LORD CHART YOUR PATH

Psalm 138:8 (NLT)

The Lord will work out his plans for my life — for your faithful love, O Lord, endures forever.

We all have the tendency to take charge of our lives instead of letting God work out His plan for us. He has a plan and a unique purpose for each one of us because He loves us. He created us with a calling that cannot be fulfilled by anyone else on earth. Nevertheless, because He gives us the choice to go with His plan or reject it, we sometimes take the wrong path.

Part of that plan is what career and type of job you will have. He will give you opportunities and will open doors, and it will be up to you to go through them. Psalm 139:3 (NLT) says, "You chart the path ahead of me and tell me where to stop and rest. Every moment you know where I am." Allow the Lord to lead your life on a daily basis for He, as your Creator, knows you. Verse 16 says, "You saw me before I was born. Every day of my life was recorded in your book. Every moment was laid out before a single day had passed." The NKJV says it this way, "Your eyes saw my substance, being yet unformed."

As you can see, God loves you and has a plan already laid out for you. All you have to do is obey Him and walk it out. I encourage you to get on the track God prepared for you, both for your work and your home life. Pray what David prayed on Psalm 139:24 (NLT). "Point out anything in me that offends you, and lead me along the path of everlasting life."

316

ONLY FEAR GOD

Isaiah 8:13 (NLT)

Do not fear anything except the Lord Almighty. He alone is the Holy One. If you fear him, you need fear nothing else.

Living in these days fear can creep into our lives in every area. The world is full of fear. There is fear of losing our jobs, fear of losing our families, fear of terrorism, accidents, thieves, bad health, etc. The list goes on and on. But the Bible tells us the only thing we have to fear is God. Fear is a reverence and respect for God, not the worldly fear as we know it.

We cannot live our lives in fear because it paralyzes us. We become unproductive, inefficient, and simply unfruitful. Yes, we are living in a scary world, in a place where there is no stability, consistency, honesty, loyalty, or faithfulness. At the same time, there is no fear of consequences for doing wrong. People don't know what integrity is anymore. But, for those same reasons, we must fear God so He keeps us safe and so His judgment doesn't come upon us. God cannot tolerate sin and, even though He is a merciful God, there comes a point where His judgment comes to rectify and correct.

The Lord is our only hope. He is our refuge and He will protect us from the enemy's attempt to destroy us. If we fear God, we don't have to fear anything else.

TAKE YOUR TROUBLES TO THE LORD

Psalm 120:1 (NLT)

I took my troubles to the Lord; I cried out to him, and he answered my prayer.

As you read through the Bible, you will find God continually asks us to take our troubles to Him. Why is that so hard for us to do? It seems we only go to Him for the big problems and only after we have exhausted every other avenue of help. Psalm 121:2 (NLT) says our "help comes from the Lord, who made the heavens and the earth!"

The Creator of all wants to help you. He is your only hope and source of help. Furthermore, "He will not let you stumble and fall; the one who watches over you will not sleep... The Lord himself watches over you! The Lord stands beside you as your protective shade... The Lord keeps you from all evil and preserves your life. The Lord keeps watch over you as you come and go, both now and forever." (Psalm 121:3, 5, 7-8 NLT).

If you are having problems at work or are in the midst of making big decisions, take them to the Lord. Appropriate these promises and go to Him with all of your troubles—big and small, important and not so important. When you cry out to Him, He does and will answer always because He loves you and wants to help you.

318

THE CREATOR OF ALL CARES ABOUT YOU

Psalm 89:11 (NLT)

The heavens are yours, and the earth is yours; everything in the world is yours—you created it all.

The world is an uncertain place where change takes place on a daily, moment by moment, basis. On the other hand, God, our Father, never changes and He cares for each one of us and our everyday life.

If you recently lost your job or are going to be laid off, don't panic. The Creator of all is in control of your life. If He is powerful enough to create the heavens and the earth, He can certainly give you a new job. It's not easy to go through the experience, but with Christ you can take this opportunity to grow and get closer to Him. With His help you can overcome and have the victory on this situation.

Ask God to give you wisdom, direct you to apply to the right jobs, in the right fields, and to connect you with the right people. Your part is to look for a job, work your network, and get out there. Leave the rest to God. Remember, the Creator of the universe is with you and cares about you. He will never leave you nor forsake you. Don't give up!

319

THE LORD INDEED DIRECTS OUR STEPS

Proverbs 20:24 (NLT)

How can we understand the road we travel?
It is the Lord who directs our steps.

Sometimes we wonder what we are doing on the path we are on. We wonder: why are we in this job? Did we choose the right career? Other times, when we ask God for direction, we are not very happy with His answer. We want Him to agree with our plans instead of us being open to His direction. But we must trust His guidance because He promises us "the steps of the godly are directed by the Lord. He delights in every detail of their lives" (Psalm 37:23 NLT).

God really cares and is interested in every single step we make in our lives. He does plan and orders our steps. He knows the things to come to our lives in the future, so He prepares us and gives us the grace to handle them. When we give Him control of our lives, He prepares the way, opens doors that no man can shut, and closes doors He knows are not for us. There will be times when we will not want to take some of those steps, but we must. We can go through doors and walk on water as Peter did with Him. He is our strong rock and safety. He is our light that illuminates the way we need to go. His Word is the lamp unto our feet. With His Word, He guides us every single step, and we follow by faith, believing in our hearts that He loves us.

It is okay if we don't understand every step we make. The Lord knows what those steps are, where they will take us, and how many we can handle at a time. There are many things in this life we will not understand until we meet our Creator face to face and spend eternity with Him. There are other things we don't understand right now, but He will reveal to us later when we are ready.

Don't worry about understanding the road you are on. If you are with the Lord, He is in charge, and He indeed directs your steps.

THE LORD IS OUR GOD—EVEN AT NIGHT

Psalm 16:7 (NLT)

I will bless the Lord who guides me; even at night my heart instructs me.

When you feel directionless in your life, go to the source, the Lord. He is your daily guide. He directs your path. Because life is a daily walk, some days you may feel purposeful—you know where you're going and feel great about hearing the voice of God. Other days, you may feel as if you've lost your purpose and direction in life. If you are at that place right now, there is only one thing to do. Run to God! He will redirect you, refocus you, and remind you of your purpose. He will guide you and hold your hand as a father with his child. Trust the Lord that He guides you even in your sleep. At night, believe He will speak to your heart and continue to give you direction.

THE LORD LEADS US AND TEACHES US THE RIGHT WAY

Psalm 25:4 (NLT)

Show me the path where I should walk, O Lord; point out the right road for me to follow.

Jesus is the only way, the only road that leads us to the Father. Therefore, our first step is to seek Jesus. He can then lead us on the path we should walk. We need to ask God for direction for our lives in every area. For example: what career should we choose?

What college should we attend? What's the right job for us? Who should we marry? Where should we live? These are all personal questions we need answers to. But we also need the daily direction for every step we make in each area. For example: with our job, how can we make it more efficient? How can we become successful at it? We need wisdom to make the right decisions. With our marriage, how can we become better wives or good housekeepers? The point is God wants to be involved and is interested in every detail and aspect of our lives.

By spending time with the Lord, we give Him the opportunity to impart His wisdom in us and give us specific direction for each area. By reading His Word, we learn the truths that guide our lives. Verse 5 says, "Lead me by your truth and teach me, for you are the God who saves me. All day long I put my hope in you."

Our next step, once we get direction from God, is to act and, as He points us to the right road, we are to follow. "He leads the humble in what is right, teaching them his way. The Lord leads with unfailing love and faithfulness all those who keep his covenant and obey his decrees" (vv. 9-10).

322

THE LORD WATCHES US DAY AND NIGHT

Psalm 3:5 (NLT)

I lay down and slept. I woke up in safety, for the Lord was watching over me.

David represents a great example to us of someone who always trusted God. He meditated on His Word and trusted Him with his life. He knew how much God loved and cared for him. He knew God heard and would answer his prayers. He always went to God when he was in trouble, and God always rescued him.

David also persisted in his prayer. When he was distressed, he continued to seek God until He came to his rescue. He also told the Lord how he felt at the time he prayed. The Lord likes us to come to Him just as we are and in whatever state we are. He is always ready to receive us, hear our heartfelt prayer, and rescue us from our enemies or bad circumstances.

When you go to sleep every night, do you fall asleep knowing that God will watch over you all night and you will wake up safe? When you pray to God, do you have the confidence He will listen to your prayer and answer it? Do you trust Him with all areas of your life or just some areas? These are good questions to ask yourself often because there may be times you trust God more than others. In those times, you need to remember what He's done for you in the past and thank Him.

Live your life knowing God watches over you and protects you day and night because He loves you.

323

TRUST GOD ALWAYS. HE IS YOUR REFUGE.

Psalm 62:8 (NLT)

O my people, trust in him at all times. Pour out your heart to him, for God is our refuge.

David exhorted his people to always trust God because He is their only refuge. This applies to us today in our everyday life. We can believe the scriptures and believe what the Bible says is true. But believing that God will come through for you personally and that He will perform His Word in your life is trusting Him.

Trusting God is having complete confidence in His unfailing love for you. It is laying down your fears, pouring out your heart before Him, and knowing He is your refuge. This is a revelation of His personal love for you that you can only arrive at by spending time with Him in prayer, in quietness, in worship. Get to know His nature and have an intimate personal relationship with Him.

If there are things in your life, at work or home, you haven't trusted God with, take this opportunity to pour out your heart to Him. He is the only one who will help you for He is your refuge.

324

TRUST GOD FIRST, NOT PEOPLE

Psalm 118:5-6, 8 (NLT)

In my distress I prayed to the Lord, and the Lord answered me and rescued me. The Lord is for me, so I will not be afraid… It is better to trust the Lord than to put confidence in people.

Why is it that so many times when we are in distress we wait to ask God until we have exhausted all other avenues? We have all experienced situations we first try to resolve and fix on our own. Then when we figure out we can't do it alone, we look to other people to help us. Then when we come to the conclusion that nobody can help us, we finally decide maybe God can. Maybe He has the answer. By then, however, we are almost defeated and at the end of our rope. It would have been so much easier, simpler, and faster to go to our Father as soon as the situation came up.

He is always waiting for you to go to Him so He can rescue you. He is interested in helping you in both small and big things in your life, not just the big traumatic events. Therefore, if you are having problems at work, don't go to your co-workers or friends outside of work first. Go to the Lord first, then He will direct you to go to the right person to help you or He will interfere supernaturally for you. He will rescue you.

TRUST IN GOD, NOT IN POWERFUL PEOPLE

Psalm 146:3 (NLT)

Don't put your confidence in powerful people;
there is no help for you there.

When we put our trust in people, we are bound to be disappointed. So many times we may think just because we know the president of the company or some of the "higher ups," we can get whatever we want. It doesn't work that way. God may use those people sometimes, but our trust must be in the Lord not in people, no matter how powerful they are on this earth. As verse 4 says, "When their breathing stops, they return to the earth, and in a moment all their plans come to an end."

If you own your own company, don't put your confidence in getting those special clients who will make or break your business. Yes, treat them well, respect them, and conduct your business with excellence. But don't depend on them. Depend on God. Verse 5 states, "But happy are those who have the God of Israel as their helper, whose hope is in the Lord their God." And remember Psalm 147:11 (NLT) says, "The Lord's delight is in those who honor him, those who put their hope in his unfailing love."

TRUST IN GOD'S UNFAILING LOVE FOREVER

Psalm 52:8 (NLT)

But I am like an olive tree, thriving in the house of God. I trust in
God's unfailing love forever and ever.

Why is it that sometimes it is so difficult to trust in God's unfailing love? We believe in all His promises, but can we believe He will come through for us because He loves us? That's another story. That is trusting in God fully and without reservations.

If you're not trusting God to help you handle a specific situation at work, remember the things He has done for you in the past (either at work or in your personal life), then praise Him and thank Him for what He's going to do for you in the future. Imagine you are like an olive tree planted by the river of life and thriving in the presence of God. Spend time with the Lord so you feel renewed, refreshed, and like a conqueror. Then your level of trust will elevate to a point where you can praise Him and trust in His unfailing love always. You will then say, "I will praise you forever, O God, for what you have done" (v. 9).

TRUST IN THE LORD ALWAYS

Psalm 37:3 (NLT)

Trust in the Lord and do good. Then you will live safely in the land and prosper.

When we make a decision to seek God first, the next step is to *trust* completely in Him. He promises us we will live safely in the land *and* prosper. He, as our Father, wants to give us security, safety, and rest, in addition to material things. He wants us to prosper and be successful in every area of our lives. This includes having a successful business and career as well as a successful marriage and family.

In addition to trusting the Lord, we, as ambassadors of Christ, must do good. When we trust Him, He will direct our path and we will then be able to do good. Therefore, trust Him always.

328

TRUST IN THE LORD DAILY

Proverbs 3:5-6 (NLT)

Trust in the Lord with all your heart; do not depend on your own understanding. Seek his will in all you do, and he will direct your paths.

Life is a daily fight; therefore, we must trust the Lord with all our heart all our days. When we depend on Him for everything we do, we are putting our trust in the hands of the Master, the Creator of the universe, our God the Father. Only when we trust Him we realize His wonderful plan for our lives. In fact, when He places His perfect will in our hearts, it becomes easy to follow every step He puts in front of us.

In the workplace, trust God that you are in the right place and that you are there for a purpose. If you find yourself in a difficult situation at work, trust God to direct your path on a daily basis. Just think how much Jesus trusted God while He went through the process of the cross!

329

TRUST THE LORD AS YOUR HELPER AND SHIELD

Psalm 115:11 (NLT)

All you who fear the Lord, trust the Lord! He is your helper; he is your shield.

Is it possible to fear God but not trust Him? It must be if the Bible tells us to trust Him (to all of us who fear Him). We all have the tendency to get religious when we obey His commandments and faithfully do things as part of a program and not from our hearts.

When we trust God, we have to surrender ourselves totally and give Him everything we are. We have to trust Him as our personal helper and shield. Sometimes we believe He can be the helper and shield for other people, yet we don't trust Him with our own problems and needs.

Fearing God is one thing, trusting God is another. When we have complete trust in Him in every area of our lives, He will help us in a supernatural way and will give us peace.

If you are having issues at work, I encourage you to trust God and lay those problems down at the altar. He is interested in every area of your life. Allow Him to be your helper and shield.

330

TRUSTING GOD GIVES YOU PEACE

Psalm 4:8 (NLT)

I will lie down in peace and sleep, for you alone, O Lord, will keep me safe.

Knowing that God is in control of your life will give you peace, joy, and rest. When you go to bed at night, examine your heart and ask yourself daily, "who is in control of my life?" If the answer is "me," then stop and give that control to the Lord. Surrender to Him again. This is a daily prayer and act of trust. It is a normal tendency to take over your life and circumstances once again, after you just surrendered them to God. You must trust Him and know He will deliver you from the current circumstances you're in and He will keep you safe.

If you have a job you love, thank God for it every day. If you are asking God for a new job, also thank Him for the future job He has for you and don't get weary in believing and trusting Him. You are not alone. He will never leave you nor forsake you. When you know this, you will lie down in peace and sleep.

331

WAIT PATIENTLY FOR GOD'S VISION TO MANIFEST IN YOUR LIFE

Habakkuk 2:2-3 (NLT)

Then the Lord said to me, "Write my answer in large, clear letters on a tablet, so that a runner can read it and tell everyone else. But these things I plan won't happen right away. Slowly, steadily, surely, the time approaches when the vision will be fulfilled. If it seems slow, wait patiently, for it will surely take place. It will not be delayed."

In this verse, the prophet Habakkuk was asking God for an answer because the world around him was a disaster and he felt helpless. He decided to go up on a tower and wait for the Lord's answer. And He answered. God told him to write the vision He was about to give him in large, clear letters, on a tablet so even a runner below could read it from afar and follow it.

If you haven't asked God to reveal His plan for you, His vision for you, it's time to do it. Then, wait on Him until He reveals it to you. If the Lord has given you a vision for your life, it's time to write it down.

The second part of these verses deals with the disappointment and discouragement we all face while we wait for His vision to manifest in our lives. He says it will take time, but slowly and surely it will happen. This is a promise that we must hang on to. By faith the just shall live (Galatians 3:11 NLT). We wait in faith until the vision He has for us comes true.

Is your work part of God's vision for you? Is it preparing you and are you learning skills to pursue God's plan in your life?

332

WAIT PATIENTLY FOR THE LORD

Psalm 27:14 (NLT)

Wait patiently for the Lord. Be brave and courageous. Yes, wait patiently for the Lord.

There are times when trouble comes, we cry out to God for help and don't immediately hear an answer. When we don't get rescued right away, we tend to get discouraged. First of all, we must live a life of fellowship with the Lord. This means we talk with Him and communicate with Him on a daily basis—all the time. We can't expect Him to just be our rescuer every time we run into trouble, and then, when things are going well, He never hears from us.

When we work, it is easy to become so busy and involved with our jobs and everything else that goes on that we don't make time to spend with Him. We need to make time for God and when we ask Him for help, believe patiently that He will help us. In the meantime, we must be brave and courageous. He is a patient God. We must be patient, too, and learn to wait on Him in faith. Sometimes we are not ready to receive what we're asking for. Other times, we need to learn to endure a little more. He knows this. Just remember, God is always in control.

333

WE ARE THE APPLE OF GOD'S EYE

Psalm 17:8 (NLT)

Guard me as the apple of your eye.
Hide me in the shadow of your wings.

David's relationship with the Lord was intimate and real. He trusted God implicitly and saw Him as his refuge and a place of protection from all his enemies. David never gave up asking God to help him, to deliver him from his enemies, or to keep him safe. He had long conversations with the Lord. He poured out his heart and threw himself at His feet. He told God exactly how he felt at the moment. Sometimes he was depressed. He told God just that. Then when the Lord lifted him up, he told the Lord about his excitement. He thanked the Lord when he experienced victory and when he suffered defeat because he knew God protected him.

Do you know how important the apple of your eye is? When David asked God to guard him as the apple of His eye it was because David knew he would then be safe. God wants to guard *you* as the apple of His eye. You are His most important and perfect creation. You became imperfect because of the sin in the world.

It blesses God when you ask Him to protect you. Just as eagles protect their babies under the shadow of their wings, you are protected under the shadow of God's wings. The enemies can walk around you but won't see you. Therefore, run to God and allow Him to be your protector. End today with the song David sang when the Lord rescued him from his enemies and from Soul. "I love you Lord; you are my strength. The Lord is my rock, my fortress, and my savior; my God is my rock, in whom I find protection. He is my shield, the strength of my salvation, and my stronghold" (Psalm 18:1-2 NLT).

334

WE CAN DO ALL THINGS WHEN WE TRUST GOD

Isaiah 26:4 (NLT)

Trust in the Lord always, for the Lord God is the eternal Rock.

God tells us throughout the Bible that He is our Rock. He is the only one, the only God we are to trust. Time and time again He reminds us of who we are in Him and how He can provide for everything we need. Why, then, is it so hard for us to trust Him and to do it fully? Simply because we are human. Because we live in a world where sin is everywhere and bad things happen to both good and bad people. We get confused. It is important, however, to differentiate between faith and trust. Faith is believing in God and that His Word is true. Trust is believing that the Word of God is true for your personal life. It is knowing in your heart, beyond any doubt, that God will come through for *you*.

Trusting the Lord with every area of our lives is a daily act of obedience. The last part of verse 9 in Isaiah 7 (NLT) says, "If you want me to protect you, learn to believe what I say." We must learn first to believe what God tells us through His Word and through the Holy Spirit for our personal lives. Then we have to obey, and we cannot obey without trusting Him fully. It is a matter of the heart. He knows our heart and whether we have faith or not. When we don't trust Him, fear comes upon us because we realize we can't do anything alone.

If God has given you a big task lately, something you cannot accomplish on your own, first believe He is the one giving you this task because He trusts you to do it. Then, trust Him that He will help you every step of the way. He will equip you, surround you with the right people, and give you the wisdom necessary to do the task. Trust in the Lord always. He is your eternal Rock. With Him you can do all things.

WISDOM

ACT WISE AND SERVE THE LORD WITH REVERENT FEAR

Psalm 2:10-11 (NLT)

Now then, you kings, act wisely! Be warned, you rulers of the earth!
Serve the Lord with reverent fear, and rejoice with trembling.

Even though the verse above was directed to kings and rulers of the earth, we are all leaders of some people at some time or another in our lives. We may be leaders in our companies, community, church, political arena, or as a parent. It doesn't matter where we exercise leadership. What matters is that leaders must have the revelation of the level of responsibility involved in each position they hold. The Bible tells us to act wisely because everything we do, and the decisions we make, will have consequences and will impact others around us.

The Bible warns us to serve the Lord with reverent fear. This means to respect Him, to honor Him, and to take Him seriously. Doing business with God and for God is serious business. And He holds us accountable for our actions as expressed in the following verses: "Submit to God's royal Son, or he will become angry, and you will be destroyed in the midst of your pursuits—for his anger can flare up in an instant. But what joy for all who find protection in him!" (v. 12).

God is a merciful God. But when we willingly disobey Him and turn away from Him, we are out of His protection and on our own, at the disposal of the enemy. As leaders, we must be wise, act wisely, and stay in God's will.

BE A DECISIVE WOMAN

James 1:5 (NLT)

*If you need wisdom—if you want to know what God wants you to do—
ask him, and he will gladly tell you. He will not resent you asking.*

Making decisions is an everyday occurrence in the business world. We, as Christian women and as leaders, must be decisive. God gives us some clues to help us confirm we are making the right decision. The most obvious one is that we have peace. Many times during the process of decision making, some things just don't feel good. We don't have inner peace. That is a signal that we might be making the wrong decision.

Colossians 3:15 (NLT) says, "And let the peace that comes from Christ rule in your hearts." God can confirm your decision through people or in other ways, however, peace is the main way He chooses to use. Follow the peace in your heart and trust God that He will give you the right answer when you need it.

BE A PRUDENT PERSON

Proverbs 22:3 (NLT)

*A prudent person foresees the danger ahead and takes precautions;
the simpleton goes blindly on and suffers the consequences.*

Always be on the lookout for things that may lead to danger. This doesn't mean you live in fear but instead that you are prudent. Being prudent is not lack of faith. It means you prepare and take precautions when you see circumstances that could bring damage to you down the road. For example: you may start noticing changes at your workplace that could mean the elimination of your job in the future. Don't wait until your job has been eliminated to start calling your network of friends. Always be prepared. Keep your network of contacts active at all times. Keep your résumé updated every time you accept a new job, or annually, to add new experience or responsibilities you acquired in the past year.

God expects us to be prudent. Only then we can foresee evil and be prepared to fight it and win.

338

BE KNOWN FOR YOUR UNDERSTANDING... BE WISE

Proverbs 16:21 (NLT)

The wise are known for their understanding, and instruction is appreciated if it's well presented.

Wise people are usually well grounded, balanced, and have strong beliefs. We are used to thinking that a wise person is old in age, but in reality, wisdom doesn't have to do much with age. It has to do with the level of understanding, discernment, and experience that a person has. It is also important to know that wisdom is a gift from God. Therefore, it doesn't matter how old you are. You can be wise.

Wisdom is applied knowledge. It is knowing (discerning) how to handle the different situations and knowing what to do when. Wisdom is also good planning, thinking ahead, and being prepared.

It takes humility to be wise. Why? Because the wise know when they know something, and they are not proud to accept when they don't know other things. It takes a humble heart to simply say "I don't know." When we seek God because we don't know what to do, we are allowing Him the opportunity to help us with His wisdom. He helps us see things from His perspective.

When we have godly wisdom, we know how to present instruction, correction, and information to others in a way that it is not hurtful. It is then well received and appreciated.

When you are getting ready to present information to your colleagues at work, ask God for the wisdom to use the right words. Ask Him to show you the way they will receive the message best. God is interested in us applying His wisdom in the workplace. It is part of being successful.

BECOME PERSUASIVE BY ACQUIRING WISDOM

Proverbs 16:23 (NLT)

From a wise mind comes wise speech; the words of the wise are persuasive.

Every business person wants to be persuasive. Our goal is to convince the public our products and services are better than the competition. Yet some individuals are much more successful than others at this skill. Why? There are several reasons. One reason is persuasive people are self-confident, fully believe in their product, and know it inside and out. Another reason is their message comes from the heart. We need these keys both in the workplace as well as our spiritual life.

In business, we must research, learn, study, and practice our speech so it is delivered with self-confidence. When we make a speech from the heart, it comes out with passion; our beliefs and convictions are revealed. We come across as an honest, truthful person who sincerely believes in what we are saying and really want to help our customers. This is persuasion.

Spiritually, we also need to be self-confident in our relationship with the Lord. We have to spend time reading the Word, researching, learning, and studying so we are first fully persuaded of the love of God for us. When we know God personally, nothing can change our opinion of Him. We will have a fire burning in our hearts that will inevitably come out and convince others. This is persuasion.

When you combine both the business with your spiritual persuasion, you become a wise, successful, persuasive woman that will touch many lives for God.

340

CHOOSE THE PEOPLE YOU CONFIDE IN CAREFULLY

Proverbs 25:19 (NLT)

Putting confidence in an unreliable person is like chewing with a toothache or walking on a broken foot.

We all have somebody in our lives that we feel comfortable sharing our deepest problems and personal issues with. The question is: is the person we are confiding in reliable? Is he or she going to keep the confidence and confidentiality of what we shared? We must be careful in choosing who we share our personal issues with. This includes our successes. Sometimes the very person we trust turns on us suddenly because of envy. The Bible says putting confidence in an unreliable person is painful because of the damage they can do to us.

Information is powerful. It gives power to the people we choose to share our information with. Information can destroy a person's life and a company. There are people who seem trustworthy on the surface but then turn around and betray your confidence. They first make you feel comfortable by sharing a few personal things with you to make you open up to them. Then they use the information you give them to taint your name and your reputation.

Ask God to give you wisdom and discernment to choose the right individuals in whom you can confide. Then don't forget to pay attention to His response. We all need people we can talk to and share concerns with, but we must be careful when choosing that person. At the same time, don't share somebody else's secrets and issues that they have confided in you. You are then gossiping and sowing that seed, which you will indeed reap later.

Finally, don't forget you always have Jesus as your best friend. You can talk to Him out loud. He will listen and will always respond to you. He will give you peace in your heart, discernment, and guidance on how to deal with every situation. In Him, you can fully trust and pour your heart out without fear or reservation.

341

DEEPER KNOWLEDGE COMES WITH TIME ALONE WITH THE LORD

Mark 4:33-34 (NLT)

He used many such stories and illustrations to teach the people as much as they were able to understand. In fact, in his public teaching he taught only with parables, but afterward when he was alone with his disciples, he explained the meaning to them.

The Bible tells us Jesus taught the things of God through parables. Why? Because He could only teach as much as the people were able to receive and therefore understand. God is too deep for us to fully comprehend His things or Himself with our human minds. We first must have an open mind and heart to receive His teachings and understand them in our hearts through our spirit. The Lord takes us one step at a time in His knowledge, one layer of revelation at a time. As we grow, He reveals Himself to us a little more. It is a life-long process until we join Him in heaven.

We should notice, however, that when Jesus was alone with His disciples, He explained the deeper meaning of His teachings.

As the disciples walked with Jesus, they drew closer to Him and were able to understand deeper things of God's Kingdom. The same applies to us today. The only way God can teach, reveal, and entrust us with more knowledge is by us spending time with Him—alone, with no worldly distractions, and with our attention fixed only on Him.

Set aside time from your busy schedule to meet with the Lord, just you and Him, alone. He is faithful and will not only be there waiting for you every time but will also make sure you don't get behind in any of your other responsibilities. He will multiply your time.

342

DON'T IGNORE CORRECTION

Proverbs 10:17 (NLT)

People who accept correction are on the pathway to life, but those who ignore it will lead others astray.

Proverbs 3:12 (NLT)

For the Lord corrects those he loves, just as a father corrects a child in whom he delights.

Sometimes God uses our spouse, our boss, a parent, or a close friend to bring correction to our lives in a certain area.

Don't be proud and reject correction because it may be exactly what you need in order to go to your next step in your career or in your personal life. Always receive correction with an open mind and heart, then take the correction to the Lord in prayer and let Him work in your life. He has a way to do it with love, mercy, and tenderness that no one else can. If you ignore correction now, you may be responsible for leading other people astray later.

343

DON'T BE AFRAID TO PLAN

Proverbs 3:21-22 (NLT)

My child, don't lose sight of good planning and insight. Hang on to them, for they fill you with life and bring you honor and respect.

Many Christians nowadays don't plan for the future, thinking Jesus is coming soon. They view planning and preparing as lack of faith. But that mind-set is not wise. We are to live our lives as if Jesus is coming today, spiritually speaking. Until He comes, we are to occupy, multiply, have dominium of, and steward God's creation. The Bible says to not lose sight of good planning and insight, for they will fill us with life. When we don't plan, we are choosing to let things happen in our lives and lose control. We are to plan good plans with God's wisdom and guidance. Lack of planning brings uncertainty and fear. Planning brings peace, certainty, security, honor, and respect.

If you are a planner, those who watch you will see you as a wise person. Then you'll have an opportunity to share your wisdom and where it comes from. Proverbs 2:11 (NLT) says, "Wise planning will watch over you. Understanding will keep you safe." "You can lie down without fear and enjoy pleasant dreams" (Proverbs 3:24 NLT).

By planning all aspects of your life, you take control of your life and responsibility for your actions. But it also means you choose to give that control to God and let Him guide you. With God as part of your planning, you can't go wrong because you have God's will for you as your plan. And even though the enemy may try to change and confuse those plans, the Lord will give you wisdom "and you will know how to find the right course of action every time" (Proverbs 2:9 NLT).

Don't be afraid to plan. Ask God for the wisdom to help you. Plan your life with the main purpose of bringing glory to Him.

344

GET CONNECTED WITH WISE PEOPLE

Proverbs 13:20 (NLT)

Whoever walks with the wise will become wise; whoever walks with fools will suffer harm.

The world has many foolish people and few wise people. Part of being wise is to look for other wise individuals and associate with them. If you don't have wisdom, ask God for it and He will gladly give it to you. All He asks for is someone with a pure heart and pure motives to use His wisdom. One way God gives us wisdom is by connecting us with others from whom we can learn. Proverbs 14:7 (NLT) says to "stay away from fools, for you won't find knowledge there."

Becoming a wise person is key in becoming a successful person. When we have wisdom, we get a knowledge and understanding of things that are supernatural. In addition, we get a special discernment that is unknown to the foolish. Proverbs 14:33 (NLT) says, "wisdom is enshrined in an understanding heart; wisdom is not found among fools."

Ask God to connect you and cross your path with wise, godly people you can associate with. Ask Him for people that can help you grow in your walk with Him, as well as in your career. He may send you one or more persons to help you in both areas. Then you need to help others become wise. Don't hoard the knowledge, pass it on and share the wisdom of God with others.

345

GET WISDOM AND LIVE BY IT

Proverbs 4:7 (NLT)

Getting wisdom is the most important thing you can do! And whatever else you do, get good judgment.

Solomon reminds us continually in the Proverbs he wrote about how important it is for us to get wisdom to be successful. The first step is to want and seek wisdom more than any other gift we may want from God. God used His wisdom to create everything, including His plan of salvation. "By wisdom the Lord founded the earth" (Proverbs 3:19 NLT). Proverbs 4:12 (NLT) says, "If you live a life guided by wisdom, you won't limp or stumble as you run."

Wisdom, knowledge, understanding, and judgment are crucial to our success in every area of our lives. How do we acquire those gifts? First, by asking God to give them to us, and then we can apply them in our everyday lives. We consult with God on every step we make in our lives. We allow Him to guide our steps by His wisdom. We give the gift of wisdom the importance it deserves and treasure it as one of His most precious gifts after salvation. We keep the gifts mentioned above growing and developing by staying in touch with the Lord and living a godly life.

When God entrusts us with the gifts of wisdom, knowledge, understanding, and judgment, we must be thankful and use them to give Him glory in everything we do. God can really use us when we walk in His wisdom and love. The workplace needs us to acquire these gifts and put them into practice so we *can* make a difference.

346

GIVE AND SEEK GODLY ADVICE

Proverbs 10:21 (NLT)

The godly give good advice, but fools are destroyed by their lack of common sense.

Proverbs 12:15 (NLT)

Fools think they need no advice, but the wise listen to others.

Through the course of our lives, people will come to us for advice in various areas. We, as godly women, must give good advice. How do we do it? By being prepared and going to the source of wisdom—the Word of God. Lack of common sense is lack of God's wisdom. Wisdom is knowing how to apply the knowledge we have.

The workplace is the perfect opportunity to seek and give advice. The next time someone asks you for advice at work, seek God first and ask Him for wisdom to give the appropriate advice. The same way, when you need advice, be open to listening to others. God speaks to us through people, but be careful whom you seek advice from. If you want godly advice, seek it from godly people. Then take those suggestions or that advice to the Lord in prayer and go with what gives you peace in your heart.

347

GOD, NOT WEALTH, BRINGS TRUE HAPPINESS

Ecclesiastes 5:10 (NLT)

Those who love money will never have enough. How absurd to think that wealth brings true happiness!

I Timothy 6:10 (NLT)

For the love of money is at the root of all kinds of evil.

Almost every person, if not everybody, desires to have money in this world. Many buy lottery tickets, gamble at casinos, hope to have a rich relative leave them a large fortune as inheritance, or dream of being a successful business owner. There is nothing wrong with having money or wanting money to live a good life, provide for our families, and help others. But the moment we start loving money, our hearts' motives may change and money may eventually replace God's place in our lives. Money has the ability to attract us to it, attract us to the things of the world, and to take us away from God. I believe the main reason money has that ability is because it can give us all the things of the world to a point where we think we no longer need God.

Ecclesiastes 7:11-12 (NLT) say, "Being wise is as good as being rich; in fact it is better. Wisdom or money can get you almost anything, but it's important to know that only wisdom can save your life." Wisdom takes us to the tree of life. It takes us to God where we find abundant life here on earth and eternal life in heaven. I believe wealth is a gift from God, but we must be mature in the Lord to handle and manage it for Him. It takes great effort not to get attached to money, but there are ways we can do it. When we put God first in our lives, dedicate our hard work to Him, and use our financial wealth to further His Kingdom, He entrusts us with material wealth. Giving, instead of hoarding, is the key.

Therefore, seek God with all your heart, not money, and give to wherever God leads you knowing He will never ask you to give what you don't have. Then you will find true happiness.

348

HIRE YOUR EMPLOYEES WISELY

Proverbs 26:10 (NLT)

An employer who hires a fool or a bystander is like an archer who shoots recklessly.

The success of a company depends entirely on the employees they hire. Therefore, the hiring process should not be taken lightly. It is crucial that the appropriate homework be done before and after interviewing a potential candidate. If a company hires the wrong people, it can cost the company money in training, major mistakes may be made, and if employees are ill-intentioned, they could bring the company down.

There are two major areas you need to look at when hiring potential employees. The first one is the person's character. Is the candidate a person of integrity, honest, truthful, and with no personal hidden agenda? How can you know if the candidate has all of these important character traits in one interview? You don't. But you can ask God to help you ask key questions that will reveal a person's character. As long as you ask everybody the same questions, and they are within legal guidelines, you should be okay in not discriminating against any candidate.

The second major area is the skills and abilities of the candidate. Don't make the mistake of hiring someone for a position just because they are nice. On the other hand, don't look only at their credentials, but also their personality. If they don't fit the position and you hire them, you are setting them up for failure and you will be frustrated. Therefore, do your homework and ask God to send you the right person to fill every position you need in your area.

LEARN TO DISCERN CRITICISM AND PRAISE

Ecclesiastes 7:5 (NLT)

It is better to be criticized by a wise person than to be praised by a fool!

Taking criticism is difficult, especially when we have worked very hard on some project and we are proud of our results. However, we can't grow without criticism. How do we improve if nobody dares to tell us anything because they know what our reaction will be? The key is to know who the person criticizing you is. If it's coming from a wise person, receive the criticism and make the appropriate changes. If it's coming from a person you don't trust or has the reputation of being a fool, then disregard it. The question is, how do we know what to receive, what to disregard, who is wise, and who is a fool? Sometimes we will know right away just by knowing the source, the person who criticized us. Other times, we will have to take the criticism to the Lord and ask Him to help us discern its validity.

We need to always be open for correction, especially when it comes from the Lord. He knows how to deal with each one of us without hurting us. Sometimes He uses people close to us to speak into our lives so we can improve.

On the other hand, receiving praise is easy. We may receive praises from fools or people who say things to gain favor with us, not because they mean it. We must watch out for those praises and not take them too seriously. Verse 7 says, "Extortion turns wise people into fools, and bribes corrupt the heart." We have to treat praises the same way we do criticism. We take them to the Lord to help us discern and to protect us from being hurt from criticism or becoming proud from praise.

350

Let Wisdom Enter in Your Heart

Ecclesiastes 10:2 (NLT)

The hearts of the wise lead them to do right, and the hearts of the foolish lead them to do evil.

God wants us to be wise. He wants to give us His wisdom because earthly wisdom is the same as foolishness. It takes us down the wrong path, leads us to do evil, and ends in destruction. The Word of God tells us to ask Him for wisdom. It is a gift He is willing and ready to pour out on us when we ask. But just as with other gifts, He can only give it to us if we are trustworthy. How do we become trustworthy in the eyes of God? By being faithful with all the other gifts He entrusts us with, by putting them to use for His Kingdom, and by developing them.

When we have godly wisdom we know what is the right thing to do every time. Godly wisdom gives us self-confidence, inner peace, and a knowing beyond doubt that we are doing the right thing. We are wise when we recognize we get wisdom from Him and when we ask Him what to do in every circumstance. Being wise is recognizing that our job, company, friends, relatives, or even our church are not our source—only He is. All those things and people are gifts from Him we must treasure and appreciate.

Ask God to pour out His wisdom into your heart. Ecclesiastes 8:1 (NLT) says, "How wonderful to be wise, to be able to analyze and interpret things. Wisdom lights up a person's face, softening its hardness." Proverbs 2:10 (NLT) says, "For wisdom will enter your heart, and knowledge will fill you with joy."

351

LISTEN TO CONSTRUCTIVE CRITICISM AND GROW

Proverbs 15:31-32 (NLT)

If you listen to constructive criticism, you will be at home among the wise. If you reject criticism, you only harm yourself; but if you listen to correction, you grow in understanding.

Nobody likes to be criticized. There are two kinds of criticism: constructive and destructive. We must learn to discern if we're getting one or the other. If you know the person who is giving you the correction as someone who loves you and cares about you, then accept it as constructive criticism. Learn from it, thank them, and move on.

On the other hand, if the criticism comes from someone who hardly knows you or is ill-intentioned, then drop it and move on. If you are not sure, then ask God to help you discern and confirm the correction.

It is wise to accept constructive criticism. God will put people at work sometimes to help you develop in your career. He will also send people in your family or friends to help you mature. Don't get offended and blow them off. Take these opportunities to grow in understanding.

LIVE YOUR LIFE WISELY

Colossians 4:5-6 (NLT)

Live wisely among those who are not Christians, and make the most of every opportunity. Let your conversation be gracious and effective so that you will have the right answer for everyone.

Those who are not Christians are watching everything Christians do. They observe our work ethic, how we treat people at work, how we treat our neighbors and family, and how we live our lives. Paul, in his letter to the Colossians, is advising them to live wisely. This means we need wisdom to live a Christian life.

Now more than ever we must be an example. This may be the only witness those around us have of a Christian lifestyle. Every conversation we have must be effective and productive and glorify God rather than undermine Him. The Lord will give us the right answer for every situation when we walk in divine wisdom.

OBTAINING FAVOR FROM GOD AND MEN

Proverbs 3:3-4 (NLT)

Never let loyalty and kindness get away from you! Wear them like a necklace; write them deep within your heart. Then you will find favor with both God and people, and you will gain a good reputation.

Loyalty and kindness in the workplace are a rarity these days, yet God tells us to never let them depart from us. We are to wear these traits all the time and wherever we go. God wants us to write and record them deep in our hearts. Indeed, this must be our way of life—both at work and at home—because only then will we qualify to have favor with both God and people. When we have favor with God, He opens doors of opportunities no man can shut. Furthermore, He gives us favor with people also, the kind of favor that amazes and intrigues others.

Therefore, cultivate the qualities of loyalty and kindness in your life. When your colleagues see these traits in you, they will trust you more and it will create a good reputation for you—something everyone wants to have. When you have favor along with a good reputation, you can influence more people for the Kingdom of God.

354

PROVERBS—THE BOOK OF WISDOM

Proverbs 1:3 (NLT)

Through these proverbs, people will receive instruction in discipline, good conduct, and doing what is right, just, and fair.

God gave us a manual full of instructions and guidelines to follow. In the Bible, we not only find His commandments but also real life tips and wisdom nuggets we can use every day. The book of Proverbs was written by Solomon, a man known for his wisdom. When King Solomon started his reign, he specifically asked God for His wisdom to lead His people and to be a good steward of the riches he was entrusted with. God was pleased with his request because He knew his heart, so He granted him his request and blessed him with godly wisdom.

The book of Proverbs teaches us God's wisdom, not Solomon's. It has instructions on what to do in every situation in life—from how to raise our children and have a successful marriage to how to conduct business on a daily basis. It sets the expectations of Christian behavior. It tells us how to choose what's right all the time, to be fair and just leaders. Verse 2 tells us the "purpose of these proverbs is to teach people wisdom and discipline, and to help them understand wise sayings." God wants us to have His wisdom; He wants us to ask Him for it so He can grant it fully to us.

I encourage you to read the entire book of Proverbs and to ask God for His wisdom. You will gain a new understanding of the things of God and your life will be changed. You need His wisdom to make your daily business decisions as well as those in your personal life.

PURSUE WISDOM WITH ALL YOUR HEART

Proverbs 1:23 (NLT)

Come here and listen to me! I'll pour out the spirit of wisdom upon you and make you wise.

In Proverbs 1:20, Wisdom cries out on the streets looking for people and can't find anyone who is willing to listen and become wise. God wants to pour out His Spirit of wisdom upon us but we have to desire it. We have to search for it and appreciate it like the most valuable treasure we could ever find or have. Wisdom is a treasure because it is by wisdom we understand what it means to fear the Lord, and we gain knowledge of God (Proverbs 2:5 NLT).

The Bible exhorts you to "Tune your ears to wisdom, and concentrate on understanding. Cry out for insight and understanding. Search for them as you would for lost money or hidden treasure" (Proverbs 2:2-4 NLT). Therefore, make an effort like never before to pursue wisdom. Seek it more than your career, job, or business.

356

RESPECT ADVICE AND YOU WILL SUCCEED

Proverbs 13:13 (NLT)

People who despise advice will find themselves in trouble; those who respect it will succeed.

Why is it that sometimes it is hard to receive advice? There are areas in our lives where we don't mind seeking advice from others. There are other areas; however, we are not as open to it. Usually, those are the areas closest to our hearts or our fields of expertise. For example, if we do gardening and we know we are not experts at it, we don't mind asking our neighbors and friends how to grow a particular fruit or vegetable. However, if we are experts in the field and we are the ones usually giving advice on how to grow plants, we may be afraid of asking for advice.

We can also apply the example of the situation above to our work. If we feel we should know the answer because it is what we do, we get defensive when people freely give us their advice. Yet we don't seek it for fear of disapproval. We are afraid of what others will say.

Asking for help is humbling. It is admitting we don't know everything and that we don't have all the answers. But the Bible tells us if we reject or despise advice, we *will* (not may) find ourselves in trouble and those who respect it will succeed. If we want to be successful we must be humble, ask for advice, and respect it when we receive it. Usually, those who give us advice sincerely care for us and want to see us succeed. God will put people in our lives to help us and give us advice. Many times that person is our boss, a colleague, or our neighbor. We must be thankful for those individuals and ask God to help us recognize who they are.

357

REVERE GOD AND FEAR HIM AND YOU SHALL HAVE WISDOM

Psalm 111:10 (NLT)

Reverence for the Lord is the foundation of true wisdom. The rewards of wisdom come to all who obey him.

Wisdom is a gift and God is ready to give it to all who ask. However, He won't give it to those who don't revere (hold in the highest regard, worship, respect) Him because they will misuse it. God's wisdom is a treasure we must protect and use responsibly. It is one of His most precious gifts to us.

We revere God by being faithful and obedient to His Word. When we obey Him, He rewards us with all His blessings—one of them is wisdom. Reverence for the Lord is having fear of the Lord. Psalm 112:1 and 3 say, "Happy are those who fear the Lord. Yes, happy are those who delight in doing what he commands… They themselves will be wealthy and their good deeds will never be forgotten."

In the workplace you must have wisdom to be successful at your job, no matter what field you're in or what type of job you have. Every person needs to be wise to make the right decisions on a daily basis. Therefore, have reverence for God, and you will have the gift of wisdom and its rewards.

SEEK GOD'S WISDOM

Proverbs 2:6-7 (NLT)

For the Lord grants wisdom! From his mouth comes knowledge and understanding. He grants a treasure of good sense to the godly. He is their shield, protecting those who walk with integrity.

Each day at work we encounter numerous situations that require us to make decisions. Many of these decisions can be challenging. In fact, sometimes we struggle with knowing when to act and when to make the correct decision—at the right time. However, when we seek God's wisdom, He grants it to us as a gift. Once we ask, we must remember to stop and listen for His response. As we gain His knowledge and understanding, things become clearer and we know what to do. When we walk in His wisdom, we become women of integrity, with no hidden agendas.

Therefore, when people ask you why you are so wise, don't forget to give the glory to God.

SEEK GOD'S WISDOM ABOVE ALL THINGS

Proverbs 8:11, 17, 35 (NLT)

For wisdom is far more valuable than rubies. Nothing you desire can be compared with it… "I love all who love me. Those who search for me will surely find me…" "For whoever finds me finds life and wins approval from the Lord."

Do you want the secret to a successful Christian life? Get wisdom. Seek wisdom above all things from the Lord. I say a successful

Christian life because you cannot obtain the wisdom of God without first becoming a Christian. God promises us that if we seek wisdom, we will surely find it. His Word tells us that when we do find it, we win approval from the Lord. We learn to fear the Lord and then the knowledge of Him comes to us.

With wisdom, you will know what to do in every situation, in every area of your life. With wisdom, you will be able to use every talent and gift God gave you, and you will prosper.

Ask God for wisdom today. Desire it more than anything else in your life because nothing else compares with it. Your success in life depends on it.

360

SEEK TO HAVE A GOOD REPUTATION

Proverbs 22:1 (NLT)

Choose a good reputation over great riches, for being held in high esteem is better than having silver or gold.

The decisions you make on a daily basis will reflect your character and create your reputation. It is your choice to do what's right every time. Consistency is vital to building your reputation. You will either be known as a person of character—someone who always chooses to do what's right regardless of the consequences—or as a person who compromises her beliefs in order to please everybody, fit in, or do what is easy or convenient.

Don't compromise! Do what's right. If you don't know what to do, ask God for wisdom. Go to His Word to seek the answer. You have the Holy Spirit who is the revealer of truth and is willing to give it to you when you ask.

361

SEEK WISDOM AND YOU WILL KNOW WHAT IS RIGHT, JUST, AND FAIR TO DO

Proverbs 2:9 (NLT)

Then you will understand what is right, just, and fair, and you will know how to find the right course of action every time.

When we ask God for wisdom He will grant it to us—every time. It is His promise that we will know what to do in every situation.

Ethical dilemmas are common in the workplace. How do we know what's the right thing to do—every time? How do we determine what's fair and just? Will we lose our jobs if we do what's right? This is when we must first go to the source of wisdom, God. Then we need to choose to do what is right, regardless of the consequences.

Proverbs 2:8 (NLT) says "He guards the paths of justice and protects those who are faithful to him." Therefore, we must do what is just, fair, and right and let God protect us, protect our reputation, and take care of us.

THE WORDS OF CHRIST MAKE YOU WISE

Colossians 3:16 (NLT)

Let the words of Christ, in all their richness, live in your hearts and make you wise. Use his words to teach and counsel each other.

We all want and need wisdom. God tells us in order to obtain wisdom we need to ask Him and He will gladly grant it to us. But we also have to do our part, which is to read His Word. The words of Christ are all recorded in the Bible. When we read the Word and meditate on it day and night, His wisdom comes to us. We also have the Holy Spirit who gives us wisdom to apply to our personal lives and specific situations. We are to use His words to teach and counsel each other, but we can't accomplish that kind of mentoring relationship if we don't possess wisdom.

If you want to be known as a wise woman at work, this is the secret. Pursue wisdom, knowledge, and understanding.

TO LEARN, WE MUST LOVE DISCIPLINE

Proverbs 12:1 (NLT)

To learn, you must love discipline; it is stupid to hate correction.

During our walk with the Lord, He continues to teach us new things and correct us in the areas we need to grow. It is always difficult to accept correction, yet correction is the only way we learn and change. It's the same with our children. We have to continue to discipline them until they get the message. For example: We have to tell them to not cross the street without looking; otherwise, they could be hurt. It may take several times of correction until they get it.

We all have areas where the Lord has to continually discipline us. The quicker we accept His correction, make the adjustments necessary, and basically pass the test, the quicker we will move on to the next level of learning. Remember, this life is a journey of learning to prepare us for eternity with God. Therefore, to learn, the Bible says we must love discipline.

364

WALK IN WISDOM

Proverbs 28:26 (NLT)

Trusting oneself is foolish, but those who walk in wisdom are safe.

As we grow in our careers, gain experience at our jobs, and become more successful because of our hard work and commitment, we will have the temptation to trust ourselves too much. The Bible says it is foolish to do so. First, we cannot forget it is God who gave us all the gifts and talents we have. Secondly, He is also the One who gave us the opportunities to succeed. So let's not forget to give Him the glory for all of our successes. Thirdly, when we walk in His wisdom we are safe because we know we are doing what He told us to do. God's wisdom is beyond our comprehension, and He will grant it to us when we ask Him for it. Part of being successful is having God's wisdom in our lives.

WISDOM COMES TO THOSE WHO ARE HUMBLE

Proverbs 11:2 (NLT)

Pride leads to disgrace, but with humility comes wisdom.

Proverbs 16:5 (NLT)

The Lord despises pride; be assured that the proud will be punished.

God can work with any person, despite all their imperfections, except a proud person. God turns away from proud people. He will not pour His wisdom into a proud heart because people often fall in the trap of elevating themselves above others. God is looking for humble, repentant hearts He can use for His purposes. God's master plan is one—to get people saved so they can spend eternity with Him in heaven.

As you succeed in life, don't allow pride to enter your heart. Success can be anything such as getting promoted at work, receiving a raise, improving your lifestyle, starting your own company, or getting married and having children. The enemy will use the smallest, unimportant things, as well as big successful events, to make you feel superior to other people. He will give you the idea that you can succeed alone—by your own efforts and smarts—without God. It is in those moments when pride enters your heart. You must rebuke it, surrender your life to the Lord again, and thank Him for your success.

Being humble doesn't mean having self-pity and low self-esteem. It means you know who you are in Christ. It is a knowing that He is the One who gives you strength to do what He's called you to do.

366

YOU CAN BE YOUNG AND WISE

Ecclesiastes 11:9 (NLT)

*Young man, it's wonderful to be young! Enjoy every minute of it.
Do everything you want to do; take it all in. But remember that you
must give an account to God for everything you do.*

Being young is wonderful. I haven't met one person yet who wants
to be old—and I doubt I ever will. But many old people want to
and yearn to be young again.

Youth represents strength, life, health, beauty, smarts, and
many other positive things. Notice, however, we don't usually associate wisdom to youth. On the contrary, the words old and wise
go together in our society. When we are young we think we know
it all. Why is that? I believe it's a lack of maturity and experience.
Only as we get older, we realize how little we know and how much
more we have to learn.

We must teach our young people to seek the wisdom of God.
Imagine what youth can accomplish with the weapon of wisdom
against the enemy of the world! Very few young people are wise.
I believe that's for two main reasons: one, because they don't ask
God for wisdom, and second, and most importantly, because wis-
dom comes with experience and maturity with the things of the
Lord. Wisdom is a gift from God, and we must be trustworthy to
be able to handle it. Otherwise, we misuse it or waste it.

If you are a young working woman, ask God for wisdom and
use it for Him. Remember also, the more gifts you have, the higher
the responsibility. Seek to be called young and wise in your life.
Enjoy your youth, but know that one day you will give account to
God for everything you did in your life. Know also, that when you
repent of your sins from your heart, God forgives you and wipes
your slate clean.

Index

ENCOURAGEMENT

FAITH

FAITHFULNESS

OBEDIENCE

SUCCESS

WISDOM

About the Author

Marcia (Marci) Malzahn is a wife, mother, writer, and speaker in addition to being a successful executive, entrepreneur, and business professional. She started two businesses, climbed the corporate ladder, and has experience both in the for-profit as well as the non-profit world.

Considered a business leader in the Minneapolis/St. Paul community, Marcia was the recipient of several awards including "25 On the Rise," given by the Minnesota Hispanic Chamber of Commerce to successful Minnesota Hispanics under the age of forty. Marcia was also named one of the "40 Under Forty" awarded by the *Minneapolis/St. Paul Business Journal* to the top forty professionals in the area under the age of forty. Marcia holds an Associates of Arts degree from North Hennepin Community College.

Marcia's passion and mission is to encourage, motivate, and inspire women to be successful and balanced in every area of their lives. She and her husband, Tim, live in Minnesota, with their two children, Nicole and Patrick.